SACRAMENTO PUBLIC LIBRARY

D0975230

THE GIRL
IN ALFRED HITCHCOCK'S
SHOWER

Titles by Robert Graysmith

ZODIAC

THE SLEEPING LADY

AUTO FOCUS: THE MURDER OF BOB CRANE

UNABOMBER: A DESIRE TO KILL

THE BELL TOWER

ZODIAC UNMASKED

AMERITHRAX

THE LAUGHING GORILLA

THE GIRL IN ALFRED HITCHCOCK'S SHOWER

Zodiac, Zodiac Unmasked, and Auto Focus have been made into major motion pictures by Warner Brothers, Paramount, Phoenix Pictures, and Sony Pictures.

Most Berkley Books are available at special quantity discounts for bulk purchases for sales promotions, premiums, fund-raising, or educational use. Special books, or book excerpts, can also be created to fit specific needs. For details, write: Special Markets, The Berkley Publishing Group, 375 Hudson Street, New York, New York 10014.

THE GIRL IN ALFRED HITCHCOCK'S SHOWER

A MURDER THAT BECAME A REAL-LIFE MYSTERY
A MYSTERY THAT BECAME AN OBSESSION

Robert Graysmith

BERKLEY BOOKS, NEW YORK

THE BERKLEY PUBLISHING GROUP
Published by the Penguin Group
Penguin Group (USA) Inc.
375 Hudson Street, New York, New York 10014, USA
Penguin Group (Canada), 90 Eglinton Avenue East, Suite 700, Toronto, Ontario M4P 2Y3, Canada
(a division of Pearson Penguin Canada Inc.)
Penguin Books Ltd., 80 Strand, London WC2R 0RL, England
Penguin Group Ireland, 25 St. Stephen's Green, Dublin 2, Ireland (a division of Penguin Books Ltd.)
Penguin Group (Australia), 250 Camberwell Road, Camberwell, Victoria 3124, Australia
(a division of Pearson Australia Group Pty. Ltd.)
Penguin Books India Pvt. Ltd., 11 Community Centre, Panchsheel Park, New Delhi—110 017, India
Penguin Group (NZ), 67 Apollo Drive, Rosedale, North Shore 0632, New Zealand
(a division of Pearson New Zealand Ltd.)
Penguin Books (South Africa) (Pty.) Ltd., 24 Sturdee Avenue, Rosebank, Johannesburg 2196,
South Africa

Penguin Books Ltd., Registered Offices: 80 Strand, London WC2R 0RL, England

This book is an original publication of The Berkley Publishing Group.

The publisher does not have any control over and does not assume any responsibility for author or
third-party websites or their content.

Copyright © 2010 by Robert Graysmith.
Text design by Tiffany Estreicher.

All rights reserved.
No part of this book may be reproduced, scanned, or distributed in any printed or electronic form
without permission. Please do not participate in or encourage piracy of copyrighted materials in
violation of the author's rights. Purchase only authorized editions.
BERKLEY® is a registered trademark of Penguin Group (USA) Inc.
The "B" design is a trademark of Penguin Group (USA) Inc.

FIRST EDITION: February 2010

Library of Congress Cataloging-in-Publication Data

Graysmith, Robert.
    The girl in Alfred Hitchcock's shower / Robert Graysmith.—1st ed.
      p. cm.
    ISBN 978-0-425-23231-6
    1. Psycho (Motion picture :1960) 2. Renfro, Marli, 1938– 3. Models (Persons)—California—
Biography. 4. Hitchcock, Alfred, 1899–1980. 5. Serial murder investigation—California. I. Title.
    PN1997.P793G73 2010
    791.43'72—dc22   2009037949

PRINTED IN THE UNITED STATES OF AMERICA

10 9 8 7 6 5 4 3 2 1

To James Ellroy

ACKNOWLEDGMENTS

Thanks to Frank McGinn, Alexis Gutierrez, Palle Madsen, and Tony Hardin of Amazing Fantasy; Brecht Andersch of Kayo Books; LAPD Detective Rick Jackson; Jason Ramirez; Sean Murphy; John Pakula, MD; and LAPD officer Christian R. Shaw for his kindness at rush hour; Beau Beausoleil, Andrea Hassiba, Eric Flaherty, and Randy Beucuf of Overland Books; Issa and Jay of the Sunset Barber Service; and, of course, the wonderful Joel Gotler, Thomas De-Trinis, Leslie Conliffe, Sarah LaBrie, and Jeane Wong, and my brilliant editors Candace B. Levy, Michelle Vega, and Natalee Rosenstein.

AP Online. November 7, 2001, Los Angeles: A handyman convicted of strangling two women, including the actress who appeared as Janet Leigh's body double in Alfred Hitchcock's *Psycho*, was sentenced Tuesday to life in prison without the possibility of parole.

CourtTV.com. April 3, 2007: She wasn't a huge Hollywood star, but she was an important part of *Psycho*; she served as the stand-in for Janet Leigh during the infamous shower scene . . .

Cold Case File: Police crack a cold case of murder when a mysterious woman calls to say that her boyfriend is the killer, and the murder of a woman in 1996 provides clues to the murder years ago of a stand-in for Janet Leigh in the movie *Psycho*.

Body Double: When movie buffs think of *Psycho*, the first image that comes to mind is the shower scene. Fans knew the stars, but few people realized they saw snippets of a performance by . . . one of Janet Leigh's "body doubles" for the chilling shower-slay scene in Alfred Hitchcock's classic film *Psycho*. Now it was her own murder that had been played out with shocking brutality.

Celebrity Sleuth: It's an amazing coda to the most affecting screen death ever. For over ten years, Marli/Myra's 1988 rape and strangulation in her West Los Angeles home had gone unsolved.

For over forty years I kept her photos, as obsessed as the detective in Laura *who fell in love with a dead woman's picture. But as I wrote the beautiful redhead's story, a nagging doubt entered my mind. What if, like "Laura," she was still alive and someone else had been murdered in her place?*

THE GIRL
IN ALFRED HITCHCOCK'S
SHOWER

Chapter One
Stylized Murder

lfred Hitchcock had cornered the stunning red-haired nude on Stage 18-A and was chatting her up. Always a bit of a prude, he still had a lascivious schoolboy attitude toward women in general and nudity in particular. Adolescent in late middle age, Hitchcock could still be goggle-eyed about sex and was making the most of this rare opportunity to be close to such an unclothed beauty.

Psycho was a reserved set, formal, controlled, polite, and exceptionally appropriate in tone. All the crew wore dress shirts, dark trousers, and neckties. Even the on-set strong-arm brigade—charged with rebuffing any interlopers—wore Brooks Brothers. As always Hitchcock was attired in a black Mariani ensemble, crisp white linen shirt, and slender black Italian tie (he never wore a wristwatch or rings). Wardrobe supervisor Rita Riggs usually wore Givenchy-like tunics and skirts, leather gloves, and Capezios with short leather heels. For Hitch, the external decorum of dress had become a fetish. In the midst of all this formality, the "sunbather" or "nudist," as Mr. Hitchcock called the gorgeous redhead, was extraordinarily underdressed.

"I recall her sitting quite nude," Riggs said later, "except for this crazy little patch we always put over pubic hair, talking with Mr. Hitchcock. I watched Mr. Hitchcock, the model, and the crew one morning standing around having coffee and doughnuts and thought: 'This is surreal.'"

The tableau was reminiscent of Manet's notorious *Le Dejeuner sur L'Herbe*, which depicted a nude female bather in the company of two fully dressed men. A hundred years ago, *The Luncheon on the Grass* had become a rallying cry for the rebellious young Impressionists. The comparison was fitting. Over a week's time, Hitchcock intended to assemble an impressionistic forty-five-second montage of quick cuts, close-ups, wild angles, and flashes of naked flesh, each lasting only two to three seconds. Hitch hoped the quick staccato cuts on the screen, indicative of a relentlessly stabbing knife, would galvanize his audience as never before.

It might as well have been midnight on the movie set of deep shadows, though it was already approaching 10:00 A.M., Friday, December 18, 1959. Everyone spoke in hushed tones or whispered, but that was out of respect for Mr. Hitchcock, who was held in great reverence by his crew and stars, many of whom would willingly work for him for free (at least if the frugal Mr. Hitchcock had his way). As far as they were concerned, it was an honor just to be included in this production, though they were being paid scale. Hitchcock, who estimated a thirty-day shoot, was paying his television unit as if *Psycho* were a single half-hour episode of *Alfred Hitchcock Presents*. It was an experiment: Could he shoot a feature film under the same conditions as a television show?

Silhouettes of grips moving on the gantries and special overhead scaffolding were barely visible, but every man above was keenly interested in the set below. It was like every movie set—dust-free air, the gentle hum of air-conditioning, generators, black cables snaking everywhere, and huge, unwieldy cameras—except for the exquisite model whose bare skin glowed warmly in the dusk. The woman who was Janet Leigh's body double paraded around the set stark naked, which was new to all of them and, in those repressed times, shocking. Such women always cause a shock when first encountered, so blinding are they in their elegance, naturalness, and beauty. One of the redhead's photographers wrote she had "an impressive body; her face sports a constant and wondrous smile." Others thought she didn't smile enough, but that only added to her mystery.

The redhead surveyed Hitchcock with a bold, direct gaze. "Your eyes are very green," said Hitch.

"I think of my eyes as blue," she countered, "but my mother thinks they are green. Once I had to renew my driver's license and, being that my eyes are sometimes blue and sometimes green, I didn't want to write down 'blue-green.' So I wrote down 'oceanic.'" The redhead formed the word *oceanic* slowly, red lips barely parting. It was amazingly sensual. She had a slender, arched neck and the classic lines of a great beauty and was full-bosomed with pink nipples. In the cool air they stood erect from unusually firm breasts. While filming *To Catch a Thief* in Cannes, Hitch had similarly ogled vivacious French actress Brigitte Auber. "She had a casual way of wearing a blouse," screenwriter John Michael Hayes recalled, "which exposed her bosom frequently and Hitch of course was delighted with her." But the redhead was much, much better.

Seen from behind, her buttocks were taut and slightly boy-like, but from the front, her hips seemed more fully curved in contrast to her exceptionally flat stomach. As she moved in her stretching exercises, she arched her back where muscles rippled like those of a disciplined dancer. Her legs were long, a dancer's legs, well toned with a fine swell of calf and trim ankles.

Hitchcock methodically studied her feet—well manicured and a perfect size seven and a half, he estimated, and he knew his feet. He licked his lips. The size of her feet was important. They would show in close-up during the Shower Sequence. Hitch had a serious thing about feet. "Haven't you ever heard about a foot fetish, my dear?" he once replied when an actress asked about his interest in her feet.

Robust, energetic, and breezy, the redhead exuded health and wholesomeness. Her carriage was erect, graceful, poised, and as limber and lithe as a cat's. She was the ultimate outdoors person—a deep-sea fisherman, bareback horseback rider, motorcycle rider, and mountain hiker who spent her days swimming, sunbathing, playing nude volleyball, or

posing under hot lights. She spent her nights parading in elaborate costumes and on nightclub stages in Vegas or Miami or Manhattan.

She paused in her stretching, both arms above her head, fingers
reaching toward the rafters where soft murmurs and sighs of apprecia-
tion emanated from the workmen. There were even sharp intakes of
breath from those who had no business up there. She waggled her fingers
at the unseen men, lowered her arms, and confidently placed one open
hand on the long curve of her hip. To Hitch, the redhead was perfectly
sunny faced and radiant, but costumer Rita Riggs, who had the sharpest
eyes in the business (second only to Alma Hitchcock's), found a flaw. A
faint spray of barely concealed freckles showed across her nose and more
trailed across the hollow of her breasts. Wearing the robe had worn off
some of her body makeup. "Makeup!" Riggs whispered. A thin young
man scurried up with a battered kit and corrected the imperfection. His
hands shook a little as he leaned over her breasts, which shook deli-
ciously from the application of his tiny sponge.

"This first morning," the redhead recalled, "I had to be in Makeup
at 5:00 A.M. The whole process lasted about five hours (though it got
shorter as the days went on). Off-set, two men worked on me, both full
makeup and wig to match Janet Leigh's hair, but gray because this was
a black-and-white film." The short wig they fitted onto her hid the long
fiery-auburn locks that made her such a highly sought photographer's
model. Lensmen hinted she had "a bit of a temper" to go with the bright
red hair that cascaded to her shoulders.

Hitchcock's nudist had a mind of her own but little vanity. Hitch was
a most unhappy man because of his restricted diet (his blood pressure
and weight kept him from enjoying the gourmet foods he craved) and
two recent box office flops (*The Wrong Man* and *Vertigo*), his determined
attempt at fine art. Hitch suspected the redhead might even be fun. He
envied her since he had very little fun outside of work. Hitch found the
nudist's coloring a most attractive feature. Her warm, healthy color, she
assured him, was "just a golden tan," the result of her Scottish, English,
Welsh, and German ancestry. What a shame this symphony of pale reds
and pinks, greens and pure pale whites on a predominant golden field
would be lost in his film. The redhead would have been great in color,

but *Psycho* was a throwback, shot in black and white (as was Hitch's anthology television show) to make the blood and subject matter less gruesome. It was also economical. It had to be. Hitch was bankrolling the movie himself, something no director likes to do, though some do agree to pay a percentage of any overages. With *Psycho*, Hitch was on the hook for all the cost overruns and forgoing his usual $250,000 salary.

He had to admit the redheaded nudist had something—an indefinable quality no different from the portrait over the mantel in the famous 1940s noir film *Laura*. Laura's painted image had so enthralled the detective sent to investigate her murder that he had fallen in love with a dead woman. In the end, Laura had turned up alive. In the noir genre, Hitch's *Vertigo* was the closest film to *Laura*. Both had a death and resurrection plot and an obsessive detective in love with a figment of his imagination.

"Even in a city swarming with beautiful girls," one photographer remarked of the redhead, "it's rare to find one with such all-round physical perfection as this twenty-three-year-old whose natural charm and intelligence make her supple thirty-six/twenty-three/thirty-five contours doubly appealing." She stood five feet, three and three quarters inches barefoot, the same height as Janet Leigh and three inches shorter than Hitch. More important, her figure approximated the star's spectacular thirty-seven/twenty-two/thirty-five curves, one of the reasons she had been hired as the star's body double. Such curvaceousness had its difficulties: Leigh had difficulty buying swimsuits: "If I fit on the bottom," she complained, "the top was too small." In spite of her voluptuous figure, Janet Leigh had a boyish butt like the redhead's. The redhead's breasts were just as sharply curved so that her nipples (like Janet's) rested just slightly atop her breasts rather than exactly on the tips. Janet Leigh's waist (officially listed as twenty-one inches) had filled out an inch. The redhead's was smaller and, though doubling for the thirty-two-year-old star, she was considerably younger. Four years earlier, at age seventeen (already a beauty queen and TV advertising model), she had graduated from Monrovia High a year early. Since then she had been a magazine cover girl and a chorus dancer at the El Rancho Vegas Casino Hotel, the International Hotel in Miami Beach, and the Latin Quarter in Manhattan.

Marli Renfro, the redhead's stage and modeling name, was a perfect name for stardom. Four syllable names like hers were usually composed in Hollywood with the right letter count to fit on theater marquees. Alan Ladd's was. Her name also had a rhythm that made it memorable. It was only slightly altered from her true first name, Marlys (pronounced *Mar-Less*). In childhood, her closest friends had nicknamed her Mouse, Marlys Mouse, and Marli Ruffles. But for *Psycho*, her name didn't matter. Her identity was to be kept secret. Around the Universal-Revue lot she became known as the "Mystery Girl."

Hitch had confided to *Psycho* screenwriter Joseph Stefano in preproduction that he feared he was going to face an obstacle with Janet Leigh. "She's very self-conscious about her breasts," he said. "She thinks they're too big . . ." Janet had been anxious during the opening scene in a Phoenix hotel room just standing around the set in her brassiere. Frankly, Hitch said, she should not have been wearing a brassiere at all. "It would have been more interesting if the girl's bare breasts had been rubbing against the man's chest," he said with an impish smile. Hitch considered her costar, handsome John Gavin, an "awfully cold fish," who drained away the last drop of sexual chemistry between himself and Janet. To remedy this, Hitchcock had whispered to Janet, as the Rock Hudson look-alike lay on the bed, that she should take matters "in hand." "You wouldn't believe it," Hitch told Stefano. "Mr. Gavin had an erection during the bed scene."

The first time on-set makeup man Jack Barron discussed the Shower Sequence with the director, Hitch revealed he was going to attempt to convince Janet to do the scene in the nude. It didn't surprise Barron that Leigh wasn't having any part of it. "As time went on, [Hitch] said he'd try 'for the European version,'" Barron said, "but she refused." According to Marshall Schlom, the on-set script supervisor, "Some directors would announce 'You will do nudity,' but he wasn't about to make Janet uncomfortable or touch anything distasteful on the screen."

"Of course, Mr. Hitchcock never asked me to do the scene in the nude," Janet reported in her memoir, "because showing nudity on the screen was simply out of the question." She also denied saying her breasts were too big. She called them a blessing from God.

Janet had nothing against nudity. She believed that imagination is much stronger than what you can see, and of course, she was right. Hitchcock understood her reticence and promised that they would cover her up as much as they could for the Shower Sequence and get it over with as rapidly as possible. "I want no problems or embarrassment for Janet," Hitch said and, in spite of a recurring cruel and vindictive streak he sometimes unleashed on his leading ladies, he actually meant it this time.

Because he was casting a star, Hitch knew the nude scenes were going to be difficult. While the censors still wouldn't permit nudity in Hollywood motion pictures, the laws had been recently relaxed, largely through the efforts of *Playboy*'s dynamic young publisher, Hugh Hefner, who had successfully sued the U.S. Post Office. Screen nudity ran against the rigid morality of the time and the inflexible prudishness of a nation founded by Puritans. Even the Salem witch hunts had continued in the 1950s with the persecution of the "Hollywood Ten" and the sacrificial victims of Senator "Tailgunner Joe" McCarthy. Hitch would probably "double" Janet, but he still wanted options for costuming and makeup if she was willing to go nude or partially nude.

"I want someone whose job it is to be naked on a set so I don't have to worry about covering her," Hitchcock told Stefano, who considered Hitch's use of a nude body double to be shrewd and absolutely essential. Hitch had had a rubber torso specially made for the nude shower scene, but decided he wasn't going to use it. "I used a live girl instead," he said later, "a naked model who stood in for Janet Leigh."

A few days earlier, Mario Caselli, a frequent *Playboy* contributor, had been photographing Marli Renfro, one of his favorite models, in his Hollywood studio. "I worked a lot with Mario," said Marli. "For years he did the covers of *TV Guide*. I was working in a shoot with him in [a] brass bathtub and he kept wanting me to smile and I didn't smile in any of my photos. I wasn't sullen. I just didn't see anything to smile about." When Marli did smile, it was pleasant and with dimples.

The redhead had secured Caselli on her own, without an agent, but recently had been considering obtaining an agent for acting jobs. "I didn't need one for modeling," Marli reasoned. "I didn't want a large agency because I would get swallowed up. I didn't want to get a small one that didn't know what they were doing. So I ended up not having an agent at all. Ambitious? I just sort of flitted along, really." That morning Caselli just happened to mention a job at Universal International. "UI is looking for a model for a movie they're doing," Mario told her and suggested she call and go for an interview, which she did.

"I don't remember who I spoke with initially," she said, "but he was a 'producer type.' I got an appointment the next day, went in, talked with him. Everything was fine and he took me on the set.

"I had to strip down for both Janet in her trailer and for Alfred Hitchcock on the sound stage." While Hitch was studying her, Marli was studying him. He looked so much as he did on TV that she could almost hear the strains of Gounod's "The Funeral March of a Marionette," Hitch's well-known theme music. "I was and am a huge fan of Hitch's and would have worked for free," she said. It was a common sentiment, and one Hitch encouraged.

"That same day, I was hired as Janet's double for the shower scene in *Psycho*. Originally I was hired for two, three days, but as filming went on it turned into almost one-and-one-half weeks." The parsimonious Hitchcock had hired Marli at a total cost of $500, though Janet Leigh, who seemed a little resentful of her, sniffed that it was only $400. "When I started modeling, like everyone else I got ten dollars an hour," said Marli. "It wasn't long before friends of mine told me, 'You've got to charge more.' So I went up to twenty-five an hour and a hundred and fifty a day."

The night before the shoot, actor Vince Edwards, an old friend of Marli's, had asked her out to dinner. "I told him I couldn't go," she said, "because I had promised artist Betti DiJulio, a friend of my parents, that I would pose for an oil painting and I had the *Psycho* shoot in the morning.

" 'Well, why don't I drive you?' he said.

"So Vince and I drove down to Manhattan Beach in his powder blue convertible." Edwards, who had acted on *Alfred Hitchcock Presents* and in Kubrick's *The Killing*, would be the biggest star on television (as hard-edged doctor Ben Casey) by this time the following year. "We got there and Betti says, 'Well I'd like to have you nude for the oil.' I looked at Vince for a minute. He looked away, shrugged and I finally said, 'Okay,' and I did. There weren't any jokes or anything like that while I was posing. I wouldn't have put up with that." After hours in makeup the next morning, Marli was ready for her scene. "The makeup artist, a very nice man, walked with me to the sound stage. I had been there for my interview and knew what it looked like and knew what to expect."

As Marli walked to the sound stage, passing actors in costume and workmen carrying scenery, her white robe cinched tight at her waist, she suffered a moment of nervousness. What was it going to be like appearing nude in front of so many clothed people in public—other actors, camera crew, electricians, grips, the script girl, the director Mr. Hitchcock, and various producers? She wondered if the screenwriter Joseph Stefano or even Robert Bloch, author of the novel *Psycho*, would be there. Ahead she saw a sign that loudly proclaimed: CLOSED SET—NO ADMITTANCE. RED LIGHTS FLASHING!!! "I relaxed a little then," she said. "Everything was going to be all right. Wrong! We open the door, walk in, and what do we see? To our right they had a couple of bleachers set up about half-full with the press and media [LA *Mirror* film critic Dick Williams and journalists from the LA *Times*, *Variety*, and *Hollywood Reporter*] and the actors from various shows being filmed. So much for CLOSED SET!" Marli was irritated. There was a flash of that fiery temperament.

"My first thought was that they were thinking that I was a stripper and was going to put on a show for them which I am not about to do. I wasn't a stripper, I was a chorus dancer. So I thought I'd dispel that notion. I decided that everyone else would react to my behavior so I made up my mind to treat the whole business as the most natural thing in the world. It was really easy because, of course, everybody was expecting a stripper, with a lot of nonsense about 'unveiling' for the big scenes. So of course they were all off guard when I just approached the whole thing as a simple, natural job." She laughed at the memory.

"I go to where I'm supposed to be and when I'm called upon to do my 'bit' I just took off the cotton robe and started doing stretching exercises and ignoring everybody." Marli interlaced her fingers, turned her palms out, extended her arms, and gently twisted her torso back and forth at the waist, keeping her knees slightly flexed. "How boring they must have thought. It wasn't long before the bleachers were cleared."

The Mirror's Dick Williams, sitting in the bleachers, considered Marli's approach a classic demonstration of the right attitude. "It made the nudity legitimate, not something dirty," he wrote, thinking she was like the girl next door. As much as Marli disliked being called a stripper, she disliked even more being stereotyped as "the All-American Girl." "I don't fit into any category," she said. "I'm just Marli Renfro."

She studied the set, or actually one of two on Stage 18-A. It was four "wild" walls, really no more wide than the six-foot tub, so tiny Hitchcock could barely get a camera in there much less the three prop men he would need with the nude body double. Altogether, the entire set couldn't have been more than twelve by twelve. To allow Hitchcock to place his cameras without restriction, film designers Robert Clatworthy and Joseph Hurley's four-walled set had detachable, breakaway walls. He could shoot the shower and tub unit either separately or attached to the larger, full set of the bathroom, a set six feet from the other tub wall to wall. The studio mill had constructed a special scaffold, a raised platform necessary for many of the shots, and the crew tried to imagine the portly Hitch up there.

The bathroom set was packed with highly reflective surfaces, dazzling white plastic tiles, a shower with a translucent curtain, and a soiled toilet with a ring around the water level to make it even more objectionable to the censors. Every bit of metal had been polished. It was the way Hitchcock liked his bathrooms. But the blinding whiteness would give the film's cinematographer, Jack Russell, Hitch's TV cameraman, problems and cause one of Hitchcock's rare reshoots. His usual cinematographer Robert Burks, who had begun his collaboration with Hitch while making Strangers on a Train in 1950, would shoot all of Hitchcock's subsequent films with the sole exception of Psycho.

Everything about Production #9401 was a mystery. On November 11, 1959, Hitch's second unit crew had captured the first footage of Psycho, shots of Highway 95 doubling for the Phoenix highway. Second unit cameraman Rex Wimpy's name on the clapboard preceded every shot and the code name "Wimpy" made an excellent, ready-made subterfuge.

Hitch wanted the prying eyes of reporters kept away from *Psycho*, but because he had a devious mind, he did all he could to excite their interest. First he placed an empty chair on the set that had "MRS. BATES" across the canvas back and posed in it. It was such an effective ploy that established actresses applied for the nonexistent part of Norman Bates's mother.

"The presence of Miss Renfro is solely for a rearview scene of Miss Leigh," Hitch assured the assembled press in the bleachers this Friday morning. They bought it. "Hollywood moviemakers have always been deliberately coy," scrawled Williams, balancing his reporter's notebook on his knee, "when filming bath, shower, or pool scenes in which the feminine star supposedly bathes in the nude. The press agents announce the set is 'closed' to everyone except the crew, then manage to slip all the correspondents—and often the photographers as well—onto the scene. It's all a harmless game, because the bathing lady always wears a flesh-colored bathing suit. But Alfred Hitchcock dispensed with this usual procedure while filming a shower scene for the latest shocker. He needed a brief rearview scene of Janet Leigh in a shower, he explained, with no distracting shoulder straps or bathing suit or bra. So he had hired a professional model accustomed to posing nude for art classes. She was so business-like and nonchalant about her bareness during the preparation and shooting of the scene that all snickering, covert peeks and grins totally disappeared among the crew."

Marli was a member of the Sundial Club, a traveling Los Angeles nudist organization that moves to different venues. She was natural about being nude because she was accustomed to the wholesome idea that there is nothing obscene about the human body. Marli, who had heard the director could be aloof, found Hitchcock to be always cordial and friendly. "He did all he could to make me comfortable," said Marli. The pleasant atmosphere relaxed her just as it had with Vince Edwards the night before. Hitchcock went to his chair and plumped down. Marli studied the roly-poly figure carefully folding his London *Times* and placing it within reach on a little table. He looked around for familiar faces. So did Marli. She knew Riggs and Helen Colvig, the wardrobe supervisor, but on-set makeup artist Jack Barron and effects supervisor Robert

Dawn were nowhere in sight. For the nude scene they had been replaced by body makeup *women*. Actor Anthony Perkins, who was to play Norman Bates, was also among the missing.

In his short novel, Robert Bloch describes the character Norman Bates as a fat, middle-aged, alcoholic motel owner who looks after his ailing, demanding mother. But in early May, Stefano had drastically altered Norman in his film script, making him a younger, more appealing character, a nervous big kid who is brooding and clumsy. Norman would be another of Hitch's sympathetic villains like Raymond Burr in *Rear Window*. Hitchcock read the screenwriter's description—"late 20s, thin and tall, soft-spoken and hesitant . . . something oddly touching in his manner," and looked up at Stefano with a grin. "In other words, Joseph," he said, "you're talking about Anthony Perkins. Well, that's who I would like to play it."

The twenty-seven-year-old Perkins owed Paramount a picture and had signed on blind, without reading the script. Like Hitch, Tony had a reputation for being standoffish, occasionally cruel, but Marli had a way of making people feel they had known her for years. She was certain she and Tony would get along when they finally met.

Perkins was due in New York to attend run-throughs of *Greenwillow*, a Frank Loesser musical slated for Broadway at the Alvin Theatre. His co-stars, Ellen McCown, Pert Kelton, and Cecil Kellaway, had already delayed rehearsals to accommodate Tony's *Psycho* filming schedule. This delay had alienated the homophobic Loesser, who would retaliate by forcing Perkins to sing his big solo number, "Never Will I Marry," in a register too high for his natural baritone. Tony, understandably keyed up, was under a lot of pressure to get back to Broadway before the start of final rehearsals on December 31.

"Look, I've got to take some of these rehearsals, and . . . and . . ." Tony nervously stammered to Hitchcock.

"Go ahead, we don't need you for this," Hitch replied coolly. He liked Tony immensely, considered him an intellectual equal, and even took suggestions from him on how to play the homicidal boy next door. It was Tony who suggested Norman have a habit of eating candy corn like a bird.

The real reason Hitchcock allowed Perkins to fly to New York for his play was this: "Tony, who is excessively shy around women should be spared unnecessary embarrassment or discomfort around a nude woman," he said. "It just wouldn't be very nice." When Tony heard what Hitchcock had said, he remarked, "That was sweet of him. Typical of his generosity. Whether imaginary or based on fantasy, still it was awful nice of him to have the idea." Hitch knew those rumors concerning Tony and actor Tab Hunter held some truth.

Just as Janet Leigh had a body double, so did the male star of *Psycho* in his drag role as Norman's dead mother. "In my novel," Bloch wrote, "following Freudian precepts, I made Norman Bates a transvestite who dressed up as his mother in a wig whenever he committed those crimes. Much to my surprise, I discovered that the actual killer dressed up also, but he allegedly wore the breasts and skin of his mother . . . who had died twelve years previously. He had kept her room inviolate and untouched since that time." Margo Epper, a twenty-four-year-old stunt double (who are used for dangerous sequences) was selected to double in the shots of Mother stalking toward the shower curtain with a raised knife. "You only have to see the film to see that the silhouette coming in that door has as little resemblance to me as any silhouette could," said Tony, who was six-foot-two. Yet, of all people Hitch could possibly have chosen, Epper, a horsewoman like Marli, came the nearest to having Tony's square shoulders and slender hips.

"I worked with Perkins's double a few times, all in the shower," Marli said, "but I wasn't aware that Tony's stunt double had a stunt double until later." The silhouetted Mother Bates behind the shower curtain was Ann Dore, an uncredited actress who handled all the shots involving physical contact with the terrified victim. And there was yet another Mother double, Mitzi, a little person used for physical scenes involving an overhead view on the stair landing inside the Bates Mansion.

For Mother's demanding and rancorous off-stage voice, Tony sold Hitch on his Montana friend Paul Jasmin. "He does this great old lady voice," Tony said enthusiastically. "Listen to this tape." For years Jasmin had hoodwinked other actors with bogus telephone calls using his character Eunice Ayers, "a no-bullshit Marjorie Main-kind of rawboned backwoods gal." Jasmin was hired. His shrewish vocal characterization would be spliced and mixed with the voices of versatile movie and *Dragnet* radio star Virginia Gregg and actor Jeanette Nolan. Including Tony Perkins, it took seven people to create Mother Bates. Hitch would do anything to outwit the audience, which he loved to do and never more so than in *Psycho*. He was going to make a rut in that garden path as he led them down it. There would be surprises behind every hedge.

Because Hitchcock had accepted Stefano's first draft, the final script with only four minor sets of revisions made between October 19 and November 15 was not the multicolored script commonly seen on film sets. Scripts are often changed—yellow or first preliminary green, blue pages for the first change, pink for the second, yellow for the third—until they have exhausted the rainbow and have to start over with white. Revisions on blue paper were inserted in the final script, the final white. Revisions to the revisions were done in goldenrod. Stefano's script was snow white.

In Hitch's mind, the film was already done on paper. Filming to him was the boring part. The enjoyable part took place in his office as he broke up scenes into distinct shots, sketched them out and laid out the entire picture. As he once told screenwriter John Michael Hayes: "All we have to do now is go on the set and make sure they do what we've given them."

Wisely, Hitchcock held back the last pages of the script from prying eyes. He rarely referred to it while shooting. "I know it by heart," he explained, "just as an orchestra conductor needs not to look at the score." Before beginning, Hitchcock had sworn everyone on the set to secrecy about what little they did know, including stars Janet Leigh, Tony Perkins, John Gavin, and Vera Miles. "When we started to work," said Miles that first morning, "we all had to raise our right hands and promise not to divulge one word of the story." Hitch also required Paul Jasmin to be on-set most days so he could get a feel for the atmosphere, but the voice actor remained unenlightened since he too was forbidden to read the final pages.

On her first morning, Marli discovered the script embargo included her. "Yes, Hitch pledged everyone not to mention the ending to anyone," she said. "Keep your lips sealed about the surprise ending!" he said and as the others had, Marli raised her hand and promised not to tell, knowing how shocking it was to kill off the leading character halfway through the picture, and then remembering with a shudder she was playing that character.

All this morning rubberneckers had congregated outside Stage 18-A as if it were the payroll window. "I think Hitchcock deliberately hired the model," Janet Leigh reported of Marli, "partly to plant the seed in people's minds that the picture had nudity. He had started to manipulate the audience before the film was even in a theatre and got glee from teasing the pros, the non-press, the sophisticated, and the naive. He knew his rumor would eventually become the Gospel truth . . . to such an extent that when the viewer came out of the movie houses they would swear on the Bible that they had seen nudity, gushing blood, and weapon penetration. Such was Alfred Hitchcock's gift."

Hitch demanded tight security. Rita Riggs saw the press and photographers outside dying to come on-set. "Mr. Hitchcock fed them precisely what he wanted them to know," she said, "and they actually felt privileged." Soon he had all of Hollywood talking about the "strange, disturbing movie" he was making. The formally dressed guards at the doors of the closed set pounced on those who managed to slip in and escorted them out with a polite, "No photos! No visitors! Thank you very much." But his gatekeepers were not foolproof. The unauthorized gawkers on the gantries above were evidence of that. Janet Leigh, while worried about her own privacy, wasn't too worried about Marli's. "Being a body double," Janet said, "she is accustomed to being nude, it being all in a day's work." Janet also had a stand-in who, unlike body doubles, was always dressed and used for non-filming purposes such as lighting adjustments while Leigh was elsewhere.

Even fewer off-set knew the film's surprise ending and Hitchcock wanted to keep it that way. Though Bloch's hardcover *Psycho* had sold 10,000 copies, those were mostly gone. Hitch, who had skimmed the novel over one entire weekend at his house on Bellagio Road in Bel-Air, had snapped up any remaining copies. In April, Fawcett Publications had rushed out paperbacks that whipped through nine printings by summer, but now those were mostly gone because Hitch had bought those too.

His serious illness in 1957 and that of his wife, Alma, the following year had prepared Hitch for instant death as had nothing else before. Only the suddenness of the shower murder "coming out of the blue" had appealed to him about *Psycho*. Nothing more. "Naked in a confined space," Bloch had reasoned, "we feel we're alone and then—well, a sudden intrusion is a *very* shocking thing." Now a simple shower bath had taken on an ominous quality and, in Hitchcock's hands, art.

Hitch hired designer Saul Bass for thirteen consecutive weeks' work to design the titles and paid him $2000 more to storyboard the Shower Sequence. Bass's storyboards laid out "a purist notion" of bloodless murder (except for a close-up of the victim's bloodstained hands reaching for her slashed neck), a series of repetitive motions but little activity. "After all," Bass told author Stephen Rebello in his groundbreaking book on *Psycho*, "all that happens was simply a woman takes a shower, gets hit, and slowly slides down the tub. Instead, [we film] a repetitive series of motions: 'She's taking a shower, taking a shower, taking a shower. She's hit-hit-hit-hit-hit. She slides-slides-slides. She's hit-hit-hit-hit. She slides-slides-slides.'"

On December 10, Bass had used a spartan set to shoot test footage. "I used the stand-in for Janet to shoot it ["If I did test footage," Marli said, "I don't remember it, as it was no big deal."] and at the end of the day had her stay a little longer." He set up a key light and used a leased Eclair camera, one of the five Orson Welles had convinced Universal to purchase for *Touch of Evil*. The handheld camera contained a spring-loaded magazine which allowed him to shoot twenty-five feet of test footage and chop it together to see if his concept would work. It did, Bass thought, but he would have to cut just above the nipple to get by the censors. "Forty or sixty cuts was just a very new idea stylistically." He used a rapid-cutting, staccato montage technique to deliver an impressionistic, rather than linear view of the shower murder so "the audience won't know what the hell is going on."

Hitch approved Bass's test footage and, adverse to give compliments except through Alma, privately admitted Bass was the best designer bar none. After he showed Janet Leigh the miniature sets he had built of every scene, Hitch laid out Bass's storyboards and explained how he was going to shoot the scene. "Every move was planned before a performer even talked with him," Janet wrote. "The storyboards detailed all the angles so I knew the camera would be there, then there. The camera was at different places all the time."

"Do I need to prepare anything?" she asked.

"No," said Hitch. "We'll cover up as much as we can and we'll never show any actual stabbing." Finally, he laid down his one inviolate rule. "My camera is absolute," he said, explaining that he told his story through its lens. "I need you to move when my camera moves; stop when my camera stops. I'm confident you'll be able to find your motivation to justify the motion . . ." After poring over the Shower Sequence storyboards—the most significant component of *Psycho* and one that would require maximum coordination from his collaborators—Hitch estimated approximately eighty camera setups would be needed for less than fifty seconds of screen time. Before beginning principal photography for the shower scene, he locked down every predictable element and banned anything unpredictable from the set. The daily production sheet for the Shower Sequence read: Int. Bathroom—Cabin One, 11 days.

On Monday, December 14, Janet Leigh, clad in a bathing suit, rehearsed the crucial Shower Sequence. Master illustrator Joseph Hurley and production designer Robert Clatworthy had hastily constructed a mockup shower (really only two flat walls and a bathtub) on the huge Phantom Stage. When Hitchcock auditioned the shower, things went terribly wrong. The tub didn't drain properly, the paint wasn't completely dry, and the shower spray sent it splashing all over the place. When Hurley and Clatworthy walked onto the darkened stage they saw the wardrobe girl wiping off Hitch's blue serge suit with a towel. "Fellows," Hitch said in a deadpan monotone, "this is quite inadequate. I believe this falls under the heading of the Raised Eyebrow Department." Janet in her bathing suit didn't work out, so on Tuesday, December 15, Hitch put out a call for a body double. The next day, Mario Casselli told Marli about the *Psycho* job. She auditioned on Thursday and was hired. The Shower Sequence filming began in earnest on Friday, December 18.

This first morning of the Shower Sequence, Marli waited on Stage 18-A as Hitch read his paper and told amusing stories, mostly naughty. He was interesting, even charming, and she was comfortable in her nudity. The set was comfortable. Hitchcock, who had a tendency to sweat, hated heat and hated cold and so the temperature was always kept moderate. The shoot had originally been set for 9:00 A.M. and it was now well after 10:00 A.M., though no one seemed in any hurry. Hitch had gotten to work by 8:30 A.M. His limo driver had picked him up (Hitch had never had a license) and driven him over the hill to North Hollywood to the impoverished Universal-Revue lot (they were $2 million in debt). Two years earlier, MCA had purchased the Universal Studios lots, the former Taylor Ranch, for their television branch, Revue Studios. When Hitch filmed prologues and epilogues for his TV show, ten at a time, he made the same trip.

Normally, he worked out of a luxurious office in the Paramount Producers' Building on Melrose, but Paramount had refused to finance *Psycho*, and even claimed all their sound stages were filled. Hitch could see they were not. So he personally put up over $800,000 to pay for *Psycho* himself. As sole producer, he would defer his director's fee in exchange for a percentage and 60 percent ownership of the negative, and prepare *Psycho* at Paramount, who would promote the film as the last of his five-picture commitment to them. For greatest efficiency and speed Hitch imported the TV crew from his CBS program to Revue Studios. He intended to prove that, like reigning exploitation kings Roger Corman and William Castle, he could make a low-budget, quality box-office hit at a small studio and do it in black and white.

From his limo, Hitch saw his Shamley Productions lodged in a modest bungalow along winding paths on the rustic Revue Studios lot in North Hollywood. He enjoyed working on the tight little island where most everyone had a British accent. He could observe well-manicured flower beds, waddling ducks, and leaping rabbits from its windows and hear the roar of traffic on Lankershim Boulevard, the site of the used-car-lot scene in *Psycho*. As his car moved along, he surveyed the vacant sound stages of this "lowbrow House of Horrors."

His driver swung wide onto Laramie Street, a thoroughfare named for a Revue Western on NBC-TV, and reached a rangy hillside just off Laramie on the back lot. In a vacant area next to Singapore Lake (renamed Falls Pond), loomed the Bates gingerbread house, or at least its left and right facade, all Hitch needed to film. His crew had cannibalized stock buildings on the Universal lot to keep costs down but it still cost Hitch $15,000. "California Gothic," he called it, having seen similar architecture with wooden watchtowers in downtown Santa Cruz near his Scots Valley ranch. Assistant director Hilton Green thought the fictional Bates house was supposed to be located up around Tulare, California. But his mansion had a complicated pedigree. First, Hitch's set-building architects had been inspired by the Hotel McCray on Beach Hill on Front Street as well as the Berhheim House at Broadway. The mansion's massive door, an exact reproduction of the Crocker House's door in San Francisco, had been constructed for another movie. The front of the house and its tower had been used for the *Harvey* house on Colonial Street. A final inspiration for the creepy Victorian was Edward Hopper's stark painting of an Iowa house called *The House by the Rails*.

The interiors of the Bates house were on Stage 18-A *and* on the Phantom Stage, which offered enough height for Hitch's planned aerial views. The shower and motel rooms—"12 rooms, 12 vacancies"—were separate sets so close that when Marli walked to the door she could see the ominous house on the hill from the set.

Finally, they got down to work. Hitch had thought about every shot beforehand so he wouldn't have to waste everybody's time thinking about what to do next. The first setup was finished. "Cut—print!" Hitch said crisply. "Let's move on." And the grips and set decorator leaped into action because they knew what the next shot was going to be. By 4:30 P.M., Hitch had made up for the time he had spent chatting. "The final straw came," reporter Williams noted on his pad, "when director Hitchcock, placing the model for her shower scene, toted a tape measure from camera to shoulder and coolly held it there while the cameraman noted the distance."

"I found it no different"—Hitchcock yawned—"than if she had been wearing a floorlength Hawaiian muumuu."

Before Marli knew it, her first day of actual filming was over. Hitch never worked past 6:00 P.M. and, with his television crew, worked even faster than usual. He started home without a word, still fuming that he wouldn't be able to do his expensive four-mile-long helicopter shot over Phoenix, which tracked uninterrupted to the open window of Janet Leigh and John Gavin's seedy hotel room. Janet was fresh from Orson Welles's *Touch of Evil*, which held the current record for the longest tracking shot in movie history. Hitchcock, with his passion for trick shots, had intended to outdo the "Boy Wonder," but the period's camera equipment was not advanced enough to accomplish his difficult shot. All right, then he would outdo Welles with his Shower Sequence. He would show them all.

Even Hitch's unit manager, Lew Leary, said of the Shower Sequence, "There is no way Hitchcock is going to get away with this scene." Oh, really, Hitch thought. Well, he would show him. He would show that French upstart, Henri-Georges Clouzot, with his black-and-white *Diabolique* and its bathroom scene (which Hitch privately envied). He would show Paramount, for passing on participating in the making of the movie, and give his all to *Psycho*. It was unthinkable for them to be proven right in their lack of faith.

Not far away an intense, gray-haired woman was fuming, too. Mother had this crazy young son (who looked a lot like Tony Perkins) who had taken to dating elderly women and was obsessed with the upcoming execution of a possibly innocent man.

Chapter Two
Sonny and Mother

J ust over eight miles from the *Psycho* set and eight tenths of a mile from Marli's home, Mother gazed from the restaurant window and gauged the monotonous traffic crawling past on West Sunset Boulevard. At 4:30 P.M. the flow was turgid as glue, the honk of horns and screech of brakes deafening. Usually Mother enjoyed the energy of the movers and shakers, the aspiring Hollywood types fighting their way home, or to an evening screening, or to a studio to watch rushes of the latest about-to-be-released film. But lately there had been an unhealthy feel to the street. It showed in the eyes of local shopkeepers walking past her front window and in the subdued steps of the neighborhood children. Perhaps it was the shooting death of the young redhead a few doors down on the corner of North Normandie Avenue. Though the murder had happened four years earlier, it still cast a pall over this Olive Hill section on the east side of Hollywood.

Perhaps it affected Mother more strongly because Sonny had been the prime suspect in the case or perhaps it was only the hopelessness of the clawing young men and starstruck actresses in their rush to nowhere. There was something else threatening there too, like a cloud on the horizon. Along this street the Bouncing Ball Strangler, an early pattern killer, had been selecting his victims and striking with chilling, unmerciful swiftness. Sunset Boulevard and Santa Monica Boulevard run parallel for miles before bumping together just where Santa Monica intersects Sanborn Avenue, another of the Strangler's stomping grounds. Perhaps it was that more than anything else that had got folks down.

Mother was Mae Busch, the "ever lovely Mae Busch" as Sonny called her. She wasn't the silent movie star of the same name that comic Jackie Gleason used to extol on his live 1950s TV show, but still pretty well known and respected in Hollywood. Mother, a plump and normally jolly woman, was the former owner and operator of the Busch's Gardens family restaurant, had been for twenty years until her husband's death. Then they lost everything. Now she just had a share in the eatery. From the beginning, the restaurant had capitalized on the more famous name of a local tourist attraction, Busch Gardens, to attract customers.

Sonny (she sometimes called him "Junior") had lived with Mother for the last three years (and off and on before that) at 5623 Virginia Avenue, one of Mother's several apartment buildings. These days, each minute Sonny stayed with her seemed unbearable. Sonny thought she was overprotective and jealous of his involvement with any other woman, and at times her overbearingness made him feel as if she were assuming his personality and he hers.

Mother didn't know how much longer she could put up with Sonny's nervousness and the strange hours he kept. Together, the pair went together like oil and water or, more aptly, gasoline and fire. Above the din of the traffic, the clatter of utensils in the kitchen, and the murmur of diners, Sonny's nasal voice rose. He was talking to the bartender, whom he often confided in, more so than in her or the friends he pretended to have. Mother left the window and walked into the kitchen where she saw Sonny just zipping up his plaid jacket. It hung carelessly on his bony shoulders. His checkered shirt—a small, neat pattern of squares—hung halfway out tan trousers, which bagged on his wiry frame.

Sonny was stringy and undernourished, his 140 pounds stretched to breaking over a lanky six feet. He was as giraffe-necked and broad-shouldered as Tony Perkins, whom he resembled in build, height, and age, but a Tony Perkins cobbled together with mismatched pieces and held together with spit and despair. Sonny was as shy as Tony and fit Stefano's description of Norman Bates: "late 20s, thin and tall, soft-spoken and hesitant . . . oddly touching."

"Gawkiness was something Tony came more than prepared to play," star Jean Simmons said of the actor, and could have said the same of Sonny if she had ever met him. The taciturn Sonny even had the same problems with his mother that the fictional Norman Bates and the real-life Tony Perkins had with theirs (though Sonny didn't know that yet). Like Tony, Sonny was a clean-cut boy next door with the faint smile of a mother's boy and easily wounded feelings like a child. Tony, who had lost his father at age five, as Sonny had, had grown up as a repressed mama's boy. So had Norman. "She—she had to raise me—all by herself, after my father died," he says in *Psycho* in a speech written by Tony. "I was only five and it—it must have been quite a strain for her."

"She wasn't like a regular mother," Sonny would say of his own parent, and his eyes would roll behind the thick lenses of his glasses in mock disbelief and the brief trace of a crooked smile would flit about his lips. He had a powerful, thick neck that supported a small, triangular-shaped head. Sonny looked like a diamondback rattler.

Sonny made attempts to be attractive. He kept his brown hair short in a burr cut on top, where the sun had bleached it with little waves of gold, but generally it was a muddy field. He kept it longer and crop-eared on the sides, which made his ears stand out prominently. Sonny was what the police sketch artists call a macrotous type: large eared. He would have been perfectly clean-cut if a wispy mustache (like chocolate milk) was not fighting to take hold. His lips were sensual, full in a sharp, triangular face. His gauntness and hollow cheeks only accentuated the general impression of a small head stuck atop a thick neck.

He looked like an accountant, a homicidal accountant if anyone looked deeply enough, though most did not. His gold-rimmed glasses magnified two sleepy eyes—what shade of blue were they? Mother always had trouble pinpointing their color because they kept changing with the time of day and Sonny's transitory moods. His eyes were as weak as those of the fictional Norman Bates, but his eyeglasses were first class, Mother had to admit that. Sonny was proud he had made them himself as part of his job at the Hollywood Optical Laboratory on Hillhurst and Prospect. The long, low building lay nearby just above Camero Avenue, a short little street to the east.

Hollywood Optical had employed Sonny as a lens polisher for some years, though in spite of his excellent work, nobody there really knew him or warmed to him. He never brought a friend to the restaurant so Mother assumed he had none. It didn't matter. A boy's best friend was his mother. Like Mother, Sonny's co-workers considered him odd. Unlike Mother, they considered him harmless. She knew things about him that were disturbing. Though the Optical Lab parking lot was nearby at Hollywood Boulevard and North Vermont Avenue, close enough to walk in a few minutes, Mother allowed Sonny to use her car to drive to work.

Mother followed him to the front door. Sonny, ever-present cigarette dangling from his lower lip, helped himself to a handful of cash from the register and stuffed it into his pocket. He scooped up the keys to her convertible from a side drawer and went out onto West Sunset Boulevard. Through the window Mother saw Sonny looking up and down the street as if making up his mind. Work at the lab was over for the day. Where was he off to now? Another of his mysterious errands, she supposed. Sonny tossed his butt into the street and lit another cigarette. Without a backward look, he gave a little over-the-shoulder wave to Mother (he could feel her watching) and, moving on long, swift legs, walked a block away to Winona Boulevard.

Mother's red-and-white '56 Super 88 Oldsmobile was parked at the curb. He loved that car. Its oval front air intake and the long chrome strip from the trailing edge of the front white sidewall to the rear bumper made it look like a rocket and himself, a rocket man. Even with the engine off the Olds appeared to be moving. Sonny slipped behind the wheel of the convertible and, in a cloud of exhaust, melded with the crawling traffic without a look at the approaching traffic or a thought of fear for his safety.

Back at the restaurant, Mother was still thinking about him. Sonny had been trouble—always—right from the beginning, right to this second, and she saw that unchanging far into the future. It wasn't fair to her. After all she had tried to do to help him, especially after her husband's death. All of Sonny's life had been spent in this neighborhood on the east side of Hollywood, a pleasant enough place with a conglomeration of shops, Chinese and Italian restaurants, dressmakers and barbershops, and abundant sun. The most impressive elements were Hollywood Presbyterian Medical Center, Kaiser Hospital, and Barnsdall Park to the northeast.

Mother recalled with dread that, as a small boy, Sonny had been given a present of three white mice. The first thing he did when he was alone in his room was to grab their heads and tails and begin to pull. He kept pulling, ignoring their squeals and high-pitched squeaks, until he had stretched the living mice out as far as they would go. Droplets of blood clung to their whiskers and their red eyes danced in pain. Then Sonny nailed them to his bedroom wall so they would stay elongated. Later he did the same to some pigeons he had captured. With their gray, black-flecked wings spread wide, he tacked them to the wallpaper so they looked as if they were still flying. Could he stuff them? He wondered. He had an interest in taxidermy but was too lazy to pursue it.

As he grew older, Sonny tortured larger domestic animals in newer and more bizarre ways. One weekend, he tied a pet pooch to a tree in a remote section of Griffith Park where he liked to go to think and scope out the ladies. He left the animal secured to the tree where it starved to death. When the dog was not found, he killed a second pet dog and threw it in the garbage can behind the restaurant so Mother couldn't miss it. When Sonny was eleven years old, he attempted to hold up his stepfather's delicatessen with a .45, but the older man swiftly disarmed him and threw him into the street.

Sonny never finished grammar school, much less high school. "They just had to pass him from grade to grade as he got bigger and was old enough to quit," Mother said, and she would begin to cry. Sonny enlisted in the army in 1952 and, surprisingly, did very well. He had a fine combat record as a rifleman and was a first-class marksman with the First Cavalry in Korea. He had a good war record. "I saw a lot of action," he said, "and I stood up to it all." Even more surprising: After the war he reenlisted. That was a mistake. When he was ordered on winter maneuvers in Japan he obstinately refused.

"I cannot go, sir," he told his captain.

"And why is that, soldier?"

"I have lost my heavy winter gloves, sir."

For this insubordination, the captain had him thrown into the stockade for six months, where he acted out against his fellow prisoners. Sonny's army superiors, to be rid of him, transferred him to Seattle where he got into a few more scrapes. Finally, he became so contrary and difficult he was given an "undesirable discharge" in 1955 and freighted back to LA where he could do some real damage.

Upon his return, Sonny joined a gang of house robbers. In a moment of expansiveness, he told Mother that over the last few months he and his two accomplices had burglarized fifty mansions in the Hollywood area, "maybe twice that number," he boasted. Because he was telling her after the fact, there wasn't much Mother could do about the crimes. Sonny claimed he had headed the gang himself, but Mother thought he was inflating his importance. Probably he had only been a member. On this point Sonny remained close-mouthed. He never revealed the exact dates of the break-ins or the names of his two accomplices who he claimed had been captured, served their time in jail, and been released. "So what purpose would it serve to give you their names," he said with a shrug. Sonny was many things but he was not a snitch. Mother, still not convinced there was a gang at all, never did find out one way or the other.

In June 1956, Sonny began working as a dishwasher at Busch's Gardens. In August, he purchased a .32 revolver from the restaurant's bartender. Steven Ernest Shaffer, a slender thirty-eight-year-old with curly dark hair and a thick mustache, was Sonny's only friend. He visited Shaffer at his home at 2000 West Miramar Street when he paid for the gun. "Say nothing about this," Sonny told him as he stowed the weapon in his belt and, whistling, left the apartment, pulling his sport shirt down to cover the weapon. He was going to look in on a girl he liked or at least felt strange feelings for.

A few doors down from Busch's Gardens, at the corner of Sunset Boulevard and Normandie Avenue, was a little variety store. Behind the counter was a pretty red-haired nineteen-year-old coed, Eudice Erenberg. Sonny watched her through the plate glass window and saw no sign of Eudice's widowed mother, who owned the store. Eudice had taken time off from school to help her out. Sonny stood smoking and listening to the little bell jingle as customers entered and exited the shop. An hour passed, yet he didn't raise a foot to enter. Sonny often dropped in on the pretty redhead to gossip with her, though it was no secret she didn't interest him romantically. Younger women just didn't attract him—when he was sober. It was a different story when he was drunk. Then any woman would do and possibly this one, too, if the circumstances were right. There was something about the redhead he couldn't shake.

A few doors up from the variety store stood a tiny bungalow in a court. He left the shop and walked there. Mrs. Elmyra Myrtle Miller, a seventy-four-year-old widow, lived there by herself, and he went up to the door. "When my folks operated the restaurant right around the corner on Sunset," Sonny said later, "I used to drop in and see the old lady all the time." Sonny, who had known Mrs. Miller all his life, called her "Auntie" and was fond of her. He rang Auntie's door at 1450 Normandie. Occasionally, he took her out on what were assumed by practically everyone except her to be dates. It was no secret that the twenty-seven-year-old Sonny liked much older women who resembled Mother though not as plump. In spite of his deep-seated mother fixation, Sonny may have actually hated Mother. It was hard to gauge his emotions because he kept so much to himself. "If only Sonny were interested in the nineteen-year-olds instead of women over sixty," thought Mother, "but he was not. He was just too shy." Thus it came as a surprise to her when Eudice, the pretty redhead at the corner store, was shot to death in early August and Sonny immediately became the prime suspect.

The day after the shooting, Shaffer, the bartender at Mother's restaurant, read that Erenberg had been shot with a .32. He froze, recalling the gun he had sold his friend Sonny, and, fearing he might be implicated, phoned the police anonymously. He had to be careful not to become entangled with the police since he had been convicted of forgery and had a record. "Shortly before Erenberg's shooting," he told an officer over the phone, "I sold a friend a .32 revolver and he told me not to say anything, not to tell anybody. Are you interested?" They were. Shaffer provided a general description of Sonny, the fact he lived in the neighborhood and knew the victim, then hung up as soon as he could. Police swiftly figured out who the bartender was talking about and sent out an all points for Sonny.

Hollywood Station cops, who patrolled Sunset and Hollywood Boulevards and the southeastern section of Hollywood Drive, located Sonny driving aimlessly in the Olds. They pulled him over, searched his car, found the .32, and brought him down to the station on a charge of suspicion of murder. Sonny was cooperative during the hour-and-fifteen-minute-long interrogation, shy and introspective yet anxious to please, but inwardly seething with anger and guilt.

"I bought the gun to protect Mother with whom I live," he explained.

Outwardly, he appeared almost heroic in his defense of her, but Sonny knew he was in trouble. He had no alibi for the time of the young girl's death. Had he done it? There were these blank spots in his memory. Sonny couldn't tell the cops he was as much in the dark as they were, so he stopped talking. "When I first came back from Korea," he said later, "I knew I had to be careful. I knew I had that urge. I knew I had to stop it. I kept going to the library for philosophy books—Socrates, Plato, Spinoza, Hegel. I'd stay in my room all night studying, trying to find out what was wrong with me." As his gun was being tested, the cops kept Sonny in a cell. By afternoon they had the ballistic results and were satisfied Sonny's gun was not the murder weapon. Still they had their doubts about the gaunt, taciturn young man. He must have done something. He was just too nervous. There were ten other murders, those of elderly women, that had gone unsolved in the area, and police questioned him about those too. Now Sonny began to twitch a little. He craved a cigarette and his glasses had steamed up.

After he returned home, Mother was especially hard on Sonny over his arrest, innocent or not, and in spite of the fact that he had gotten the gun for her benefit. In his room Sonny found another way out. He would discover who had shot the girl and get himself off the hook. Everett Wilson, a writer for *True Detective* covering the story, had interviewed witnesses at the scene and read the police reports for two days. Along the way, he picked up a tall, gangling young man who badgered him endlessly for details about the Erenberg slaying. When Wilson wasn't forthcoming with information, Sonny stubbed out his cigarette, stalked away, and drove to the *Los Angeles Herald* offices, where he began annoying the reporters there for more information.

A week after the redhead's death, Wilson reread his notes, and they brought back the memory of the young man who had questioned him so relentlessly. Sonny something. An odd neighborhood boy. Was it just morbid curiosity on his part? What if he had been talking to the girl's murderer? After a sleepless night, Wilson reached for the phone, dialed the LAPD, and told them of his suspicions. They told him that Sonny was already a suspect in the case. With the news of Sonny's unhealthy interest in the investigation, the cops were convinced they had had the right man in the first place. Somewhere there was a second gun, and they intended to find it or get Sonny to lead them to it.

When they questioned Sonny a second time, the young man began to fear he was leading a Jekyll-Hyde existence. He couldn't tell the police he often returned home at night without knowing what he had done earlier. "I'd find myself back in my room, later," he said, "and I couldn't remember what had happened. But the noise in my head would be gone." On the knife he carried, he detected rust-like traces of something that could be blood and threw it away. Sonny felt pressure from all sides, especially from the police, who he knew continued to surveil him, and from Mother. Her round, smiling face expected so much from him, and the more she smiled, the less he wanted to give. The intense stress unleashed something within himself, but he only smiled his crooked smile and contented himself with the idea that others thought he wouldn't hurt a fly.

Chapter Three
Another Day of Stabbing

itchcock took another puff on his Flor de Allones, one of the Dunhill Cuban line (still legal in the United States at the time) and on Monday morning, December 21, 1959, resumed shooting another day of the complicated and all-important Shower Sequence. Marli Renfro doffed her cotton robe, stood nude, and waited for the whirr of the camera and rush of reliably warm water. Three men were balanced on ladders, an unsteady bucket brigade, hefting their buckets and preparing to commence their cycle of refilling the huge tanks with heated water all over again. On Friday, with the long, complicated setups, they had had to struggle to maintain a comfortable temperature for her.

Florence Dee would have done Marli's long red hair if they hadn't saddled the nudist with that atrocious gray wig; Vincent Dee would have handled Marli's costume if she had had one, not just her glowing golden skin. Costumer Rita Riggs, working uncredited but glad to have the experience of working with Hitch on a film, had taken extreme care in selecting Mother Bates's clothes from used clothing stores. Hitch had specified a small printed kind of fabric with the feeling of an older person. "I remember buying the old lady shoes in Tony Perkins's size which was large. They were the longest old lady shoes you ever saw," the Boone County native said, glad to have escaped Leadhill, Arkansas. It seemed Janet Leigh's husband, Tony Curtis, had no sooner taken off his dress (as Joe/Josephine in *Some Like It Hot*) than Tony Perkins was about to put his on. Hilton Green thought the day Perkins donned Mother's wardrobe and became her would be a very special day. Joseph Stefano, whose father had been a tailor, approved of the costume. On November 11, Helen Colvig and Riggs had dressed Perkins for a test in drag and so knew the costume would work. Janet had taken a week off while Vera Miles and John Gavin were starting their scenes.

"One time I had them make me up just like they do Janet—exactly, her eyebrows and everything," Marli said. "It wasn't for any scene. I just wanted to. And oh, I looked horrible! But Janet's body and mine are very similar."

Marli stretched, feeling out the poses she would use, fully aware there would be no extensive rehearsals and they would just go straight to it. Hitchcock, who hired only the best, didn't believe in rehearsals and usually let the actor figure it out on their own. Hitch considered directing an actor in front of the cast and crew demeaning for both the actor and the director. He instead liked to work out a series of code words and signs in advance to get what he wanted: "planned spontaneity." Right from the beginning he told Marli he was pretty much going to leave her to her own devices except in the passages where he had explicit storyboard instructions to follow. To her the storyboard looked like a huge comic strip without words, but it was easy to follow. "The storyboards for that sequence were unbelievable," Riggs said. "They shot frame by frame from them because each of them had only to look at them to know exactly what the camera would see. Cinematographer Jack Russell was using fifty-millimeter lenses and thirty-five-millimeter cameras, which give the closest approximation of the human eye and permitted him to approximate the bather's point of view.

This approach also allowed the audience to view the action as if they were seeing it with their own eyes. The theme of voyeurism and "cruel eyes studying you" permeated the entire movie. Though nude, Marli

Renfro did not feel naked, yet felt probing eyes on her as she moved around to keep limber. A crack of light appearing in the far wall attracted her attention. Someone was entering the dark, silent tomb.

Earlier that morning, co-star John Gavin read that day's call sheet and saw the shower montage was still being shot. Curious, "the stiff," as Hitch called him, decided to drop by and take a peek. Ignoring the sign that said "Closed Set," he opened the door and strolled right in. No one interfered with him. Gavin felt his way along in the darkness, tripped over a cable, then got his bearings as his eyes grew accustomed to the dim light. "I walked around," said Gavin, "and all of a sudden I noticed this girl walking around absolutely stark naked. My eyes almost fell out of my head, like a great lout." He realized that no one else was paying any attention to the beautiful redhead's stunning figure and supposed that by now everyone in the crew had become completely used to her, though that seemed hard to believe to the handsome leading man.

Marli felt the vibes on the set had improved over the slightly down-in-the-mouth tenor of last Friday. Or perhaps it was her mood that had brightened. Instead of being nervous, she now felt refreshed and excited, as if the enormity of her good fortune had finally sunk in. At 9:30 Sunday night she had watched *Alfred Hitchcock Presents*, an anthology show combining irony, suspense, and dry humor punctuated by a droll twist at the end. Hitch ended each teleplay with a disclaimer explaining that the villain didn't really get away with his crime, but that didn't stop one housewife from emulating a murder she had seen on his program the next day. The episode was about a husband who tied himself to a bed to give the impression of robbery; his motive was insurance. His wife helped make the situation more credible by slaying him when he was helpless. Author Henry Slesar knew of several episodes that had become an official part of police investigations. "Very much the same circumstance occurred," he wrote, "when we aired a story about a woman who went to a TV show and left a glass of poisoned milk for her husband to drink. The New Jersey woman who took this as an inspiration for murder was only too willing to cite the Hitchcock program as her source."

The most publicized incidence of this sort was based on Slesar's own story, "Not the Running Type." A London bank clerk watched the show and based his embezzlement of hundreds of thousands of pounds on the plot. The only problem was that the police had seen the show too and a check of recent bank deposits produced the evidence to convict him. The English press headlined it as the "Alfred Hitchcock Crime."

Watching Hitch's program had brought home to Marli the celebrity of the portly director. The title sequence she saw on her parents' black-and-white television set faded in on the economical line caricature of Hitchcock. He had drawn it himself—it couldn't be more than six or seven lines. In the opening credits Hitch, in silhouette, enters the frame stage right and steps into his own profile to intone, closing his eyes to savor each word, "Good evening, ladies and gentlemen."

As if Hitch's drawing had come to life on Stage 18-A, Hitch stepped forward, silhouetting his actual profile against the gloom of the black curtains, and said to Marli in his measured monotone: "Good morning." Though Hitchcock was a serene, many-chinned Buddha on the outside, Marli felt at heart he was a melancholy man who had insulated himself against the world with his excess poundage. Rita Riggs, as perky and upbeat as they come, agreed, envisioning Hitch as "the prince locked in the frog," who truly loved beauty so much he set out to create it. She had been the on-set costumer for Hitch's TV show, even driven him home in her VW bug one night. Rita dressed the opening and closing with him, and he was easy because he wore the same black suit, tie, and white shirt every time.

How sad he had seemed, Marli thought, but Hitch was in high spirits today. The bad weather at the beginning of principal photography and a looming Screen Actor's Guild strike had both failed to materialize. Over the weekend the rotund director had shrugged off the scalding disappointment that accompanied the abandonment of his elaborate, six-mile tracking shot for the beginning of *Psycho*. He had also discarded two trick sequences. For comic effect he had wanted to feature Arbogast, the detective, driving back and forth in front of the Bates Motel. The second tracking shot involved a 360-degree turn beginning and ending on Tony Perkins's face as he perched on the motel steps and caught sight of Arbogast driving in. Hitch contented himself that at least the Shower Sequence ended with an amazing tracking shot, possibly his best, certainly his hardest, and one requiring split-second timing.

As he had last Friday, Hitchcock spent considerable time conversing with Marli. "One of my favorite memories of the whole experience," said one crew member, "was of Alfred Hitchcock standing there talking seriously about camera angles with a naked model." Stefano noticed Marli too. "He brought a nude model, a very nice young lady," he said. Even years later his eyes would twinkle at the memory of her. "It was quite charming to see the two of them standing there talking. Hitchcock here and the naked girl there." It was the princess and the frog.

Marli listened as Hitch told unprintable stories about Hollywood, scandalous tales of famous people Marli had seen on the screen for years. The director delighted in shocking his leading ladies just before a scene by whispering the naughtiest off-color stories he could think of. "I am aware that I am equipped with what other people have called a fiendish sense of humor," he admitted.

Just ask Janet Leigh. "Mr. Hitchcock had this impish, wonderful sense of humor," she said. Several times he concealed a full-size stuffed corpse of Mother Bates in her dressing room to give her a good fright when she stumbled upon it. He gauged the effectiveness of the corpse by the volume of Janet's cries and decided by them which version of Mother to use. Prop man Bob Bone was slated to operate the mummified maquette of Mother, which the University of California Los Angeles had confirmed as scientifically accurate, something the censors had insisted on.

When Hitch was nervous, he told wicked stories to hide his shyness and often got naughty. When Grace Kelly arrived on the *Rear Window* set in an elaborate gold gown Edith Head had sewn her into, Hitch leered, "Grace, there's hills in them thar gold." He perversely delighted in throwing his leading ladies into romantic situations with his actors or screenwriters. Kelly biographer Robert Lacey wrote that when Hitch learned Grace had had a tryst with Frederick Knott, the author of *Dial M for Murder*, the director said in astonishment, "She even fucked little Freddie the writer!"

One shocking story flitting around Hollywood was about Hitch, Grace, and the telescope from *Rear Window*. Kenneth Anger wrote that Hitch had convinced Kelly to strip in a brightly lit open window while he watched through a close-up lens from across the canyon. The lovely ice blond had consented to indulge Hitch's whim "just this once." And now the impish Hitch, with *Psycho*, was going to make his audience voyeurs like himself.

"*Psycho* was the biggest joke to me," Hitch said. "I couldn't make *Psycho* without my tongue in my cheek. If I'd been doing *Psycho* seriously, then it would have been a case history told in a documentary manner. It certainly wouldn't have been in terms of mystery and oooooh, look out audience, here comes the boogy man! This is like telling a . . . fairy story. You tell it in hushed tones: 'Shh! and then the woman went up the stairs!' That's all I'm doing. And you have to have a sense of humor to do this."

They began shooting late because Hitchcock would have rather laughed, joked, and told stories than get down to work. An authority on obscure facts, he adored the origins of odd things. The first day Joseph Stefano arrived at Hitch's office to audition for adapting the book into a script, he had been forewarned by Ned Brown, his agent, about making small talk. "I don't want to do any small talk. Mr. Hitchcock," Stefano said immediately, "may I tell you how I would do this movie?"

"Of course," Hitch had said and eased his bulk back in his chair to listen. Stefano pitched the movie so vividly that the opening sequence the audience eventually saw in *Psycho* was just as he told it. Not bad for a writer with only one screen credit for a movie Hitch did not particularly like.

Screenwriter Samuel Taylor had observed that Hitch never talked about the overall story, only acted out his favorite scenes. "So for him," he said, "it was like a mosaic and when he finally got the entire mosaic put together you saw the story. Now if he didn't have a good writer there were going to be pieces missing in that mosaic."

During their longest session (Hitch was accommodating Stefano's morning psychoanalysis appointments, which were useful in crafting the Bates Mother–Son relationship), Hitch visualized the shower scene and acted out the scene that eliminated a sympathetic character—played by a star actress—one third of the way into the story. "I remember him sitting on a couch at his Paramount office where we were working this particular day," Stefano said, "discussing the murder in great detail." Hitch had come toward him, saying, "Now, we won't have her really lying on the bathroom floor. We'll show him lift the shower curtain . . ." Hitch acted out "every gesture, every nuance of wrapping the corpse in the curtain." Nothing tickled him more (and he loved to laugh) than pre-designing the murder sequence. Hitch was down on the floor when Alma flung open the door and nearly scared them both to death.

It was now 10:30 A.M. for a 9:00 A.M. shoot. But still Hitchcock didn't give Russell his first setup. At this rate, they would be four days over schedule by the completion of the bathroom scene. But as Hitch joked and related bawdy stories, he was working the sequence over in his mind. It had to be just right. After all it was his primary reason for making *Psycho*.

"Frankly we all thought he'd cut it to just show Mother coming into the bathroom," Helen Colvig said, "the knife raising, the blood, the girl falling, and that's it. We thought the bits-and-pieces montage approach lent itself to any censorship or editorial changes he had in mind. It was so outrageous for its time."

Today Hitch would first do the scene without Marli in the shower and film the initial appearance of Mother in bits and pieces. Margo Epper, Perkins's body double, played Tony in drag, and it disturbed her so much that years afterward she would still be reluctant to discuss her strange experience with Hitchcock ("an odd person to work for"). Just to recall those days made her uneasy.

"They were working on a kind of raised platform. Hitch was standing just below, looking up and telling her exactly what to do, how to do it, and repeating the smallest things over and over. I was just shown walking with the knife like I was going to stab her," she said. "There wasn't really anybody in the shower at the time, but he wanted it to be really real." As to how to tell Epper apart from the other Mother doubles, she explained, "When you see her with the knife like I was going to stab her, that's me."

Marli read over the script. The overview was straightforward—the bathroom door being pushed quietly open, then cautiously closed as a woman's shadow falls across the shower curtain, which is then ripped aside. "Hitch spent quite a bit of time choreographing the scene with Mother and me," Marli said, "filming both straight on and overhead." He adhered closely to Bass's storyboards, especially the high angle shot divided by the curtain rod that Stefano specifies in his script. The writer's imagery was like a completed film—the blur of water, a glimpse of a mad woman's contorted face, the closed curtain, the sounds of rushing water, and the front door slamming.

"Hitchcock had such a casual way of directing," Jack Barron said. "It was like he wasn't doing anything. Maybe he'd sit slumped over, but those eyes never missed anything. To me, he wasn't a director's director. I'm not an actor and I don't know how much he'd impart to them, but they'd shoot, he'd say, 'Fine,' and that was that." Hitchcock rarely stirred from his chair except to check a lighting cue. He *never* moved a camera without a good reason. He might have seemed asleep, but he was listening to the cadence of the dialogue.

"Now I want to do a two-shot," Hitch said, "so use a thirty millimeter lens . . . I think the distance will be ten feet, so you're going to be cutting right in here." He pointed to a level on Marli's torso.

"Make no mistake about it," Marli said, "Hitch directed the whole shower scene."

Saul Bass would later make some pretty wild claims. "Hitch sometimes would sit and others would stand but he directed it all." He referred to the storyboards, only rarely looked up from his London *Times*, and missed nothing. "He was there except between takes when he was in his tent working on the next shot." Many of Hitchcock's writers spoke of his need for quiet reflection on set. The only time a voice was ever raised was if someone dared interrupt his private cogitation and that voice would be Hitch's.

Now Marli stepped into the shower in the dazzling white bathroom. Hitchcock bathrooms were always spotless. In her ears was the roar of running water. She looked to Hitch for direction. "He knew exactly what he wanted to do each time," she said. "Sometimes he would leave it up to me to do what I wanted in the shower and other times he would be explicit."

After Hitch placed Marli in position for her setups, the shower scene was shot with an air of business as usual. He enjoyed the challenge of filming in a small space. His *Lifeboat* had been photographed in its entirety inside a lifeboat and *Rope* was shot in continuous ten-minute segments (all the film the cameras of the period would hold without reloading) with breakaway props and walls so the camera could follow the actors through the confined space of a studio apartment.

"While Perkins's double and I were going through the stabbing takes," Marli said, "Hitchcock asked me to scream during the scene. I did, though I didn't do any bloodcurdling screams. Mine were more like whimpers." Hitch would dub in the screams later. Janet Leigh would also have to be redubbed because the rushing water drowned out her cries too.

Years later, Hitchcock confessed to interviewers that he photographed a nude girl all the way through, covering every aspect of her stabbing. "I had the camera slow and the girl moving slowly," he said, "so that I could measure out the movements and the covering of the awkward parts of the body, the arm movement, gesture and so forth." Moving slowly, *click-click-click* like individual frames of films moving through a sprocket, was no problem for Marli, nor was holding backbreaking, joint-trembling poses for any length of time. "I don't remember there being any rest breaks," Marli said, "because there were so many breaks between each scene setting up for the next take."

Overall there were between seventy-one and seventy-eight angles, each lasting two or three seconds on the screen. No matter the screen time—two seconds or twenty minutes—it took Hitch's cameramen just as long to prepare for a setup, move the camera, and set the lighting. Since Hitch knew what his crew was setting up from the next scene in the script and his sketch, he would turn his back and light a cigar, and "talk about politics or baseball." His screenwriters considered him a delight on the set. The shoot seemed to go on forever. "But I was never fatigued," said Marli, "because I was in very good shape and used to holding poses. I found nothing Hitch asked me to do to be uncomfortable or a hardship." The script calls Janet Leigh's character "Mary," a name that had to be changed since there was a real Mary Crane living in Phoenix. Marli looked over the script.

As Mary washes and soaps herself, the small worry in
her eyes diminishes and a sense of relief comes over
her face. She has decided to do the right thing. After
the shower curtain was savagely pulled back, Mother
began to brutally stab and slash "Mary Crane."

Stefano describes her as "an attractive girl nearing the end of her
twenties and her rope."

As Janet Leigh had suggested, Hitch was too clever to convey objectionable scenes in a blatant manner. He would suggest the slashing by
the impression of a ripping knife, using sound to complete the illusion:
screaming, silence, and "the dreadful thump as Mary's body falls in the
tub." Between setups Marli noticed something odd. Barron and Dawn
had brought in two cardboard boxes. Marli, a very curious person, asked,
"What are all those bottles of chocolate syrup for?"

"Shasta just came out with chocolate syrup in a plastic squeeze bottle," Barron explained. He held one up for her to see. "It's pretty revolutionary. Up to now we were using Hershey's or Bosco from the can, but
you can do a lot more with a squeeze bottle." Barron and Dawn began
mixing the syrup with water.

"When they told me it was for blood," Marli said, "I thought it was
ingenious."

The blood was the main reason Hitch didn't film *Psycho* in color.
"That was the only reason," the director said. "With all that blood in the
bathtub, I knew very well I'd have had the whole sequence cut out—if
it had been filmed in color. It just couldn't have been done." They had
tried movie blood and even catsup, but only chocolate gave the right
consistency.

"There were two or three men who had to dribble chocolate next to
me," Marli said, "so it would land on the bathtub floor around my feet
and legs while I'm slowly circling."

"The men dribbling the squeeze bottles had to be real close to me,"
Marli said, "only a few inches away and I am moving and they're dribbling. Well, this one fellow, he was shaking so visibly—I tried to put him
at ease, but I don't think he had been around an unclothed lady before."

"That was it," Robert Bloch wrote of Norman Bates in *Psycho*. "The poor guy was actually afraid to get near a woman! When Norman helped Marion Crane off with her coat he was clumsy about it, and for a moment she felt rising irritation, then checked it as she realized the cause. He was afraid to touch her." Marion's nudity may have even been the motive for Norman's murderous shower attack. The novel's cruder, alcoholic Norman states Marion was killed because she was evil. "She had flaunted herself before him, she had deliberately tempted him with the perversion of her nakedness."

All were boy-men, in *Psycho* and in real life, who felt they had been perverted by a woman's nakedness. Like Hitchcock, they could watch, but never touch. America in 1960 was a nation of repressed, conforming men, voyeurs who secretly watched but never actually engaged a human being. It was the world of Hitchcock, a born watcher from the sidelines making films for a nation of Peeping Toms, and it was Sonny's world too.

The Shower Sequence was done in montage. "I shot some of it in slow motion so as to cover the breasts," Hitchcock said. The retarded shots were later accelerated and inserted in the montage to give the impression of normal speed. But in spite of Hitch's care, a nipple got in for a fraction of a second. Seen in individual frames, Marli's breasts are very recognizable. Her nipples are marked with two short creases, inclined on the right as / and on the left as \. So far no one had caught the "nip slip." That was not the only slip.

"My crotch patch," Marli said, "would dangle in front after numerous times in water." Hitchcock called it an antipudic, a patch that covers the private parts of the body. "I gathered up my courage and suggested to Hitch that we remove the patch entirely, but he wouldn't have anything to do with that."

"No, no, my dear," Hitchcock replied. "We must have it at all costs."

Chapter Four
Thad Brown

APD Chief of Detectives Thaddeus Franklin Brown had promised himself to capture the Bouncing Ball Strangler, though that was not the name the long-sought killer of ladies was known by . . . not yet. That description would come in mere months from the first living witness in the case. Until then the powerful strangler-rapist remained a question mark to the investigators. All Brown knew was that elderly women were being raped then strangled, usually around colleges (the Southside University District), on Hollywood Boulevard, or along Sunset Boulevard by Busch's Gardens. It was such a big case that both Central Homicide and Hollywood Station were involved and putting in long hours. The homicide case had staying power, a kind of numbing endless quality. Such a tough nut to crack irritated Brown.

Seated behind his desk, Brown, known as "the detectives' detective," leaned back in his swivel chair and took a puff on his pipe. He just as often smoked cigars but believed he looked smarter with the pipe. Methodically, he drummed his fingers on his desk and thought hard how to solve the riddle. Why was a rapist selecting older women as victims and then killing them? That was extraordinarily rare. In fact the rape of the elderly was practically nonexistent, but when it occurred he had to admit it often turned deadly. Only very young rape victims had a higher murder rate, but then they weren't usually killed first and *then* sexually assaulted.

It was difficult to figure why a rapist would seek out a senior victim. It had to be an issue of anger and power because the level of violence visited on the victim could be explained only if she were symbolic to the rapist killer. Perhaps the elderly women reminded him of his own mother. Brown made a memo to get hold of the exact statistics on such crimes, but he was certain it had to be less than 1 percent. Yes, he would capture the strangler as a present to himself and to the people of LA. He studied the picture in a silver frame on his desk and centered it.

Though an unassuming man, Brown was known to millions across the nation from the *Dragnet* radio show as Sergeant Joe Friday's boss. Not everyone gets a new job and hears it dramatized on national radio, as Brown did on December 15, 1949:

"See the transfer list?" Sgt. Joe Friday's partner says one inclement morning. "New Chief of Detectives."

"I heard there was a new Chief, Thad Brown," Friday says. They go into Chief Brown's office.

"It's a great way to start off as your new chief," Brown tells them, "call you back on a rotten morning like this."

"Glad you got the job, Chief," Friday says.

"Yeah, congratulations, Chief."

"It's hard to follow a man like Ed Backstrand," says Brown. "Gonna need your help."

"You got it," Friday says. Then narrates: "Ben and I left Thad Brown's office, picked up Lt. Lee Jones of the Crime Lab and drove to the West Adams district."

Brown, a powerfully built fifty-seven-year-old with a high, receding forehead, looked older than he was and a little like a Kansas general store grocer. His rocklike jaw, straight lips, and steely eyes indicated his toughness. He was a taciturn man, difficult to read, quiet speaking, but his unwavering gaze could be intimidating. A lot of suspects had wilted before that gaze. His voice was deep and gravelly (when he used it) though his commands were delivered in the polite form of a suggestion. Fable has it that he once asked a policeman to leap from the top of City Hall and the officer was halfway down before he thought about inquiring about the reason for his plunge.

Brown was a no-nonsense kind of guy, yet overall, an optimistic one. In his private life, he held one simple rule above all: "Treat others as you like to be treated yourself, provided they merit such treatment." He had gotten that from the Bible. His on-the-job credo was simpler, just "hard work and common sense." Brown absolutely believed that if one followed that axiom every case could be solved. Why couldn't this one? The assaults were unusual by their very nature. Obviously, something was setting the killer off. How else to explain the long gaps between attacks? Was it something he read or a film he had seen?

Brown, who it was said possessed "a steel trap mind," realized that they were looking for someone who did not fit into his peer group, probably a young man who was sexually inadequate or unattractive. They should be looking for someone who had problems with the opposite sex, had no friends, and probably lived with his mother. This Mr. X would have a criminal history but probably one of petty thefts and misdemeanor incidents. From experience, Brown knew in all likelihood the strangler lived within six blocks of his victim. That had been the case in over 50 percent of the murders he had solved, and of those, about a third lived on the same street as their victim. Focus the search on the neighborhood, he had ordered his men. They had, but came up empty.

Brown removed his dark-frame glasses and rubbed his eyes. There were dark semicircles under them. He fingered his famous snub-nosed revolver and put it in his desk drawer. His impassive face gave away little of his emotions, but it wasn't hard to guess he was feeling low. The Bouncing Ball Strangler had been hanging over Brown's head for four years, though it was only recently that public pressure to crack the case had leaped all the way to the top and was making his seat a bit hot to sit in. The LAPD had no clues so far—four years and no clues in a city that averaged one murder every three days. He had to solve those, too (and they were just as important), but these crimes stood out because they were the work of one man and against a particularly defenseless type of victim.

As chief of detectives (thirty-four years in the department, nine years as head of homicide, and now deputy chief), Thad helmed a Homicide Division made up of sixty detectives assigned to the fourteen square miles of Central Division and its 160,000 residents. But homicide was only a small part of his job. He also supervised the auto theft, burglary, fugitive, bunco, narcotics, and robbery divisions, even the capture of fugitives. He commanded the 653 officers and thirty-nine civilian personnel of the Detective Bureau. After work, he often helped a young policeman in minor trouble or comforted an officer's widow. A decade earlier, he had been in a tight competition for the chief's position with William H. "Sonny" Parker, now the fortieth chief in LAPD history. Brown had lost out, though his qualifying scores were second only to Parker's.

Chief Parker had joined the force on August 8, 1927, and then passed the bar three years later. He and his wife, policewoman Helen Schultz, had a home near Silver Lake. Parker was strong on police professionalism and autonomy from civilian administration, primarily as concerned internal affairs, but he tended to be cynical or, as he put it, "a realist." He understood that corruption of a police force was inevitable. "Even the LAPD has to recruit from the human race," the chief said with resignation. Parker's cops were quick to anger, and he had gotten bad press from that. A year into Parker's administration, a bloody Christmas scandal led to more civilian accountability and a cry to curtail police brutality, especially in the black neighborhoods, and remove Parker.

Brown respected Parker as an attorney and public speaker, but not as a detective. "Parker never worked on the detective bureau in all his years on the force," Brown said. "As a matter of fact, outside of traffic work, he never did much police work at all. He made it pretty difficult from a detective's point of view. He took a pessimistic attorney's outlook. He searched for loopholes. You've got to be optimistic about your chances in this business." And Thad Brown was an optimist if he was anything else. How else was he so sure he was going to catch the Bouncing Ball Strangler without a single lead to go on?

In spite of his abrasive relationship with Parker, Thad had reconciled himself to the fact that he would probably never be chief. He once told Parker, "Bill, I'll do the work and you do the talking, and if I'm half as good at working as you are at talking we'll both be in business."

As chief of detectives, in command of the Detective Bureau as deputy chief of police, Thad's door was always open to policemen in other states and jurisdictions. He often loaned his men out to pore over MO cards and question witnesses and suspects outside LA. Brown had a file of personal contacts and confidential informants who could accelerate any investigation he chose to focus on. Today he was thinking about those four unsolved murders of elderly ladies and wondering if any of his snitches could help. Probably not. The Bouncing Ball Strangler worked alone.

Thad was born on December 7, 1902, in Greenfield, Missouri, the son of a local storekeeper who ran the Gray's Point store. At fifteen he quit school to work for seventeen and a half cents an hour in the zinc and lead mines near Joplin. In 1924, he married and, with his bride, made the long drive in a 1923 Dodge touring car to California, where he worked as a ranch hand, hod carrier, plasterer, oil-field hand, swamper, and tractor driver. One icy day while toiling in the San Gabriel Mountains in the winter of 1926, Thad got sick of the lack of job security and filed to become a policeman or a fireman.

Famed Detective W. A. "Pappy" Neely convinced Brown to join the LAPD. On January 11, 1926, Thad became a policeman, Badge 869, only three days before the fire department also accepted him. He attended the sixth police academy class at the Seventy-seventh Street Station and walked a beat in the downtown area. His first job was directing traffic at Seventh Street and Broadway. Assigned to the Watts Substation, he joined the Watts Chamber of Commerce in 1928 and spent most of his first twelve years on the force cracking ten whiskey stills a day, enforcing the ill-conceived Volstead Act that was later repealed.

"It was in the 1930s and I saved an innocent man from a murder trial, and maybe from execution," Brown reported. "This cabdriver lived in a third-floor apartment at Third and Columbia. He had a Murphy

bed. It pulled down and you couldn't open the front door without raising the bed. No one could get in that room with the bed down." He told
how the cabbie awakened one morning and discovered his wife on the
floor. "She had fallen out of bed. He picked her up. She was cold, and
he pulled her tongue forward to give her artificial resuscitation. It didn't
work. When he realized she was dead, the cabbie carried her to a couch,
lifted the bed and left to call an ambulance." The coroner discovered
she had died of suffocation and, because of bruise marks on her neck,
called it murder. "Hell," Thad said, "that man did not kill his wife, and
I have to prove it. It doesn't ring true." His investigation revealed the
woman had epilepsy, something she had concealed from her husband.
Her sister had once saved her from choking to death on her tongue
during a seizure. And the bruise marks? Brown learned that the dead
girl had a friend training to be a chiropractor and the friend admitted
practicing on her and bruising her neck shortly before her death. "And
everyone saw it as a clear-cut murder," Brown said. "Everyone but me."

In 1934 Brown was transferred to the homicide squad downtown
and three years later made sergeant. He became a lieutenant in 1940,
and for the next two years worked Detective Bureau assignments. After
Pearl Harbor, Chief C. B. Horral named Brown as the LAPD's liaison
officer with the armed forces and charged him with guarding refineries
and shipyards against sabotage. Thad used a rumrunner's boat he had
confiscated to patrol San Pedro Bay. In 1943, when crime surged 13 percent and seventy-eight murders were committed (because so many police
officers were overseas fighting), Brown was made captain of inspectors in
command of the Homicide Division and started solving those cases. He
was made inspector in 1945 and deputy chief in 1946. For the first three
years as deputy chief, he commanded the Patrol Bureau but in late 1949
took over command of his "first love," the Detective Bureau. By now he
had worked all the famous murder cases of the time—William Edward
"the Fox" Hickman (hanged for killing a child) and the unsolved murder case of William Desmond Taylor, the silent-movie director, a case
Brown had inherited from his predecessor. Recently, he had reopened
his investigation of Taylor's murder. Director King Vidor was trying to
solve the case to make a film of it, and Thad was giving him a helping

hand. It was a dirty case involving a crooked DA or two, and Vidor was convinced he knew who did it.

Sometimes Thad used tough tactics to get the truth—such as in the case of Albert "Eddie the Sailor" Dyer. In the summer of 1937 Dyer, a school crossing guard, lured three little girls into the woods and strangled them one at a time. To keep Dyer from being lynched by an outraged mob, Brown had him taken directly to the Los Angeles jail for questioning. Dyer was questioned for hours but denied the killings. Finally, Thad threatened that if he didn't tell the truth he would take him back to Inglewood and let him explain the discrepancies in his story to the lynch mob. Dyer confessed and was hanged at San Quentin the following year. By then not even Dyer's wife believed in his innocence. No one claimed his body.

In 1947, Brown arrested Louise Peete for murdering two of her husbands (though he suspected she had been responsible for the deaths of four other individuals). The only time the fury beneath Louise's calm self-possession and poised exterior erupted was when Thad, as chief of the Homicide Squad, stolidly testified at trial to a conversation he had had with her. "Why don't you tell the truth!" she screamed at him from the defense table. "Why are you lying, you bastard?" In 1947, she became the second woman in California history to be executed by gas at San Quentin.

In 1955, Thad arrested Barbara Graham, a weak, self-indulgent murderer. She was executed the morning of June 3, 1955. He nabbed L. Ewing Scott (convicted of killing his wife, though her body was never found). Most famously, he tried to solve the case of Elizabeth Short, "the Black Dahlia." In a confidential conversation Brown disclosed to Jack Webb, "We know who killed the Black Dahlia. The case was solved. [Her killer] was a doctor who lived on Franklin Avenue in Hollywood."

His homicide team's responsibilities included train wrecking, treason, bigamy, and unlawful assembly. Thad, though, mainly handled assaults, attempted murder, kidnappings, homicides, and rapes. He waited for the phone to ring. The answer would come. It always did—in the form of a tip or freak traffic stop. He waited for that ring and willed the killer to make one mistake, just one. He had to. Nothing came past his desk, and at the end of the day he got in his car and drove to his house in Northridge and the comfort of his wife, Lil, sons, Pete and James, and daughter, Betty Lou. Perhaps tomorrow they would get a little closer to this monster who had remarkable staying power and amazing luck and who seemed so unbelievably cruel.

Chapter Five
Illusion

"**M**arvelous country," Hitch enthused to Marli. "Miles and miles of vineyards." He spread his short arms to describe the area between Santa Cruz and Los Gatos and as if to encompass the nude redhead. He loved the region sixty-seven miles south of San Francisco so much that in 1940 he had bought a two-hundred-acre mountaintop estate ranch there as a tax write-off, then purchased the vineyard at the end of Canham Road too. As a wine connoisseur, Hitch kept his cellar in the Vine Hill area near Scotts Valley stocked to the rafters with French wines (Montrachet primarily) and local domestic vintages, mostly from the new vineyards in Napa. Marli, a constant traveler, a voracious reader, and a lover of classical music, also appreciated fine wines.

Eventually, the on-set conversation turned to Caryl Chessman's impending execution on San Quentin's Death Row. It was a topic of outrage and concern all over the world. "The day Chessman is executed," the foreign press wrote, "will be a bad day to be an American." Appeals were speeding to Governor Pat Brown, who publicly favored the condemned man's release and had already stayed the execution once.

Chessman, a master of prolonged court maneuvering and the author of several successful books, had managed to stave off his execution for years. Now it looked as if his delaying tactics had come to an end. Many thought the condemned man innocent. Hitch's recent film *The Wrong Man*, based on the true story of Christopher Emanuel Balestrero, a New York musician wrongly accused and tried for armed robbery, dealt with the same issues of misidentification. Hitch had an extensive collection of nonfiction crime literature and had even written a mystery story for *Look* in 1943. *The Wrong Man* had been a box-office failure, and he was giving true crime a wide berth for the time being. Yet wasn't *Psycho* also a true story?

Yes, Hitch told Marli, *Psycho* was adapted from a book based on a true story by a frequent contributor to his television show, Robert Bloch. He considered sketching the story of the cross-dressing maniac who had inspired Norman Bates, then decided it was not proper to speak of such disgusting horror to a beautiful young lady. Although Marli had never read Bloch's novel, she did read true crime. "The first book that got me into reading nonfiction as a serious pastime was while I was in Vegas," she said. "The book was Meyer Levin's *Compulsion*, on the Leopold/Loeb case in Chicago. After that I read quite a few books on Clarence Darrow who was the Plaintiffs' attorney." According to Hitch, *Psycho* represented "a brave new world in which we are becoming conditioned to suspect our neighbors and expecting the worst."

"As if such ghastly creatures could ever be real," Marli replied at the suggestion that *Psycho* was real. "Was the world truly as dark as that?" She lived in a world of sun and sparkling water; of casinos, dancing, and galloping horses; and of handsome men, but the world that had inspired *Psycho* and created a Caryl Chessman and a Bouncing Ball Strangler smelled of cordite and blood. Marli could never have imagined the flailed bodies hanging from pulleys and the "Mother suit" worn by the man who was the real-life source material for Bloch's novel. Neither could Hitch's audience, and that's why he was going to be able to frighten them to death. "There is no terror in the bang," he said, "only in the anticipation of it." *Psycho* was the greatest audience participation film of all time.

In every respect Hitch was not directing the actors as much as he was directing the audience. It was a talent that gave him fiendish glee. "They thought the story was about a girl who stole $40,000," he said. "That was deliberate. And suddenly out of the blue, she is stabbed to death. Now, a lot of people complained about the excessive violence. This was purposely done, because as the film then proceeded, I reduced the violence while I was transferring it to the mind of the audience. By that first impact, the design of the film was very clearly laid out. So that the audience, by the time we got toward the end when the girl [Vera Miles] was going over the house, wandering, they didn't particularly care who she was . . . They will yell LOOK OUT! . . . So I was transferring by establishing the violence strong in the beginning and then got less and less violent as the film went on, thus letting their minds carry."

Hitchcock considered *Psycho* to be the most cinematic picture he'd ever made. "Because there you had montage in the bathtub killing where the whole thing is purely an illusion," he said. *Psycho* was all about illusion, which delighted Hitch. "You see *Psycho* was designed, first of all to lead an audience completely up the garden path . . . *Tell* the audience that something awful is going to happen—then let them work themselves into a lather anticipating the payoff."

The greatest illusion in *Psycho* was a piece of film not more than four or five inches long filled with bits and pieces, flashes and slashes that were each on the screen for a fraction of a second. Hitch told all the action in terms of pieces of film. The entire scene was only about a minute and a half. "That's all," Hitch said, and yet what a minute and a half.

The violence was implied, expressed only by contrasting angles and those fragments of celluloid, yet Hitch was able to convey the illusion of complete nudity and violent stabbing through their juxtaposition. "We have two kinds," he said. "We can have the pieces of film that are put together to create an idea, or the pieces of film that are put together to create an emotion. Now the bathtub scene was an emotional putting together of film . . . an expression of extreme violence."

Hitch studied the shower stall to see if he had overlooked any unpredictable element. He needed a POV shot to heighten audience identification with Janet Leigh's character, Marion. He wanted to show water pulsing out of the showerhead straight toward the camera creating a sunburst. It would be as if she were looking up at it. But the showerhead was so old-fashioned, the crew couldn't control the spray. The cameraman was stumped. "If we shoot right at it," he said, "how are we going to keep the lens dry?"

"How much time passed while they worked that out?" Marli was asked later. It was hard to tell, she said. The bathroom was so bright it dazzled her eyes, and she felt lightheaded. She was brought back to her senses when Hitch came up with an amazingly simple solution she thought was very logical. "Put the camera there with a long lens," he said, "and block off the inner holes on the showerhead so they won't spout water." Using the longer lens, the cameraman could get back a little farther, shoot a little tighter, and while the water appeared to hit the lens, it actually sprayed past it from the special rig. Men on both sides of the shower got soaked, but Hitch got his shot.

Marli later heard that Hitch had constructed a showerhead six feet in diameter, but didn't recall such a thing. Hitch had built similar devices in the past, such as the giant revolver in a huge plaster hand in *Spellbound* that fired directly at the audience, a burst of red in a black-and-white film.

Margo Epper, of course, performed Mother's entry and made the stabbing motions as directed. To accelerate the brilliance of the gleaming porcelain and polished chrome, to make everything look sharper, Hitch had used an intense high-key light. But the strong light generated so much reflection from the highly shined bathroom surfaces Hitch so prized, it created a second problem. His goal was to simultaneously conceal Marli's nudity and keep Epper's face hidden because bright light would reveal she was not Mrs. Bates.

```
CUT TO:
MARY—ECU
As she turns in response to the feel and SOUND of the
shower curtain being torn aside. A hand comes into the
shot. The hand holds an enormous bread knife.
```

As Hitch completed the last shot of the day, he was mildly concerned Epper's face might be visible. "I'll have some film for you to see at noon," said George Tomasini, Hitchcock's editor. The mild-mannered giant, who would die young, was the only member of Hitch's feature film crew to come over to *Psycho*. Tomasini, who had begun his association with Hitch on *Rear Window* and worked on the disaster of *The Wrong Man*, had been hired primarily for the shower scene. When actor Michael Douglas was sixteen, he had used his father Kirk's influence to get a job at Universal while Hitchcock was shooting *Psycho*. At lunchtime, he and his mates liked to congregate in the editing room to watch outtakes from the Shower Sequence. The crew didn't run dailies until the end of the day, but Hitch usually saw them first at noon. "We'd be sitting there, eating sandwiches," Douglas claimed, "going, 'Stop it there! Wow!'"

"I think that will be all for today," Hitch told his crew at 5:00 P.M. He rarely stayed past 6:00. After the late start, he had done from fourteen to eighteen setups that day, an astonishing amount of work for any director. He rose, the day's work done, walked to his car, and was driven home without a suspicion he was crafting a film like none ever before. He was a far greater artist than he knew.

"The day was nice and warm," Marli said. "When I was all through and Hitchcock had left, I went back to the set in a turtleneck jersey and long-sleeved dress. Though I was very warm, I thought I would dress nice to show everybody what I look like without that horrible wig. In the dresses I buy I don't like just one note. I like a bunch of designers, a real variety so it's hard for me to pick a favorite. I dressed at the forefront at the time. I bought a lot of my clothes at Jax in Beverly Hills. For swimsuits I wore Rudi Gernrich, his wool-knit swimsuits."

Marli walked around the gleaming bathroom set for the next half hour, taking it all in and hoping someone would see how fashionable she looked. But everyone had left. She could see the California gothic on the hill at the top of the flights of stairs and admired the exterior of the motel. On the first day, it had all seemed unreal, but this evening the set seemed so realistic it was starting to make her uncomfortable. The deep shadows of the sound stage hid so much and every sound of her heels echoed on the hard floor as if there were a second person in the darkened room with her.

Several hours later in the editing booth, Hitch's vague fear was realized—the brilliant illumination during Mother's entrance into the polished room plainly revealed Epper's face. Tomasini called Bel-Air to deliver the bad news to the director. This wouldn't have happened if they had shot this scene in the morning. "If something was wrong, we knew about it immediately, right after lunch," Tomasini said.

Hitch the perfectionist never reshot a scene, but he would have no choice this time. After all that meticulous preparation and hard work the Shower Sequence with its attendant headaches might put him behind schedule. All the cost overruns were coming out of Hitch's own pocket, which was the worst torture of all for him.

Chapter Six
Prep Work

Nine miles away, Sonny was undergoing his own meticulous preparation, one fraught with as many headaches as those facing Hitchcock. He already had recurrent physical headaches of his own and didn't need more. Sonny popped two aspirins and began scouting the areas around Sunset Boulevard where he felt most comfortable. He was gathering equipment to ensure he wouldn't make a mistake when he set out in earnest. He had a habit of going far away from his Olive Hill section only in straight lines as if that were the only way he could find his way back home to Mother. On the second day of the Shower Sequence, Sonny dressed in his favorite tan sport jacket, which was a little frayed at the cuffs, and one of the short-sleeved striped shirts he favored and that Mother had ironed for him. The shirt was still warm. He turned her picture to the wall and went out.

He climbed behind the wheel of Mother's two-tone Olds convertible. The white top and red sides were immaculate. He could feel its considerable power as he started the engine—240 gross horsepower that could be boosted. The oval speedometer and clock face were more stylish than the round ones on the '55 Olds. The Jetaway Hydra-Matic transmission did its work smoothly and Sonny pulled into traffic. The dual exhausts, which increased horsepower 7 percent and torque 6 percent, began to rumble pleasantly. He gave a blast on his horn and got by a slower driver. His reconnaissance mission had begun.

He drove to a pawnshop on West Hobart and Hollywood Boulevard where he had seen a pair of handcuffs in the front showcase last week. He wasn't concerned that the broker would remember him. Who would ever believe such a methodical, ineffectual man, a quiet, friendless lens-crafter in thick glasses, could ever be dangerous?

The handcuffs were still there, covered lightly with dust, so he tapped on the glass, indicated to the pawnbroker what he wanted and bought them. He gave a shy smile, slipped the package into his pocket and walked away making sure no one was watching. Just around the corner, he hid the cuffs in his car, then drove several miles away to search used bookstores along Sunset. At first he was not sure what he was looking for, then gradually the books he required, as if by magic, tumbled from the shelves into his hands. During Sonny's manic periods, he read constantly. Among the books on philosophy, psychology, and criminology was a real prize. He wondered how the volume had found its way to Hollywood and what good fortune for him that it had. He studied the gray cover: *Fighting Crime—The New York Police Department in Action.*

He drove home and at every break over the next week boned up on police techniques and searched for ways he might evade capture for any future crimes he might be inclined to commit. The book was great, but he found his most important acquisition a few days later, a real treasure. In bold capitals the pamphlet's cover read *LAPD Radio Code Signals.* The LAPD had come up with an ingenious system, one he had to appreciate. Officers communicated in a clipped number code to conserve air time and transmit information as quickly as possible long before the police simulcasts on bureau and citywide frequencies.

Sonny lovingly turned the slim volume over in his huge hands. The rounded muscles in his neck worked. He lit a cigarette, took a deep drag, and began to underline and dog-ear the first page of the pamphlet. When he had done that he memorized every number and its meaning. It was quite a job, and Sonny was not yet sure he had mastered it. He would have to put himself to the test. In his room, he recited aloud: "211—Robbery; 311—Indecent exposure; 390—Drunk (male); 390W—Drunk (female); 415—Disturbance; 459—Burglary; 484—Theft; 502—Drunk Driver . . ." And again, "211—Robbery . . ." Sonny quickly learned that A was a patrol unit, X was an extra patrol, W was a detective, and Z was a volunteer officer unit. Simple, once he put his mind to it. Sonny had a pretty good memory.

He turned his attention to the next page: Code 1—Acknowledge message or more simply "Answer your radio!"; Code 2—Urgent (no red light, siren) but respond to the location while obeying all traffic laws; Code 3—Emergency (red light, siren) which means you are exempt from traffic laws; Code 4—No further units need to respond and you should return to patrol; Code 4 Adam—Sufficient help at the scene though the suspect is still at large and in the vicinity; Code 5 had to do with stakeouts and meant that marked police cars had to avoid that location. Code 6 Adam—Out for investigation and may need assistance. Codes 12 through 14 dealt with major disasters, which Sonny most certainly was. Code 100 interested him the most. This code meant that mobile units were in position to intercept a fleeing suspect and might forewarn him. He triple underlined that.

At night Sonny roved the streets looking at women, not young women, but women as old as Mother, much older than himself. She was not like regular mothers. There was a strange twist to their relationship that no one suspected. Though he didn't keep Mother in the fruit cellar like Norman Bates, their shocking secret nearly equaled that of *Psycho*.

Lately, Mother had made his life unbearable in her kindly, friendly way. If it came to getting tossed out of her home (which he strongly desired, yet feared at the same time), he might have to press the issue. He had to be forcibly put out on his own—the only way he was ever going to be set free. Mother had plenty of other property, including apartment houses in the area, where he could live if he were on his own and she was warmhearted enough to be sure he could live in one. At last he would be able to take the women he met in bars to his own place and not just theirs or in his car. With a room of his own, he would have the freedom to pursue the urges that periodically overwhelmed him. That night, he waited until Mother was asleep and then slipped out to rove the streets. This time he went on foot and left the Olds in its space. Sonny returned after the bars closed accompanied by his bartender friend, Ernie Shaffer.

The following day, Sonny purchased new knives rather than sharpen the ones he habitually carried. (He had once stabbed a man to death in Korea when he was serving in the military.) He anticipated the release of *Psycho*, which he anxiously waited to see and which, according to one poster, featured a butcher's knife. Before then there was something else he had to do that he would never reveal to anyone, especially Mother.

Chapter Seven
The Winking Girl

The next day, Thursday, Barron blackened stuntwoman Margo Epper's face with something that looked to Marli like coal dust. Within a few strokes, Epper's face was effectively concealed and would no longer reflect the brilliant light of the bathroom. The shot of Mother's entrance was redone and the mistake rectified. There would be another glitch toward the end, one that escaped even Hitchcock's eagle eye and that of his cinematographer. It would be Alma Hitchcock, Hitch's strong right arm, who caught it, but it would be Hitch's quick-wittedness that undid the complication with a magical wave of his hand.

The crew loved Thursdays because that was Hitchcock's night to go to Chasen's with "Mom," Alma Hitchcock, and that meant they could be home by 4:00 P.M. "Hitch shot chronologically," Marli said. He liked to start on page one and go straight on, so in watching the shower scene you see his progress. "Sometimes he told me what to do exactly. Other times he told me basically what to do and if he liked it—fine; if not he told me to do something else. Each take was slightly different and I tried to be creative. I tried to move slowly and to feel out the pose."

Hitch made adjustments in the shower. This close to Marli, he could appreciate her coloring. Her skin was not blue tinged as was common with redheaded women with green eyes. While their skin tends toward pale alabaster, Marli's glowed with radiant health. It had an indefinable hue—red and yellow yet stepped down so it was not readily apparent but filled with sunlight accented by her flaming hair. Yes, that was it. He was looking at the sun. That made perfect sense. Marli was a spiritually based nudist, and the sun had worked its way into her pores on her extended visits to the Sundial traveling nudist camp.

"In the course of handling a nude girl," Hitch revealed later, "I actually used a nude girl, but I shot her in slow motion, and turned the camera slow as well, so that when it's projected at normal speed this slow motion is speeded up. I made her work very slowly because I wanted the breast, the bare breast to be conveniently covered with the struggling arm at the right moment. Doing it with rapidity, you could never time it right . . . But that's nothing to do with the technique, that was only a means of achieving that covering up, you see."

"We put the knife against her belly and then pulled it back," recalled Hitchcock of Slashing Scene, Shot 116. On that page he had scribbled in his own hand, "The slashing. An impression of a knife slashing, as if tearing at the very screen, ripping the film." He used a fast motion reverse shot to give the sense that the knife enters the girl's abdomen.

Asked about the scene later, he said, "I think it was the stand-in. No knife ever touched any woman's body in that scene. Ever." But frame-by-frame analysis revealed that the knife pierced a naked midsection just south of the navel. "Hitch used a retractable knife," Janet Leigh wrote. "In fact he held the knife himself because he knew exactly where he wanted that to be for his camera. But his editing brilliance made you sure you saw something else, right?"

"Speaking of the knife," Marli said, "the placement of the knife was Hitchcock's dig at the censors. At that time you couldn't show a belly button, even the bikinis were worn above the navel. But mine is shown getting stabbed! The shower scene was one way Hitch got one over the censors as my belly button is shown, but he had too many other things occupying the viewer's mind to notice. I do believe that that could be one of his greatest pleasures derived from Psycho.

"Everybody is shocked by the whole scene. I especially was shocked by the whole scene. Other than Hitch, I didn't know anyone else who I talked with who worked behind the scenes. Janet wasn't very nice to me. She wasn't mean, just standoffish. Marty Balsam and Vera Miles were friendly. Vera had just finished a movie [*Five Branded Women*] where she had to be bald and so wore a wig for Psycho. She remarked that she wished she could be bald all the time—it was so comfortable." So on the Psycho set there were three wigs: Marli's gray "Janet Leigh" wig, Vera's real-life wig, and Mrs. Bates's old-fashioned bun wig that would rest on Tony Perkins's head by the end of the month.

"Several times I had lunch in the commissary," said Marli, "and went with whomever was going. I got quite a few looks while I was there. I knew they were imagining that I didn't really have any clothes on under the cotton robe that I wore when not working. There was only one time I remember Hitch elicited any humor directed toward me. After the stabbing in the shower, I'm sitting down on the floor of the tub and had to reach my hand out to grab the shower curtain to drag myself up which pulled the shower curtain down. I was groping. And Hitch says, 'No! Stop!' Then he says, 'I just want you to go out there and do it very slow and grab the shower curtain.'"

But Marli was self-conscious about grabbing the curtain. "My ring finger on my right hand was cut off when I was three years old," she said, "and I've always favored it. We were in Texas very north of Dallas, in the country and it took an hour to find a doctor. The whole finger just after the last joint was just hanging by a couple of layers of skin. We finally just cleaned it up, dipped it in cod liver oil and put it on a splint and wrapped it up. I have all my feeling. My finger reattached itself completely, though there are a few lingering effects. My nail is thicker and it's calcified at the bone. My knuckle goes in and it's not as strong as the other knuckles."

When they wanted a close-up of her right hand coming forward to grasp the curtain after the stabbing Marli had to say something. She got up out of her sitting position at the bottom of the bath tub, held out her hand and pointed out the imperfection to Hitch.

"How did that happen," he asked her. "Did you blow it off picking your nose?"

"The ring finger on my right hand was cut off at the tip by a lawn mower when I was three and it's noticeable," she said.

"Sit back down and don't worry about it."

Marli was in the shower so much that her skin was beginning to furrow. Janet would suffer the same pruning. "We did four to six takes of me rising out of a sitting position in the shower and falling over the edge to land in exactly the same position," Marli said. She carefully remembered each pose exactly in case Hitch wanted her to re-create it. She had amazing control over her body and could hold a pose indefinitely, having kept in perfect shape playing volleyball twice a week and fishing in cold mountain streams. "I tried very hard to duplicate myself each time. It was remarkable that I could." Those long hours of holding and repeating a pose for photographers Sam Wu and Peter Gowland had schooled her well.

Chapter Eight
Dressing Nude Janet

A s Christmas 1960 approached, Janet Leigh found herself distracted as she wrapped presents. "The question consuming me during the day," she wrote, "was, 'What to wear in the shower?'" On-set costumer Rita Riggs and supervisor Helen Colvig were stumped too. For the Shower Sequence, how could they suggest nudity and at the same time remain within the strict censorship bounds of the time? Janet had to appear nude without being nude.

Leigh had been a surprise choice for the role of Marion Crane and not Hitch's first preference. From the beginning, he had wanted the biggest star he could get—for the extra shock value—and had considered Eva Marie Saint, Lana Turner, Shirley Jones, and Hope Lange. But Hitch was a real bargain hunter and since Janet Leigh, like Tony Perkins, owed Paramount one last film to complete her contractual obligations and since Lew Wasserman personally represented not only Hitchcock but also Janet and her husband, Tony Curtis, Hitch could have her cut-rate. According to John Michael Hayes, screenwriter on four consecutive Hitchcock films, he was very cheap. "He didn't pay much and never complimented you for anything. If you did it well, that's what you were paid for."

Wasserman, then the head of MCA, the most powerful talent agency in Hollywood, had become Tony Curtis's agent in 1952. "With Lew Wasserman as my mentor doors opened at the slightest touch," Tony rhapsodized about "the most honorable man" he had ever known. He knew Lew loved Alfred Hitchcock (and had been the driving force behind his TV show and lucrative multi-picture deal with Paramount), and Hitch loved Lew in return. Tony was at a party one evening watching the two men conversing. "Lew was sitting there in his horn-rimmed glasses with his long legs crossed," he said, "while Hitch was perched on his seat— all five-feet-seven-inches of him in that famous pear shape. To look at them these two men could not have been more different, but they were bounded by the power of their intellect."

In October, Hitch tucked a copy of Bloch's novel (at that time the script was still uncompleted) into a manila envelope and sent it to Janet. It would at least give her the essence of the story. He had also enclosed a short note:

> *Please consider the role of Mary [later changed to Marion]. In the completed script Mary will be improved upon and, of course, the descriptions of the characters will be completely different. As you know, Tony Perkins is going to play Norman Bates.*

That Perkins was to be in the film was a deciding factor, but Janet would have taken the part in any case. "I didn't even have to read [the book], but I did," she said, "only because the opportunity of working with Mr. Hitchcock was enough for me . . . I was very intrigued, it was so different." She found *Psycho* such a departure and an unusual approach to a movie that she just had to see how Hitchcock was going to work his magic. The director never liked to repeat himself and this was certainly a drastic departure from his earlier films. Janet had immediately dialed MCA and told them, "Yes." Like Marli, Janet would have done the film for free and, like Tony Perkins, had taken the part without reading a script.

Now how to dress Janet Leigh without dressing her? Rita Riggs, who had picked out Janet's wardrobe at Jax in Beverly Hills (Marli's favorite store), lugged in a huge stack of magazines with strippers on the cover. She thumped them down on the coffee table. She smoothed her full skirt, gave a shake of her long dark hair, which today was cinched with a bright ribbon into a pony tail, and sat down. It was still early. Rita hated to get up in the morning but still managed to be perky and enthusiastic first thing. She and Janet began to thumb through the pages, searching for a solution to the nudity problem. In a decade of work in the industry (though she was not yet thirty) it was Rita's first experience with nudity for a film, and she was having a little difficulty learning how to handle it. But it was a humorous endeavor.

"It's hysterical," Leigh said, tossing the magazines aside. "Hardly practical." Both women were stifling laughter. Janet picked up the thick catalogs and leafed through. All she found for sale were an endless array of spangles, feathers, and birds of paradise suitable for a Tropicana showgirl and a mind-blowing assortment of ingenious metal pasties and colored pinwheels such as strippers wore.

"The giggles Janet and I had out of sheer shyness," Rita said. "I was very aware of not only Janet's but Mr. Hitchcock's shyness, so I approached the job by thinking, 'How would I feel?'" Rita agreed it wasn't right that such a big star, a beautiful woman with children, should have to expose her whole body to the camera. Both women studied Bass's innovative storyboards for the Shower Sequence. Janet observed that one angle would show "an arm here, a tummy there, shoulders down to the great divide, legs, back." She looked at Rita. "Why, complete nudity isn't necessary for *Psycho* at all!" she said. "It just isn't Hitch's style. Doing the scene actually in the nude would have negated how clever and subtle he was at suggesting things." Rita only had to glance at the boards to realize Hitch never needed "to show the entire body, but, say, a nude back, or breasts almost down to where the nipple begins."

As Rita experimented she recalled a light flannel with adhesive backing called "moleskin" that might work. "If we had to see a part of a breast, say, under the crook of an elbow," she explained, "I would sculpt moleskin, then glue, cover, and trim away until it was just the amount of the body that was needed was visible." Flesh-colored moleskin over both her breasts and over the "vital part" would accomplish their aims. Janet considered Rita's solution brilliant. The application of moleskin would be time-consuming, but not invasive. Rita came to think of the moleskin as a sculpture and got faster at the process as she got into it. Rita also used nude body stockings and panties that were cut and sometimes glued. "Janet, who was a terrific sport and a wonderful professional throughout, was never nude."

When Saul Bass heard Rita had covered Janet's private parts with nude-colored moleskin, he reportedly found the entire procedure ridiculous. "Little square gauze on her nipples," he said. "I mean, it was more erotic than if she were nude!"

Janet was still worried about on-set security, a constant source of trouble since the day Marli had done her first scene. Peeping Toms crept in whenever they wanted, in spite of Hitch's security patrol. "Even though I wore the moleskin . . . I was still pretty much . . . on display," Janet said. "I didn't want strangers lurking around, hoping to get a peek in case of any accidental mishap. If anything did slip up at least only my friends would get a look." As an added precaution Riggs erected screens around the set during filming to further protect Leigh's privacy.

"I was right there on the set the entire time the shower scene was shot," Marli said. "Janet was very modestly dressed when I saw her perform. She wore a bathing suit that is straight across the top and is a full suit to her butt. The color is a light tan/skin color with a sheen to it. You'll notice that the camera, when shooting Janet, never strays too far below her collar bone. She could have been wearing a strapless, sequined evening gown for all anyone would know. As I've said, "If you don't see Janet's face, it's me—hands, feet, legs, back, belly button, back of head, etc. . . . .

"Even if Janet did try to do the shower scene wearing moleskin later, which I have a hard time in believing, all those scenes wound up on the editor's floor, with the only ones she did in front of me ending up in the final cut of the movie. For her to say that she bared it all for art is ludicrous. What a crock. And using flannel? In the water? In warm, not hot, water? Unbelievable, insane. My crotch patch was made up of some kind of thin rubber-like material, not moleskin, with a little bit of stretch in it."

Janet wrote in her memoir that while she was in the tub looking up toward the showerhead, she had been surprised by how many gaffers were on the overhead scaffolding. "I hadn't seen that many technicians up there even during elaborate scenes on the huge stages, let alone one person in a tiny bathtub. And each one must have had two or three assistants."

On December 28, Janet didn't find it hard to scream during the Shower Sequence in close-ups showing her response to her attacker. She was "damn frightened" when Mother threw open the curtain. And then another problem. Janet's screams couldn't be heard over the roar of the rushing water. Well, Hitch would just have her overdub them. Marli and Ann Dore, the stand-in for Mother who handled all shots involving physical contact with the frightened victim, were filmed in the afternoon. The actual slashing was filmed the next day.

"The next series of shots depended on the cutting to startle and terrify," Janet wrote, "which is why he was so careful about following the storyboard. We had to do it over and over." The many days in water were trying for everyone because there were so many repeats of the same action, taken from different angles, or difficulties with a balky camera or klieg light.

Gossip around the Revue back lot was that Hitchcock had pumped ice-cold water out of the showerhead to get a shocked reaction from Janet when Mother entered the bathroom. "Nonsense," Janet said. "The temperature was quite comfortable." At Hitch's request, the three crewmen kept the water as hot as possible, which caused the biggest problem and the most delays. "Abruptly, I felt something strange happening around my breasts," Janet wrote later. "The steam from the hot water had melted the adhesive and I sensed the moleskin peeling away from my skin. What to do? Spoil the shot and be modest? Or get it over with and be immodest? I opted for immodesty . . . and no one noticed my bareness before I could cover up. I think!"

Hitch grew impatient after the trimmed, glued-on moleskin contraption covering her breasts was detached by the shower steam during an apparently successful take. "At that point, with that shot," she said, "I didn't give a damn." Rita would get in the shower with Janet to replace the moleskin only to have the water wash it off again as the camera rolled. After this had happened a number of times, Hitch sat there twiddling his thumbs clockwise. When he got more irritated he switched to counterclockwise twiddling, only faster. "Oh, come now," he said, "we've all seen more than that at the beach."

"I never saw Hitch get upset or raise his voice," Marli said, "let alone stalk off the set."

Hitch could be intimidating without raising his voice. "Once, in the middle of *Psycho*, the film ran out in the middle of a take," wrote Russell Taylor. "Nothing was said, absolutely nothing, but the set was enveloped in an atmosphere of dread for the rest of the day."

Janet wrote that wearing the moleskin made her skin raw when they peeled it off, so Rita had to remove it between shots to give her skin some relief, and that was time-consuming. Russell also had to light each setup and move the camera from shooting straight down to straight up to cross angles to the water. It was as tedious for Russell as it was for Hitch and Janet.

After three hours of running water, nudity, and wipe-offs of the moleskin Hitch got up and walked away because he was so exasperated. He did this a few times. No one had ever seen him get as angry on the set or get up as many times before. "With the nudist," he grumbled, "it went so much more smoothly."

"I was in the shower so much that my skin was beginning to look like a wrinkled prune," Janet said. Filming was easy "until the last twenty seconds" when she had to express total horror as her character was being slashed to death. The end of the Shower Sequence was also the most difficult. "On my slide down the tiled wall and collapse over the edge," she related, "I had landed in the most awkward position— my mouth and nose were squished against the side of the tub." The next setup was a cut to the dead body, lying half out of the tub, the head grazing the floor, one eye wide open and one arm lying limp along the floor. Hitch initially had Janet fitted for contact lenses that prevented her from blinking, but the ophthalmologist told him that she might suffer eye damage without at least six weeks to accustom her eyes to them. "You'll just have to go it alone then, old girl," Hitch told her. As the camera pulled back on a close-up of Janet's "dead" eye gradually to show more of the tub, then more of the shower bathroom, she was not allowed to swallow or breathe.

The traveling dolly required such split-second cueing that Hitch needed dozens of retakes between setups twenty-two and twenty-six. During each pass, the camera had to slide past Janet lying nearly nude and shivering on the bathroom floor holding her breath and maintaining a death stare through sheer willpower. As splashing water settled on her face, it trickled into her nose and eyes and made her want to sneeze or blink. It amazed onlookers that the star was able to retain such a high degree of concentration.

"I was impressed at how Janet Leigh never blinked during the close-ups of her staring straight ahead," Marli said, "and sliding down the side of the shower and then again at the end with the close-up when she's dead."

"I could feel the damn moleskin pulling away from my left breast," Janet wrote later. "I knew the lens would not pick it up—that part was below the top of the tub. But I knew the grip in the balcony would get an eyeful. By that time I was sore where I was pressed against the ungiving porcelain—my body ached and I didn't want to shoot this again if we didn't have to. So I decided not to say anything—the hell with it I said to myself. Let 'em look!" There was no autofocus in late 1959 and the operator had to manually change the focus as the camera traveled. Hitch snapped his fingers loudly to indicate to Janet that the camera had gone past her face so she could breathe and blink again.

Exhausted, Janet went home at 4:00 P.M., though Marli and Ann Dore continued working for another two hours on December 30.

A complicated dolly shot always excited Hitch. The mechanical dolly had been designed to enable the cameraman to film the scene as one unbroken shot. "He was not like some directors," Marshall Schlom said, "who think, 'Okay, I've dreamed up the most difficult shot. Let's see if the crew can do it.'" Hitch would explain how it would work. With so many technical aspects, though, making the Shower Sequence dolly shot look like one continuous take would be difficult.

Just after the stabbing, the dolly would open on a full screen close-up of the lifeless eye of Janet Leigh.

```
CAMERA FOLLOWS away from the body, travels slowly
across the bathroom, past the toilet, and out into
the bedroom. AS CAMERA approaches the bed, we see the
folded newspaper [in which the stolen $40,000 is hid-
den] as Mary placed it on the bedside table.
```

Finally the camera travels to the open window, actually a screen with projection backing and projector on the stage throwing an image of Tony running down the stairs from the backlot house toward the motel. It all had to be perfectly timed so it was the same exposure in the printer. The single continuous shot, actually three different shots, would be optically composited on a single piece of film by the postproduction team.

"Shooting the shower scene was never seen by us as more than getting all the bits and pieces together purely for shock effect," Hilton Green said. "The fragments that we photographed were sort of stored away, but Mr. Hitchcock had a general idea of how he wanted to make the idea progress."

"It took us seven days to shoot that scene," Hitchcock later told François Truffaut, though Rita, years later, estimated the entire sequence at three *weeks*. "There were seventy camera setups for forty-five seconds of footage. I used a . . . a naked model who stood in for Janet Leigh. We only showed Miss Leigh's hands, shoulders, and head. All the rest was the stand-in . . . [S]he had a gray wig on for the black-and-white. Naturally the knife never touched the body." But Hitchcock had misstated the facts. Though the knife point had only briefly touched Marli's stomach and been withdrawn, he had been the one who held the knife. It felt comfortable in his hand.

Chapter Nine

Sonny

Triggered by severe stress, a person sometimes escapes from an emotionally charged situation into a calmer existence. During such a psychogenic fugue one part of the personality can split off from the other and take on another identity. Sometimes the assumption of a new identity can be very elaborate with all the trimmings—a new job and new set of personality characteristics, even a new place to live that the subject may not later be aware of. In such a fugue a person might establish a complex social life without ever questioning his inability to recall the past. In most cases, the fugue is of such a brief duration that the individual does not recollect what took place during his headlong flight from his usual life. It is as if the mythical person had completely vanished from the face of the earth.

In the case of multiple personalities the original individual, while seldom aware of the existence of the others, is aware of lost periods of time while another identity comes out under stress to walk around in the world. Sometimes the voices of the other identities may filter through into their consciousness. Dissociative disorders remain among the most poorly understood clinical syndromes, but could be the result of a massive repression dating back to unacceptable infantile sexual wishes. In adulthood, these yearnings increase until they are expressed as an explosive, impulsive sexual act at the moment of highest stress and then forgotten.

The pressure grew on Sonny until it was more unbearable than ever. He feared he would suffer another loss of time that he couldn't account for. But he could think of no way to guard against it and drown out the noise in his head. "It was like static on the radio at first," Sonny said later. "Then it got to be a high screaming sound. It would be pounding in my head." The tension had been at its worst four years ago when the pretty redhead at the corner variety store had been shot dead. He had been the number one suspect until, unexpectedly, there had been a break in the case, and Sonny was off the hook. All the tension left his body at once like water spiraling down the drain. Hungry to know what had happened, he called Wilson, the reporter covering the case for *True Detective*. He knew all about it.

"San Diego cops," Wilson told him, "grabbed up one Robert Lee Nichols, a petty crook with a record, down at the docks. It was just a fluke arrest. They only wanted to ask him about some minor infraction. He not only didn't put up a struggle, but confessed that he had shot a red-haired girl in a failed stickup in Los Angeles on Sunset Boulevard in 1956. Nichols didn't know her name, but that girl had to have been Eudice Erenberg. It was the only case like that."

Nichols went to prison for life, but cops were still interested in Sonny. So was Wilson. Certain he had not seen the last of Sonny, he filed his notes away with the notion he might need them again someday when another fluke arrest might be made.

Wilson's file on unsolved LA female homicides grew fat. About all the crimes he noticed a similarity. So far ten older women had been found nude and strangled in their lonely apartments. There was an impression in their beds as if someone had been sleeping beside their corpses—their killer? If not, who? If so, why?

On January 31, 1956, he had added the name of Barbara Jean Jepsen to his records. Someone had throttled her and violently raped her. Over the next year, police linked three more murders to hers, and Wilson made a file for each and numbered them:

1. Mrs. Ruth N. Goldsmith was killed on April 4, 1957.
2. Mrs. Esther Greenwald was murdered on August 19, 1957.
3. Fifty-year-old Helen Jerome was slaughtered on August 26, 1958.

Helen Jerome? Wilson knew that name. He looked it up in the *Los Angeles Herald* morgue. Jerome had been a well-known British stage actress before she came to Hollywood to make several films, but was most celebrated for her adaptation of Jane Austen's comedy of manners *Pride and Prejudice*. Jerome's 1936 stage version at London's St. James's Theatre starred Celia Johnson and Hugh Williams. The more famous film version four years later, based on Jerome's stage adaptation, starred Greer Garson and Laurence Olivier with a script by Aldous Huxley and Jane Murfin.

Wilson read over all the stories about her, a simple manila file. Jerome's corpse had been discovered in her hotel room on North Las Palmas Avenue just off Hollywood Boulevard—nude and strangled. She may have been the loneliest of all the older victims, having tasted fame and success, then been forgotten. If Sonny had left Busch's Gardens restaurant, driven one block on Normandie, and turned onto Hollywood Boulevard he could have driven the two miles west in a dead straight line to Jerome's hotel in about eight minutes. Sonny tended to drive in a direct line whenever he went anywhere. He rarely strayed far.

Many of the strangulations and rapes of elderly women had occurred along Hollywood Boulevard and Sunset Boulevard. In his office, Wilson studied the map. He took a pencil and traced the route. Beginning in the east at Sunset Boulevard, Hollywood Boulevard runs northwest to Vermont Avenue, straightens, and runs due west to Laurel Canyon Boulevard. It was a familiar area not only for the Bouncing Ball Strangler but also for Sonny in his cruising Olds. Wilson noted that the murders had begun precisely when Sonny returned to Los Angeles after being drummed out of the service. The shambling, shy young man could not be connected to any crime outside of obtaining an unregistered gun from the restaurant's bartender, Ernie Shaffer. Wilson did not know about the robberies Sonny had committed.

The Jepsen, Goldsmith, Greenwald, and Jerome rape-murders remained unsolved. And then a year later, Linda Martin, twenty-one, a University of Southern California (USC) coed, was found stabbed and nude, another victim with the same MO, but much younger than the others, in what was now a string of similar murders. Wilson had looked over the map of USC, flanked by South Vermont to the west, Exposition Boulevard to the south, South Figueroa Street to the east, and West Jefferson Boulevard to the north. The victims were four elderly women and one young woman. Could they all be victims of the same killer? It didn't make sense. It was almost as if there were two stranglers at work, pattern killers as they were coming to be known. Wilson considered investigating further, but more freelance assignments from the magazine diverted his attention. Then there were changes in his life, a chance to write a book, and he never got back to Sonny.

And that was the way events stood just a few weeks after Marli Renfro entered Hitchcock's shower. LA was a dangerous place to be and not one but two killers might be stalking its streets. Unless it was one killer who didn't know he was the other.

Chapter Ten
Tony and the Cleanup

Tony Perkins's fastidious cleanup of the bathroom ate up another three days of shooting time. Hitch liked his nervous energy. Tony, who had lost his father when he was five, was more frantic than usual, nervous ticks and stuttering in full swing. The young actor was working under double deadlines. First, the *Psycho* deadline; the other, the beginning date for rehearsals of his Broadway musical, *Greenwillow*. Tony had returned from New York without much hope for this "whimsical fantasy of love altering destiny set in a quaint imaginary village." It was all a hopeless mishmash based on an incomprehensible novel. Tony, conscientious to the quick, felt every second he was working on the set that he was desperately needed back at the Alvin Theatre by December 30. But director George Roy Hill and producer Robert Willey had privately pushed the official opening date back to March 8, 1960. On the set of *Psycho*, things were going better for the gangling young man. He loved being there and was adored in return.

"The crew always referred to Mother and Norman as totally separate people," Tony wrote. "Mother always has her own 'backstage' persona, as it were. It's just not acknowledged that Norman is Mother. It's just not how people want to see it—neither audiences, nor the people who work on the crew."

While Janet Leigh thought Tony had "a wonderful sense of humor, wonderful . . . very dry, you know? He was not Norman Bates. But he was so brilliant that the people said, 'Yes, you are. You are too, Norman Bates.'"

Joseph Stefano was a little more perceptive. "It was clear to me early on," he said, "that he was becoming Norman Bates."

With his dark good looks, Tony was brooding but charming with his stammering and disaffecting quirkiness. Though he had been playing romantic leading men and currently was a teenage heartthrob, he lacked confidence in his appearance. Tony detested his small head, overly thick neck, spindly physique, and the noticeable hunch in his spine. Where the shy, detached Perkins shined was on set in between takes when he played clever word games with the cast and crew (the only time he didn't retreat to his dressing room as a recluse).

It was during these games that Marli realized how bright Tony was and what a highly intelligent game player he was. Tony had a flair for games and charades between scenes that he had demonstrated as far back as his first film. On one of his pictures, competition got so intense during an Ad Lib game that Tony dumped a bucket of water over Shirley MacLaine's head and called the actress "one of the meanest people he had ever met."

"But Tony Perkins and I got along great," Marli said. "Tony and I, along with the wardrobe lady, Rita Riggs, and his double, played word games, namely 'Ghost,' between scenes. I still remember the word I beat him with. I got Tony with *genus* which means a grouping of organisms having common characteristics distinct from those of other such groupings." Or in philosophical terms, genus is a class of things that have common characteristics and can be divided into subordinate kinds. Marli was thrilled with her victory because she was very taken with Tony.

"He asked me out," Marli recalled. "But I was dating another guy, a nudist like myself, so I told him, 'I'm dating someone. Thank you anyway.' And I think he was really hurt. But Tony was very, very nice and any other time, who knows?" He was also isolated and lonely, pursued by as many demons as Norman Bates. When Robert Bloch visited the *Psycho* set no one noticed or spoke to him. He glimpsed Tony Perkins, equally alone, walking with his head lowered among the desolate row of motel rooms.

Tony's fastidious polishing to clean up after Mother in the bathroom had everyone rooting for Norman Bates and identifying with him, which was exactly what Hitch intended in his manipulation of the audience. As Tony scrubbed, the strong illumination that had vexed them during Mother's entrance worked for the Bathroom Scene by backlighting Tony and his own intrinsic oddness and emphasizing the bizarreness of Norman Bates. When it came time for Norman to wrap Marion's body in the opaque shower curtain, whomever was inside (even though you don't see a close-up) had to be nude.

"I'd rather not be nude," Janet Leigh said.

"There's no reason for you to be because you can't tell who it is anyway," Hitchcock said. "We've got someone else."

"There was a nude model, absolutely for several reasons," Janet said. She explained that Hitch had to determine the density of the water and translucency of the shower curtain so that you couldn't see whether someone was nude or not. "You can't tell that unless you see someone nude; to know when to cut it off, where you don't want to see it. Also, there was a scene where he drags the body, wraps the body in the curtain, and then takes it to the car. I did not do that." She would not do that.

So it was Marli Renfro inside the curtain that Tony Perkins carried out. "Every scene I was in was shot completely on a set," Marli said, "even when he carried me out to the trunk of the car."

In his script, Stefano precisely dictated Norman's movements: the lonely motel keeper was to bend to wrap the shower curtain around the body (the audience seeing only the raised edges of the curtain as they are lifted and lowered) cross to the bathroom door, using his foot to pull it open, rapidly cross the porch with his burden, and "gently lay the body in the trunk."

Perkins claimed he had to keep from breaking up because Marli kept looking up at him and winking—a very endearing gesture in the midst of such violence and such a serious scene. "No, I didn't wink at Perkins when he wrapped me in the shower curtain," said Marli. "That's not true, though it should be. I'm a bit like that. Tony put his arms under me, lifted me about four to five inches off the ground and let go. That was the cause of another take in which he got a better hold of me and changed his position so he could get it right.

"Tony pulled me out toward the shower curtain. We did it just once (except for when he dropped me). Otherwise it was one take all the way through. Everything was fine by me. Other than that it was a seamless single take to the car. But when he put me in the trunk, that was a little rough and was the only uncomfortable part." How uncomfortable? "I was thinking about that. They didn't even pad the trunk. I landed pretty hard and that made me a little mad. But Tony couldn't get the trunk lid all the way down and had to push down on it and that hurt too. Right after Tony put me into the trunk, they did the Bog Scene with the sinking car."

Out of the trunk now, Marli got to watch as they lowered the Ford Fairlane into the lake, a studio set lot known as Falls Pond. As she watched, she rubbed her sore bottom and cursed the unpadded trunk. The setting was frightening enough to give Marli a few chills as they waited and waited for the car to completely sink, rooting for Norman Bates to conceal his crime. Through a system of ramps and hydraulic lifts Hitch had accomplished the delayed sinking.

With the completion of the swamp scene Tony was off and running to the airport to fly east. His heart was beating fast all the way back as he fidgeted in his seat. He made pages of notes to improve the musical, but it was all for naught. *Greenwillow* would close before the end of May after an extremely brief run of ninety-five performances. Tony thought it might be some sort of record. It was a terrible experience.

Perkins might have left, but Hitchcock still wasn't through with the dazzling redheaded nudist. He did extensive shooting of Marli for insert shots for the Shower Sequence. According to production reports, during half of the forty-two day shooting schedule as many as two, three, and four cameras were rented for the day. At least two cameras were in operation while Marli and Janet were in the shower. "Using two cameras," observed Bill Krohn, "enabled Hitchcock to accumulate material for editing not at random, but within the paradigms set up by the storyboards." Altogether there were seventy-eight pieces of film, seventy takes of two and three seconds and over ninety splices for a sequence that runs only forty-five seconds; yet it is the most harrowing forty-five seconds of footage in cinema history. Because of its complexity, the Shower Sequence was of particular concern to Hitchcock, and on December 31 he marked it for immediate editing. *Psycho* was now four days over schedule.

Schlom and Tomasini cut the Shower Sequence all day Saturday, January 1, 1960, and again all day Sunday. Tomasini had worked with Hitch for so long that he instinctively knew how to put everything together, fully aware it had been precut on paper. Hitch was a frame cutter and would get down to frames so his work had to be perfect.

Saul Bass aided in the editing over that first weekend of a bright new year. On Monday, they showed the sequence to Hitchcock and he inserted a couple more splices. According to Bass (who also claimed it was he, not Hitchcock, who had filmed the famous Shower Sequence) the first insert was of a spatter of blood on Marion as she starts to go down while the blows are being struck. Another was the flash cut of the knife going into Marion's belly.

Later, when it was safe to do so and all the fuss had died down, Hitchcock disclosed that only Janet Leigh's hands, shoulders, and head were photographed. It wasn't until Janet's 1996 memoir that she would admit that there had been a body double. After all, it was the crowning achievement of her career, at least the one everyone remembered, and Marion Crane was the most memorable character the great star had ever played. No one could deny that the reason the Shower Sequence had worked so well was because of the great humanity Janet brought to the character. Audiences were truly shocked with her brutal demise because they cared about Marion. But it had taken two people to create that performance.

"If you don't see Janet's face—its me," Marli Renfro repeated. "My arms, my hands, my back, my legs, my knees, my belly button,"—Marli laughed, recalling that on Friday Hitch had stabbed her just below her navel. He had pushed the blade in lightly at that spot and then with-drawn it quickly. It was Hitch's private joke on the censors. It meant they had to pass the shot of the navel since it was part of the murder and crucial to the plot.

That night Alma Hitchcock spotted a glitch that the keen, practiced eyes of Hitch, Tomasini, Schlom, and even Bass had overlooked. They had run the Shower Sequence back and forth in the Moviola a couple of hundred times and failed to see it. Alma told Hitch the scene was great but they couldn't use the sequence. "And why not?" Hitch asked in surprise. "What's the matter?" Alma explained that Janet, staring in a fixed-eyed close-up on the bathroom floor, had gulped (Janet later recalled it as a blink or a breath). Alma was in the habit of watching a film frame by frame from her days as a film editor. Hitch smiled and said not to worry. They wouldn't have to reshoot. It was an easy fix. The glitch could be taken out and replaced with another cut of the showerhead. Then Hitch had the shot of Janet's eye enlarged so that it appeared to be a perfect fit for the bathtub drain and its spiraling black water.

On January 11, Hitch filmed more close-ups of Janet's face show-ing her reaction to the stabbing. Then he had Marli and Ann work on the Shower Sequence again, using three camera assistants hired for the day to allow filming from three angles at once. The next day, January 12, Marli returned to the shower to do retakes that were filmed by two Mitchell BNC cameras. At the end of the day, she was finished, and so was Janet Leigh, who left the production (though she would have to return in March for yet more close-ups of her screaming).

Nine days over schedule, Hitchcock wrapped principal photography on *Psycho* on February 1 and it was all over. For Marli her amazing year was just beginning.

Chapter Eleven
The Girl on Hugh Hefner's Cover

"It had to be mid-February," Marli said, "when *Playboy* flew me to Chicago to do the cover for the September '60 issue. I was also to pose for a couple of photo layouts—including two 'plastic dress' see-thru shots of fashions of the future. When I told my friend, Dr. Ralph [Robbins], where I was going, he warned me off Hefner. 'You watch out for him,' Dr. Ralph cautioned. 'He is weird—a sexual deviant.'" Hugh Marston Hefner, in his battle against the puritanical sexual repression of the times, was not just the "Walt Disney of Sex" but a civil rights crusader. Hef's family's strict conservative Protestant religious code (he was a direct descendent of Puritan patriarchs) had forbidden discussion of sex at home. It is astonishing but Hef had been a virgin until the age of twenty-two, but after he read Alfred Kinsey's *Sexual Behavior in the Human Male* while attending the University of Illinois, he made a drastic turnaround. Eventually, the formerly shy introvert would sleep with thousands of women. "And they still all like me," he would add proudly. His best pickup line: "My name is Hugh Hefner."

"So basically I planned to stay away from Hef," Marli said, "and when

I couldn't stay away, steer our conversations to Mercedes-Benz, which he had and I wish I did." Dr. Ralph may have been right. Author Steven Watts, in an authorized biography, *Mr. Playboy*, tells how Hef once enlisted his friend Eldon Sellers into staging a foursome. Hef once tried a gay tryst (oral sex) and even shot a stag film, *After the Masquerade*, which starred Hef and a female acquaintance in masks having sex.

Marli arrived alone at the airport and was driven by limo to her hotel on the Near North Side. "*Playboy* put me up at the Mayfair just down the street from the new Playboy Club which was still under construction." Five years earlier, the *Playboy* offices had been inside a dowdy four-story brownstone at 11 East Superior Street. Seven years earlier, the entire enterprise had fit on Hef's white kitchen table in the South Side Hyde Park apartment he shared with his wife, Mildred, and infant daughter, Christie. The new four-story offices at 232 East Ohio, remodeled for $325,000, were more sumptuous.

Marli was taking in the clean lines of the modern building when Arthur Paul, a slender, balding thirty-five-year-old designer, greeted her. *Playboy*'s first and only art director had joined the magazine in early 1955 while the first issue was still in mockup. A local freelance graphics designer, Paul conceived the *Playboy* logo and impressed Hef so much he asked him to design the entire first issue. In the beginning, *Playboy*'s only employees were Hef, his close friend Eldon Sellers (who accepted stock in place of a salary and was *Playboy*'s bookkeeper and subscription manager), and Paul, who savored their "ideal editor-art director relationship of mutual respect and flexibility." *Playboy*'s core staff included the self-taught photographer Vince Tajiri (in those days the entire photo department), Joe Paczek (layout man), Jack Kessie, and John Mastro (production manager). Later rotund, cigar-chomping Ray Russell (in charge of anything with words) arrived, and on his heels, New York literary heavyweight A. C. Spectorsky (who began buying original stories for publication).

Paul's knees had to have been calloused after years of kneeling on the diamond-checkerboard carpet Hef had used as his desktop at the old brownstone. William Randolph Hearst had done the same thing, only barefoot with a blue pencil between his toes and on all fours. Hef contented himself with gesturing from the couch with the stem of his briar to direct Paul to get down and make a fix. Hef's editors, all in white shirts, black ties, and black slacks kneeled or rested on their haunches in front of the fireplace or by the air-conditioner below the window, shooting out ideas like sparks. Now Paul and the editors were taking the measure of their first *Playboy* conference table in the new building. Paul, who had studied at the Art Institute of Chicago and the Illinois Institute of Design, embraced the rigorous design ethic of Bauhaus. He also invented the tuxedo and bowtie wearing trademark *Playboy* rabbit.

Playboy's free and relaxed atmosphere allowed him to experiment with bold illustrations that captured the mood of a text, not merely a situation within it, and actually enhanced the story. To Art Paul, illustration was not decoration, but a means to enlighten the reader. By 1960 Hef had ceased buying packaged material from independent photographers (like West Coast lensman Russ Meyer) and begun to shoot his own Playmates. By controlling the selection of his subject, lighting, pose, and content, Hef was able to clearly express his vision of "healthy female sexuality." *Playboy* photographers either went to the subject or the subject came to Chicago, as Marli had. They always shot more film than needed—about 120 snaps per Playmate—and used only a fraction of those. Don Bronstein, the first staff photographer *Playboy* ever hired, had just returned to the office from shooting the nation's top college teams and players for *Playboy*'s Pigskin Preview of All-America teams—tackle Ken Rice of Auburn, Robert Lilly of Texas Christian, and so on . . . a dream assignment. Don was also photographing a lot of *Playboy* covers. In 1958 he had lensed their July, October, November, and December covers and in 1959 photographed *Playboy*'s March and November numbers. In 1960 he was assigned the *Playboy* Centerfold with Ann Davis and the September cover with Marli Renfro. "Bronstein, who photographed me, was a great fellow," Marli said. "He had real talent."

Bronstein, excited about photographing Marli, was convinced she would make a great Playmate of the Month. She had a perfect athletic body with a beautiful face, eyes, and hair. "They really wanted to have me as a centerfold," Marli said. "The problem was that I had appeared in many other men's magazines." She showed Bronstein the large portfolio of her appearances. "Later my first husband made me get rid of everything—everything," she said. "Oh, my goodness I would go to a magazine stand and I would be in four or five magazines or on the covers and I didn't model that long—just three years. Wherever I was posing for any of the photographs there was never anything lewd. I would have been out of there in a flash if there had been." Hef's fear was if the reader recognized Marli from another magazine, it would shatter the fantasy he was striving for of the obtainable girl next door. "All the *Playboy* Center-folds hadn't been models. I wanted to do it and was really disappointed when I couldn't.

"A lot of times they took a while setting up the lighting, so I just did my own hair [in a French twist for Bronstein's session], my own makeup while I waited. I always did that." Don was looking for a pleasing com-position in the frame of his ground glass when Hef entered wearing a white long-sleeved shirt and narrow black tie, a black pipe clinched firmly in his mouth. He was gaunt, good looking, intense. Hef exuded confidence, and the pipe only accentuated the already powerful thrust of his jaw. At the time, every college boy in the nation considered Hef the height of sophistication, and it was true that he knew more about jazz than most critics. Like Paul, he had extremely definite ideas about his work and was hands-on about every aspect of his magazine. Marli studied Hef as she posed, recalled Dr. Ralph's admonition, and knuckled down to work.

"A lot of times you just walked around and the photographers they just stayed in one position with the lighting," Marli explained. "Other times you're where you are and they're walking back and forth." She worked through her extensive repertoire of poses smoothly. "Why can't all models look like her?" Don Bronstein thought as she glided in and out of inventive positions. Marli had the rare ability to express a par-ticular emotion to an audience simply through her physical being. With a slight twist to her body, she added excitement to her next pose and in the next was able in some ephemeral way to transmit her personality to the viewer. Whenever you met her in the flesh, you were never sur-prised by the person. Marli was exactly like her image and that image was magic. Her strength was that while a lot of models looked similar to one another, Marli was unique and could never be mistaken for another. Don tried different head angles with her. Tilting her head was flattering as it made her long red hair fall away from her body. He decided to put her hair up for the cover shot so he could show her profile. When Marli tipped her head up slightly, it accentuated her partially closed eyes, and her slightly opened mouth gave her a sensuous look. When she tipped her head down her blue-green eyes dominated and seemed larger. Don adjusted the fill light of the strobe to fill in body shadow.

Finally he decided to show Marli nude from behind as if in the shower, her head tilted slightly down and looking over her shoulder at the viewer. Instead of composing his picture with a strong diagonal line, Paul centered her figure down to her lumbar region. Marli played with her hair, even placed her hands behind her head. Then she tried them folded across her midriff. They would not show in the posterior view as they were in front of her, held very loosely and barely touching. Bronstein liked that. It kept the swell of her hips unbroken and brought the viewer's eye back to her face.

After Don developed Marli's contact sheets the next day, Art Paul walked them up to Hef. The publisher was dressed casually, as always, in loafers, white socks and dark slacks, and hefting a bottle of Pepsi, one of the two dozen he drank daily. It was his favorite nightcap—with a little Jack Daniel's added. Paul laid the contact sheets out on a light table, clicked it to life, and watched as Hef went over every inch of them with a jeweler's loupe. The publisher believed every issue of *Playboy* "must be paced like a symphony. While there may be a *scherzo* of cartoons, a *largo* of literature, a *rondo* of reportage, the *allegro* in each edition is still the girls . . . they remain the main motif."

Hef was cordial, aware that because of his relentless drive and exacting nature he had a tendency to snap at his staff. These days he was making a conscious effort to commend them whenever he could. If he disagreed with Paul on a cover, he usually backed down and simply said, "You're the art editor."

The back shot was approved. Paul, excited about its golden tones— red hair, slightly redder lipstick, and orange background—showed Hef a clever concept for Marli's cover. He began drawing curved lines on a blowup like slash marks. Paul had designed the cover as a jigsaw puzzle with one piece in the shape of the *Playboy* rabbit missing at the curve of Marli's right hip. "Perfect," Hef said. And that was what Marli was—a mystery with a missing piece. Paul's concept was a way of saying who the girl was and yet was not, as if there was so much more to find out.

While Hitch and Janet had kept Marli's part in *Psycho* a closely guarded secret, it was known around the *Playboy* building. The upcoming September cover showed her in a pose that looked as if she had been surprised in the shower. After Paul left Hef got out the "bible" for the September issue and saw that he had already earmarked page twenty-eight for the magazine's review of *Psycho*.

Then Paul ran into a problem. It would be too expensive for him to get an actual die made for the puzzle cover. The difficulty stumped him for most of the evening, but by morning he had solved the problem. "So they ended up doing it as art," Marli said, "with Paul drawing all the lines in by hand. It was demanding, time consuming work but very effective and he brought it off wonderfully."

"That cover was an easy one, but the hardest picture I ever posed for was with Bronstein and it was the one with the plastic dresses we did on the second day." It would actually appear before the September issue, in the July *Playboy*. "There is a dress that is balloon plastic and it bubbles down just about to my knees and I'm standing basically with my back to the camera, about three quarter and that pose was the hardest, really. I'm a dancer and could be balanced and get it right, but he had me with my weight on my left foot and my right foot way back (it doesn't look like it's way back in the picture) and the rest of my body doing stuff. My hand is way back, I'm holding a balloon. I tell you I had a hard time.

"Getting paid at *Playboy* was funny. At the end they called me into the offices. I go in after I did the cover and two other photo shoots, one for the July issue that would beat my cover onto the stands and a second for a later issue."

"Well," Paul said. "What do we have now? What do we owe you?" At the time *Playboy* Centerfolds and cover spots received $500 for posing (the magazine in 1960 sold for sixty cents), the same amount Marli had received for many backbreaking days filming the *Psycho* Shower Sequence. The following year *Playboy* would double the rates. "We pay $10 an hour," Paul said.

"I charge $25 an hour or $150 a day,'" Marli told him.

"His jaw just dropped," she recalled. "I liked being my own agent and could be tough when I had to be."

Playboy got its money's worth, though. The September number would be a landmark issue especially for Hef—it introduced the Playboy Advisor wherein he answered readers' questions on food, drink, fashion, manners, morals, and etiquette. A joke in that issue made Marli laugh: "An artist's model is nearly always unsuited for her work."

Her striking red hair and oceanic eyes put Marli in great demand around the *Playboy* offices during the three days she was there. She met Shel Silverstein, who had gotten his start as a cartoonist in Japan at the Tokyo *Stars and Stripes*. Shel worked big on semi-translucent vellum with dozens of pentimenti and white-outs and had a lustful eye for the ladies. Sports and social illustrator LeRoy Neiman, a striking man with a huge mustache and shock of black hair, was another Chicago Art Institute alum. He wanted Marli to sit for one of his impressionist paintings. "I didn't want to sit while I was there. I was tired after of days of posing. I told him, 'No, thanks.' Then I learned they were preparing to open the first Playboy Club at the end of the month."

The Playboy Club was the brainchild of Playboy Promotions Director Victor Lownes III. Hef, who admired Vic's sophisticated humor and sexual adventurousness (five women a day was the office scuttlebutt), listened carefully to any idea he brought. Vic was often right. The initial spark for the men's key club had been Jonathan Rhoads's November 1958 *Playboy* article, "The Lock on the Barroom Door." Rhoads began his piece: "A doorman appeared beside him. 'Can't get in without a key,' he said . . ." and captioned a color photo of sexy women in velvet one-piece costumes: "The Gaslight Club captures the mood of the Gay Nineties in each of its handsome rooms . . . membership is by invitation only and there is always a long waiting list for the keys that will open the Gaslight's locked door."

The Chicago Gaslight Club in the bohemian section on Rush Street was only one of several highly successful after-hours bottle clubs in the nation. Burton Browne, a local ad executive, had opened it six years ago. Currently four thousand key holders, many Second City power-brokers and VIPs, were members. The Gaslight Girls served patrons dressed in Gay Nineties–style wasp-waisted corsets and fishnet tights. Rhoads concluded his article by writing: "Browne knew a seller's market and a solid gimmick when he saw them." So did Vic Lownes, who suggested to Hef that a key club could bring the magazine's bachelor pad image to life and diversify their brand to reach those who didn't read *Playboy*. "Readers love the concept," Vic said and dumped boxes of mail received in response to the article on Hef's desk. Hef realized *Playboy* could create its own "urban hangout," or swinging bachelor pad for the cosmopolitan man with beautiful, scantily clad young women as hostesses. "Besides," he said, "it was a great way to meet chicks."

One of Vic's girlfriends, Ilsa Taurins, took a long, hard look at Art Paul's design for the *Playboy* logo, and suggested to Vic and Hef that the waitresses should be dressed as bunnies. Hef, who thought of the rabbit as male, was initially resistant, favoring instead short nighties on the girls. Undeterred, Ilsa had her mother stitch a costume from her design. A few days later she sauntered into the half-finished Playboy Club wearing "a satin bodice, fluffy tail, and headband with large ears." Hef was sold.

Marli, who liked almost everyone, did not like the abrasive Lownes. "A little snooty-type, a spoiled young man," she said, "Vic Lownes was very caught up in himself." Much of the *Playboy* staff agreed, calling him "a brow-beater with a cruel streak," "vicious," and "brutal." Vic ruled by "outright terror," and any sign of weakness in his subordinates was a red flag to him. Occasionally, his staff would quit en masse and Hef would have to chase after them to the elevator and coax them back with promises of better treatment and raises.

But the Playboy Club was a genius idea and it was Vic's. "Right away," Marli said, "I asked if I could work at the Playboy Club and right away they said, 'Yes.' So, I went back to LA for two or three weeks to tidy up my affairs.

"After I squared things in LA, I flew back to Chicago in early March 1960 to work at the first Playboy Club in downtown Chicago. I got there about a week after it opened [on Leap Year day]." Marli exited a cab in front of 116 East Walton and saw a dazzling throng of well-dressed executives and impeccably attired young men waiting to see *Playboy* come to life for another gala night. Limos and taxis were coming and going in front of the five-story building. Cars were two and three deep. Marli felt the chill bite of a windy night as she started up the steps to the imposing front entrance. A photographer snapped a picture of Hef standing above like an emperor just as some other girls were coming up. "Let's have another picture," Hef called and stretched out his arms. "They just called us together, a bunch of us to take a picture," Marli said, "some on the stairs going up and some on the ground level with Hef. I'm to the far right. He's talking to one of his favorites." Marli was smiling one of her rare smiles. It was an exciting time at the start of an unbelievably exciting year.

For once Marli was aware of the momentous events swirling around her. *Playboy* seemed to be one happy, slightly dysfunctional family. Hef's really big all-night parties would not start until May. Now *Playboy*, with all its success, was embarking on what seemed to be an even more fruitful enterprise. Marli was glad to be associated with *Playboy*. It could be a stepping-stone—if she wanted it. "And I did," she said. She got a place living upstairs in a coach house in the downtown Gold Coast District and prepared for her new job.

"First they started me at the door of the Playboy Club taking members' keys, then I tried to get a job as a waitress but had no experience. I quit, and got a job at the Cloisters [a Near North Side Chicago jazz club on Rush Street] as a cocktail waitress. As soon as I had experience I went back to the *Playboy* as a Bunny. I didn't have a bunny outfit—I wore a black leotard until they had my costume made." The design was still in flux.

"A young lady who was the assistant wardrobe designed the essential costume," Marli said, "and she did mine on me and so I was one of the first to wear one. It was higher up in the legs (to make your legs look longer) and lower down in the back—they added the ears and the tail." The original *Playboy* costume, a formfitting leotard, resembled a strapless, one-piece, rayon-satin bathing suit with black mesh tights. It had satin ears, bow tie, and a small fluffy tail; the white collar, name tags, rosettes, and cuffs would come later. Marli's bunny shoe was a plain pump with a three-inch heel and pointed toe. The ideal Bunny stood five feet two inches and measured thirty-seven/twenty-three/thirty-two. Marli was five foot two and measured thirty-six/twenty-three/thirty-six.

Within two years Renee Blot would perfect the costume by reducing the size of the ears and adding a bow tie, shirt cuffs, and a rosette name tag on the right hip, which allowed seated key holders to see a Bunny's name at eye level. Hef was so impressed, he patented the bunny costume—the first service costume ever copyrighted with the U.S. Patent and Trademark Office and the first symbol of the coming sexual revolution he had helped start. The slightly revealing costume showed some skin, but remained innocent enough to demonstrate Hef's "Look but don't touch" policy with bunnies. He had taken another page from the Gaslight Club: Anyone who touched a waitress would be immediately expelled.

The Bunny Mother, who supervised Marli and others, not only wrote them up if they had chipped nails or scuffed pumps but gave lessons on how to refuse to tell a guy your name. Any whiff of scandal could destroy the entire operation, which promised to be successful beyond Hef's wildest dreams. The Bunnies were also not allowed to date key holders or give them their numbers, a rule the fun-loving Marli broke at once.

"When I was in Chicago, I dated a quote, unquote 'supposed gangster' I had met at the Playboy Club. We weren't supposed to date any of the customers, but I wanted to date him so I targeted him and about the third time he came into the bar he asked me out. He wasn't a thug, just real nice and we had a lot of laughs. I thought he looked a lot like John Garfield the actor." He was slight of build, about 150 pounds, with brown eyes and graying hair. She mentioned her stint dancing at the El Rancho Vegas to him and the several TV commercials she had done waterskiing and horseback riding for Ray Ryan, who owned the El Mirador and the North Shore Yacht Club, where her dad was commissioned to sell the properties. She might have told him too much, but it meant nothing to her at the time. The "supposed mobster" left Chicago, and she didn't think of the charming older man until sometime later.

"I get a clipping from a newspaper that shows a car that had been bombed," Marli said. "It's Ray Ryan's car! Down below the picture there are two people suspected of doing it and one of them was the guy I dated in Chicago—the 'gangster.' Circles within circles." Marli never suspected that he was actually a top enforcer for the Chicago mob. If Dr. Ralph had not been far away in Miami, he might have warned her because he was wise in many ways. Danger was everywhere, he might have cautioned, but for now the lights were bright, the men handsome, the women beautiful, and she was happy. She saw Hef across the room, a lovely Bunny on each arm, and smiled.

Outside the club, Bunny Scouts were busy beating the bushes of the nation's hinterlands for the most beautiful "girls next door"—attractive women between eighteen and twenty-five who would look spectacular in velvet and who would be raised by stern Bunny Mothers in the Chicago Hutch.

The Red Journal Playboy Club had two levels. The lower level had the bar—liqueurs, cocktails, cognacs, vintage French champagne— and then booths on the opposite sides. It had the first juke box that lit up with colors following the music, red for the bass and lighter ones for the higher notes. There was wood paneling and leather-covered furniture in the Living Room, the Penthouse, and the Library. In the Chicago Hutch the Playmate Bar was decorated with illuminated transparencies of centerfolds, and a cartoon corner was filled with original Shel Silverstein inked pages and Jack "Plastic Man" Cole's frothy watercolors of sexy women. Just after Cole mailed Hef a letter on August 13, 1958, he shot himself to death with a .22-caliber single-shot Marlin rifle. Hef, a cartoonist himself, opened Cole's letter the next morning and read his last words, which spoke volumes about the kind of guy Hef was:

When you read this I shall be dead. I cannot go on living with myself hurting those dear to me. What I do has nothing to do with you. You have been the best guy I've ever worked for in all these years. I'm only sorry I leave owing you . . . Thanks for everything, Heffer, you're a good guy. Kindest regards, Jack.

Marli considered the popular nightspot a terrific place to work. "The drinks were a dollar and a half (when drinks back then were normally 25 to 35 cents) and people tipped big time," she said. "I worked a lot of lunches and really liked the lunchtime crowd." Marli swiftly mastered the Bunny dip, facing away from the table, arching her back, bending both knees and setting the drink on the table with one smooth sweep of her arm. If you leaned too far over the table you would look bad from the back and much too good from the front. The Chicago Playboy Club Bunnies became known for their superior derrieres.

"The worst people—they pulled your ears, pulled your tail—hard!— were women. I couldn't believe it! Men basically left you alone. They would bring business types, and clients in and they tipped nice too." When Marli got a tip she slipped it into her low cleavage. "It was a turn-on," she said. "I thoroughly enjoyed it." Being a Bunny was being a flirt, and the costume really helped her flirt. In the VIP room the Bunnies wore blue velvet costumes trimmed in silver lame, but on the floor they dressed redheads like Marli in green, one of ten available colors. The black costumes, the most elegant of the Bunny costumes, were coveted by all the girls.

"Plus I did a lot of photo ads for the Playboy Club in the magazine in my Bunny outfit and advertising the TV show," Marli said. Within a year, the Chicago Key Club would be the busiest nightclub in the world and a status symbol just to join. A lifetime membership was $50 and that included a key. Less than 30 percent of the key holders ever used their key. Hef counted on this. The Club's revenue shored up the magazine, which was becoming the least-profitable part of Hef's empire.

The previous summer, Hef had decided to diversify further by hosting a ninety-minute "hip, swinging late evening bachelor party" on an elaborate TV studio set with a wood-burning fireplace, a fish tank, and a revolving bookcase that turned into a bar. *Playboy's Penthouse* debuted on October 24 out of the Chicago WBKB studio and was syndicated for twenty-six weeks by a loose network of twelve stations across the nation. Current Bunnies and Playmates were always in attendance as Hef, the MC, using his pipe as a prop to occupy his hands, said stiffly, "Good evening. I'm Hugh Hefner. Welcome to the party." Then they all surrounded Cy Coleman, seated at the piano, as he sang his hit "Witchcraft."

"I was on their first program after the Club opened and several times after that," Marli said. "One taping we bunnies rushed in front of the red and white camera to surround Hef. Well, at first, I was one of the first to come in; then I found myself being shoved to the back. So by the next take I was one of the last on and got a surprised look from Hef. I guess he was expecting someone else."

On his show, Hef featured controversial comedians, jazz (his passion, along with Sinatra), folk musicians, and soul artists. Pete Seeger, Ray Charles, Sammy Davis Jr., Tony Bennett, Sarah Vaughan, Nat King Cole, Harry Belafonte, and Ella Fitzgerald all performed. One guest was Dr. Michael Davis, a hypnotist, who could put almost anyone under. *Playboy* had the first national TV program where whites and blacks sat and partied as equals. Black performers didn't just entertain (Nat King Cole didn't even sing) and walk off but joined the party, chatting and laughing and drinking Scotch and soda in clouds of cigarette smoke. This favorably impressed Marli, who was still shocked by her spring 1958 trip to Miami where, for the first time, she encountered separate black and white water fountains. Once again, the personable young dancer had arrived at a crucial history-changing juncture in her amazing year. Her next meeting was even more fortuitous. The club, really just a bar with *Playboy* Bunnies serving drinks to key holders, offered entertainment by the brightest comedians, and among them was a young "sicknic" comic very unlike sweater-clad Mort Sahl and his rolled up newspaper.

Hef had first seen Lenny Bruce at the Cloisters and admired his profane language and jazz-riff vocabulary. Like Hef, he questioned the conformity of the times. Naturally, Hef made certain that Lenny, one of his favorites, was on the first *Playboy Penthouse*. Lenny did bits about almost sneezing from the champagne and having to blow his nose, a veiled cocaine reference. Bruce, who sprinkled his act with Freudian-isms like Oedipus complex, was performing once when he looked out into the audience and asked two boys who had made it big in Chicago to stand up and take a bow—"Ladies and gentlemen, Leopold and Loeb!"

"I dated Lenny Bruce," Marli said. "What fun! What fun. I wasn't with Lenny very long, maybe two or three weeks, something like that. I thought he was brilliant, I really did. I only dated him three or four times with different circles of friends." The diminutive thirty-four-old in his Brooks Brothers suit—slender, handsome, a constant cigarette cocked in his hand—had dark curly hair and arched eyebrows, and was a magnetic figure. A Long Island native, Bruce had dropped out after grammar school, worked on a farm, served a hitch in the navy (Marli had noticed the large tattoo on his arm), and seen action at Anzio and Salerno. On *Playboy's Penthouse*, Lenny, chatting up two Playmates, worried aloud that his tattoo might prevent burial in a Jewish cemetery.

"He really touched people's sensitivity," Marli said. "I went to one of his shows and was so surprised. I guess he was telling a Catholic joke and quite a few people got up and left. I just couldn't believe it. We're talking humor here. Hey, Folks! Don't take it so seriously."

Lenny, who adored movies, was working on a film, *Leather Jacket*. "I remember sitting in Lenny's front room back when he was married to Holly Harlow," said Vegas producer, writer, filmmaker, and stuntman, Jerry Schafer, "talking about going to Chicago with him so that I could bail him out when they arrested him—and of course they did." Lenny had arrived at the Chicago Playboy Club fresh from performing at Enrico Banducci's hungry in San Francisco. By October, his performance at the San Francisco Jazz Workshop would bring down the unforgiving wrath of censors upon him, land him in court, and earn him the sobriquet "Dirty Lenny." When the comic returned to Chicago in December 1962, he would again be arrested for obscenity, this time at the Golden Horn.

"It's actually a party," Lenny marveled on the show. "Yeah, it's cool with some pretty chicks serving real liquor. When I'm swinging and I feel the warmth coming up at me, I'd like to ball the whole audience."

"I went to Hef's mansion a couple of times," Marli said. She always brought along other girls from the club. Hef, who had growing social obligations, had moved out of the cramped bedroom apartment behind his office into a magnificent forty-room mansion, a limestone and brick four-story, two blocks from Lake Michigan on the Near North Side. Marli and her friends passed through the ornate iron fence fronting 1340 North State Street and saw a plaque on the door in Latin, a gift from A. C. Spectorsky, which read *Si Non Oscillas Noli Tintinnare* (If You Don't Swing, Don't Ring). Two suits of armor guarded the entrance.

The girls climbed the stairs. On the second floor, Hef had a two-story ballroom with oak-paneled walls, an open-beamed ceiling, a marble fireplace, a movie screen that dropped down from the ceiling, and a trapdoor in the floor for looking into a waterfall cave called the "Woo Grotto." Just off the ballroom was Hef's bedroom, which contained a round rotating bed, a hi-fi, plush white carpeting, secret panels, and more gadgets than 007; in fact, James Bond's creator, Ian Fleming, was visiting the *Playboy* offices right then. Fleming even had Bond join the Playboy Club in one of his novels.

"Hef had an indoor pool on one floor," Marli said, "and on the floor below he had a bar which backed up to the walls of the pool with a giant picture window so people, basically men, could watch the swimmers in the water who were mostly topless." The kidney-shaped, bathing suit–optional pool had a waterfall, underwater bar, and adjoining sun and steam rooms.

"Hef also had a study-type room where he had a hypnotist who would put girls under and have them masturbate with quite a lot of men watching," Marli said. "I know this because I was curious as to what was going on in there and hung around until I was invited in. When the hypnotist thought I was 'under' that was when he started telling me to start playing with myself, which I didn't because sex to me has always been a private matter between me and a man. Then he realized that I wasn't under after all and I left the room, my curiosity taken care of. And I still had my nine lives, or most of them at least." What would Dr. Ralph have thought?

Hef's big weekly parties wouldn't really begin until May with upward of two hundred guests partying until dawn on exotic food and fine liquors. Janet Leigh's husband, Tony Curtis, spent considerable time at the mansion. He and Hef had met in 1950 while Janet was filming *Jet Pilot* for producer Howard Hughes, who had designs on her. She lived with her parents in a little house on Sunset Boulevard until she married.

Curtis recalled how when he and Janet were first married, June 4, 1951, she would take away his dish before he was finished eating. "I thought you were done, darling," she would say. "That's how I found out how compulsively neat Janet was," Tony said. "Nothing could be out of place when she was around . . . sometimes Janet's insistence that everything be in its place made me a little edgy." While Janet was playing in *My Sister Eileen*, Tony believed she was having a fling with the film's choreographer, Bob Fosse, basing his unfounded suspicions on a vague note, but as he wrote in *American Prince*, "I couldn't be absolutely sure. Sure, I had affairs of my own, but . . . I made damn sure Janet never found out about them . . . By this time Hugh Hefner had become a good friend. To get away from Janet and Fosse, I flew to Chicago to visit with Hef. That weekend I met some very friendly *Playboy* Bunnies, and I had not the slightest pangs of guilt about having sex with them. After a week of debauchery in Chicago, I knew I was going to be all right."

Later, Tony would spend three full months with Hef at his mansion with his frequent guests Tony Bennett, Sammy Davis Jr., Ray Charles, The Grateful Dead, B. B. King, Buddy Rich, and Mel Torme. "Hef was a steadying influence on me," Tony wrote, "the kind of guy I could tell anything to and he would understand. I was so vulnerable in those days that I fell for every girl I met at the mansion. There was hardly anyone around to take them out, and Hef didn't want them floating around the city unescorted, so I always had a girl on my arm." In 1961 Curtis would become involved in a Hollywood movie about Hef's life and spend a couple of weeks in Chicago hanging around the *Playboy* offices to get a feel for Hef's operation to prepare himself. Tony envisioned a light comedy about a swinging bachelor with six girlfriends and the difficulties that ensued when they crossed paths. Hef had other ideas. When he began sending thirty-page memos to the studio, Curtis didn't even have to read them. "I just had to weigh them," he said, "to know that we're never, *ever* going to make this movie."

"When I was at Chicago," Marli said, "I went down to the hot sulphur springs in Georgia by train. We're sitting there in our seats and a couple of priests were opposite us having lunch. They brought out some wine and I thought, 'Wow, I didn't know you guys were supposed to drink.' We get down to the hot springs and it's a convention of designers of men's fashions, a large gathering. We wore our bunny outfits and had to stand in this little room, as Green is talking." Robert Lamont Green, with his wavy silvering hair, colorful ties, and elegant suits, had been the

Playboy fashion arbiter since 1958. "He's droning on and on and there just isn't anything in this room but a big wheel and so I start turning it. All the lights went out and Greenberg was livid until I figured out what I had done and turned it back."

"When *Playboy* was launched into the repressed, clean-cut America of the early 1950s," wrote the London *Times*, "it would have an impact far greater than Hefner could imagined and alongside the Pill and rock and roll, it would prove to be one of the pillars of the so-called sexual revolution of the 1960s and 1970s." Hefner's official biographer, Steven Watts, portrayed him as a genuine romantic, a sentimental optimist, and an idealist. Hef was on a quest for sex without guilt, while Hitch's devout Catholic upbringing caused him to wrestle with guilt in most of his films.

In Hollywood, editor George Tomasini's rough cut of *Psycho* was transported to the MPAA, the Hayes office, the film industry's self-censorship board. Hitch commonly gave the censors bait, which they focused on and therefore the things he really wanted to keep didn't appear to be harmful. For *Rear Window* Hitch shot protection footage of "Miss Torso" clothed to replace two topless scenes of her he had never intended to use.

With all his bait in place after the first cut, Hitch arranged a screening for Luigi Luraschi, head of Paramount's censorship department. Luraschi acted as intermediary between that studio and the Production Code Administration (PCA), Hollywood's self-appointed censorship board. "We're all looking on placidly," recalled Peggy Robertson, Hitch's personal secretary since serving as script supervisor on *Vertigo*, "but that all changed when they reached the Shower Sequence."

"Stop! Stop! My God!' Luraschi shouted.

"Yes, Luigi," Hitch said, "what is it?"

"I saw her breast."

"No you didn't, Luigi. It's just in your dirty mind. You didn't see a breast at all. Yes, we'll run it again." So they ran it again. "Well, Luigi did you see a breast?"

"No, but we're going to be in a lot of trouble with it," Luraschi said.

"We made him realize," Peggy said, "it was a perfectly charming little Sunday afternoon Shower Sequence."

Still, everyone was worried as the censors prepared to pass judgment. Hitch and Stefano had broken three taboos—shown a toilet on the screen for the first time (and been bold enough to flush it), portrayed a couple in a lunchtime liaison at a cheap hotel, and shown a woman in her bra—both black and white bras to symbolize her moods. They got away with that, but then the censors thought they saw Leigh's nipple (one was really there) and demanded its removal. "But in actual fact," one critic said much later, "only [Janet Leigh's] head, feet, and arms are seen—the rest is stand-in Marli Renfro, a nude model, whose dignity was preserved through judicial use of moleskin patches and glue." He was partially right. Marli was stark naked and it was Janet who wore the moleskin. He was wrong when he called Marli a stand-in, She was a body double, a huge difference. Hitch offered to fix the scene, but the guardians of public morals never pursued it and failed to turn up for a review screening that Hitch had arranged to demonstrate how inoffensive the scene was.

Stefano never reconciled himself to the loss of one scene—excision of an overhead shot of Marli lying over the tub with her buttocks exposed devastated him. He regretted that deletion more than any other. In his heart he had known Hitch would never get away with a nude derriere but felt, more than any other scene, it held tremendous emotional impact. "It was the only angle from the Shower Sequence that was cut," Stefano lamented. "That one shot really brought home the tragedy of a lost life," Stefano told Stephen Rebello, "so poetic and so hurtful." Was there anything "more painful than to see that beauty murdered?"

A finished, scored, and titled version of *Psycho* wouldn't be available until March 30, just four days before Marli Renfro's birthday. Hitchcock's Mystery Girl would soon be famous without being famous. But just who was she and what were the roots of the girl in Hitchcock's shower?

Chapter Twelve
Marlys

"My dad was born in a covered wagon in 1905," Marli said. "His parents were traveling from Illinois and his mom is ready to give birth, so they stopped at this farm southeast of Dallas, owned by Boone Dougherty. They asked if they could stop there so she could have her baby. And he said 'Sure thing. And I'll tell you this: If it's a boy and you name him after me, I'll mention him in my will.' So they named my dad Jesse Boone Jackson Renfro."

Marlys Annelle Renfro was born in the Methodist Hospital, downtown Los Angeles, on April 3, 1938 at 5:56 A.M. "in the sun sign of Aries and the moon sign of Aries." When she was three, her family moved just north of Dallas to Tioga, where her paternal grandmother lived. In those days, the Renfros traveled and camped out a lot, drove up to Canada when Marli was seven and moved to snowy Big Bear Lake for a year while Marli attended fifth grade.

The family didn't have a lot of money—Marli's mother made all of her clothes (except for sweaters and underwear) and a colorful costume, which included clown makeup, for her favorite Christmas on 104th

Street near Broadway. They ate pinto beans and cornbread at least once a week, but Louise was such a good cook that Marli's friend Diane Manthey always connived to be there when she cooked that dish. "When my parents woke up they'd always play cards," Marli said. "The first person up would play solitaire (mom, dad, or me), then we would all play gin in the morning."

The Renfros moved down to North Hollywood, then to Fifty-sixth and Western in Los Angeles while Marli attended seventh grade at John Muir Junior High. Practically every day throughout the summer Marli and her best friend, Pat Meford, caught the streetcar at South Vermont Avenue and West Slauson Avenue and rode far south down Vermont to the end of the line at 117th. Then they'd walk two miles along the railroad tracks below what is now the Glenn Anderson Freeway to the stables to ride bareback over the rolling hills, doubling on Pat's horse, Mitzi. "That's where I really learned to ride horses," Marli said. "I still love horses." She eventually owned both saddle- and racehorses.

Just before Marli entered eighth grade, the Renfros bought a house in Arcadia, and her dad went into real estate. When he became the general manager of Moonridge Mountain Estates in Big Bear, the Renfros bought a tiny cabin there with a hide-a-bed in the living room. Every Friday, Marli's parents would pick her up after school and they'd drive up to Big Bear for the weekend or spend a vacation there.

When she was fourteen, Marli began to ask three or four of her girlfriends up to the cabin for a weekend while a few of their guy friends stayed nearby at Ted Page's place. Over Halloween, Marli and her friend Judy Chapman tinted their hair black like witches. "I'd been putting a bleach solution on the part in my hair," Marli said, "and when I washed out the black tint, it came out everywhere except at the lightened part which came out a beautiful turquoise." The next day when she went to classes at Clifton Junior High she wore one of her mother's handmade dresses, denim with many-colored stripes—"to match my hair."

"My dad, as general manager of Moonridge Mountain Estates," she said, "had me enter beauty contests up there when I was a junior in high school. My hair was very long then, and I won Miss Coast Federal. I won quite a few contests." Marli was aware of the politics involved in beauty competitions. "But I knew what my body was and I knew other girls' bodies, all hemmed in and all this stuff. This one contest I just wore a two-piece suit."

Marli attended Monrovia High—"green and white, go Wildcats!"— and made new friends: Preston, John, Maryann, John, Billye Sue, David, Chuck, Al, and all the rest. "Somewhere along the line I skipped a grade because I was just seventeen when I graduated," Marli said. After graduation she got a job in new accounts at Coast Federal Savings and Loan downtown.

In December 1956 she substituted for *Addams Family* star Carolyn Jones as the grand marshal in Hollywood's Christmas parade. "Carolyn had the flu or something," she said. "They dressed me in a mink coat and I waved to various and sundry fans and had a ball." Marli was then living with Republic actor John Carroll and his family. Carroll once played Zorro, a singing Zorro. "His daughter was about my age," said Marli. "John had a production company and it was my job to read scripts. Nobody could be less qualified. I not only didn't know what I was doing, but I hated English."

Her beauty contest wins got her jobs modeling on Harry Owens's Hawaii program, posing by the pool at the El Mirador in Palm Springs for their postcards and swimming and waterskiing for Lake Mojave Ranchos TV commercials where they gave her the nickname "Marli."

Her dad's company was Jack B. Renfro and Associates. He had a large office staff, about forty salespeople, working for him selling properties— $20 down, $20 a month. He entertained a lot, mostly lunches, and invited different staff to lunch. Everywhere he sold was out of the area, basically resorts. During the week, his salespeople would get leads from his advertisements and go out to the potential buyer's home, talk to them, and then meet them at the property—at Big Bear, Hollywood by the Sea, Ventura, Oxnard, North Shore Yacht Club Estates, or Salton Sea. There were times when they would take the buyers out, but usually on a Saturday night Marli's dad would have the salespeople over for dinner. "My mother was one of the bookkeepers," she said, "and they had me working the front desk, answering calls and entering payments in a receipt book."

Jack Renfro advertised heavily, spending about 40 percent of his profits advertising on *The Ben Hunter Show* on KTLA, Channel 5, and on Hunter's nighttime radio program, *Night Owls*. "He sponsored a few of Hank Williams's dances," Marli said, "and was real good friends with Hank Penny 'the Old Country Boy,' and singer Sue Thompson. He also had a kind of travel agency where he took tours down into Mexico. When my dad came out to Twenty-Nine Palms in the later fifties, he was contracted to sell a huge section of lots and named it the Ben Hunter Tract. Then, they did another further north of there, Ben Hunter Two." Her dad advertised on Jackson Wheeler's TV program; Wheeler was one of the notable personalities in southern California and sold property to a lot of celebrities—directors, cameramen, actors. Through her father, Marli got to meet a number of these celebrities. She sometimes lunched at Nickodel's on Melrose or the Blarney Castle on Western with Richard Jansen the actor and Peter Whorf the art director. "I dated Hugh O'Brien just once," she said. "He was, as expected, cold and perfectly attired. I dated Gene Norman, owner of the Crescendo supper club on La Cienega, a few times. There was a great Mexican group there who also played the lounge at the El Rancho in Vegas."

In October 1957, Marli moved to Manhattan and first lived at the Barbizon Hotel for Women for three weeks before sharing an apartment with two other girls. Her first job was for Fiat Motors, and then she auditioned for and got a job as a chorus dancer at the Latin Quarter at 2551 Broadway. "Was I ever nervous on stage?" said Marli. "When you first get on stage, yes, but after that, no. The first time I appeared at the Latin Quarter, this other girl and I, dressed in little bathing suit-type things with sequins and frou-frou around in the back. We would prance out to the middle of the stage up front, down stage, and in poems would introduce the next act and dance off. The first time you get out there, my left knee cap is going up and down. Just nerves."

She admitted she wasn't always graceful in the beginning. "Those were big time production numbers, some lasting as long as fifteen minutes. Why they picked on me, I don't know, but one time I filled in for a showgirl, wearing a huge-feathered hat and descending a steep spiral staircase, catching my heel on a step and almost tumbling down. Another time I filled in for one of the lead singers. I didn't sing but was sang to—*Kismet*—I had never been sung to before and I had the hardest time keeping from giggling when he looked into my eyes singing of his love.

"I was first hired with another lady to say the poems we used to introduce each act coming up—the singers and comedians and dancers. We had a different costume each time, just little bittie costumes. We did that for about a month, then they shelved that and both of us were hired into the chorus. That was really hard work. We had one number where the whole show was built around Can Can and Paris. For our Can Can number we wore heavy, heavy red velvet and big skirts which we undid toward the end and took those off. The whole number was right foot kicking, on your left foot and you are kicking.

"At the Latin Quarter that's where I really saw stage door Johnnys. It's something you see in the movies and then you see them in real life. I thought it was neat. One guy was just in love with one showgirl—tall and skinny (I think she was bulimic, she used to throw up after she ate), rail-thin. And he would always give her great big blueberry cheesecakes." Marli met Gary Morton at the Latin Quarter and from 1957 until 1961 saw him a few times and later ran into him when he was a guest comedian on the *Playboy Penthouse*. "He later married Lucille Ball," Marli said. "A very nice, funny man. Sometimes after the show I had a date. Other times I just went home.

"So many of the women there were married with families. I got around by bus or taxi or subway. Not often on the subway. We had a snow storm and there were very few of anything running and at the time I lived out on 17th Street near 2nd Avenue. The Latin Quarter was in the 40s. I walked all the way in the ice and cold. It was a harrowing evening for me to get home."

In May 1958, Marli moved to Miami Beach, where she got a job as a chorus dancer at the Americana Hotel and was introduced to fishing. "We went out fishing two or three times a week in the waters off South Beach," she said. "The fellow I was with down there, Dr. Ralph Robbins, a bon vivant, was a Miami Beach icon." And why was he an icon? "Because he was a celebrity," she said. And why was he a celebrity? "He was a celebrity just being himself." Just like Marli.

"Dr. Ralph had two brothers who were also doctors. One of his brother's patients was an heir to the Singer Sewing Machine fortune. She had a little home next door to the Woolworth's on this small secluded island off of Miami Beach and this beautiful all-white thirty-five-foot cabin cruiser with twin Chrysler engines. She was a full bull dyke and just worked on her boat engines and tried as much as she could to be manly. I kidded her, 'if you want to be a man, be a *gentle*man. Clean your nails.' She got a laugh out of that." She and her girlfriend took Marli and Dr. Ralph fishing. "Both were just center stage people while Ralph and I were more happy-go-lucky people. So, gee, we just got into having a good time." And Marli did have fun. She had a lusty appetite for filet mignon, medium-rare hamburgers, BLTs, meat loaf, and shrimp and enjoyed her favorite drinks—martinis, Rob Roys and Cerveza Pacifico. On her nights off, she danced until dawn.

Offshore in the winter there is a strong migration of North Atlantic bluefish schools to Florida's east coast, but in the spring and summer they spawn near Miami. At the beginning of June, Marli and Dr. Ralph went fishing in the afternoon. Marli, in shorts and a sailor hat, looking golden, impossibly sexy, listened to the churning of the twin-diesels as the craft pounded against the waves. "You leave Miami Beach and you go out into the ocean," she said, "and about a half hour later there's this place on stilts on a huge sandbar, called the Quarter Deck. Shutters, open windows, loads of decking, and a bar. I had conch dip for the first time and liked it. You could also eat whatever you caught here." In minutes the couple approached Fort Lauderdale and in ten minutes reached the warm Gulf Stream. "We had outriggers," she said.

A school of sporting dolphins passed them. In the glow of the sun, against the blue sea, Marli, very much a water person, looked beautiful. The ancient Romans had identified their goddess Venus with the sea. The Venus Anadyomene is always shown rising from the sea, wringing water from her hair and standing on a shell. The shell and the dolphin were her counterparts. Beauty and ocean always went together.

Marli braced herself on the platform in the fighting chair, like a barber's chair. "Now they buckle you in," she said, "but we didn't do that then." She hoped for a swordfish breaking the surface. She wasn't after bluefish unless they weighed less than four pounds, any heavier and their meat was dark, oily, and unpalatable. Besides, blues, whose sharp teeth could cut through flesh and small bones, can inflict serious bites to fishermen. Marli looked to the west where she saw fish feeding on the surface and then swimming away at nearly fifty knots.

Sailfish, which could be twelve feet long and weigh 220 pounds (about the same as a blue marlin), were migrating south for their winter vacation. Upper-water fish who desired tropical water in winter were going where the most agreeable temperature was. The wind was from the west, and the Gulf Stream current was running north at a little over five knots an hour in early afternoon. Marli would be dancing on stage that night, but her days were always her own, and there were many days when she didn't work at all. "Between May and December 1958 we went out fishing two or three times a week."

Around 3:00 P.M., Marli had been slow trolling with a double hook baited with fresh squid. "We're just going along," she said, "when all of a sudden my rod goes 'Whang!' At first I thought it was a shark. I had caught one just before. But the line goes out and knocks me on the floor of the boat. Thank goodness I landed there and not out into the water. We figured it had to be big whatever it was."

Now her reel began to talk, a slow steady buzz like a hornet's and growing in anger. The nylon line was walking off when Marli pushed the drag lever up to strike, and the plastic reel really began screaming like a banshee. The line ripped into the water and she felt the eleven or twelve pounds of drag grow heavier as the fish added its considerable weight. Marli tensed, feeling out the fish's strength, and began to fight. At first she feared she might be pulled over the side into the roiling water because she wasn't strapped in, but she took a more stable stance. "I wasn't too worried," she said. "The sailfish isn't really big enough to pull you over."

In a few minutes, she was exhausted, but had her catch alongside the boat where she could see it in the bright sunlight. It was dark blue with a silvery underbelly and spear—a long, pointed bill shooting dangerously from its upper jaw. Its first dorsal was hugely enlarged in the shape of a spiked sail. Marli had captured a huge sailfish.

As she lifted her catch onto deck, she had to be careful not to be speared. The fish was a beauty all right. She knew exactly what to do with it. When they got back to Miami Beach, Marli had a taxidermist mount the sailfish in time to ship to her dad for Father's Day on June 15.

Dr. Ralph invited her and another girl to come down and spend a week with him to entertain the governor of Tennessee, who Marli didn't like very much. As usual with gorgeous women, Marli preferred to be admired for her mind. She had varied interests and was intrigued by anatomy, astronomy, numerology, massage, tarot, acupressure, reflexology, and nature and was well-read and well versed in the classics. She read nonfiction and fiction—"Except for the romantic novels," she said, "where it takes the heroine six pages to decide if she's going to kiss the guy or not."

In December 1959 Marli moved back to Los Angeles to film Ford Motor commercials for the *Tennessee Ernie Ford Show*, model advertising layouts for various companies, and work at her parents' office. She also did some posing for Mario Casilli. It was through Mario that she heard that casting was going on for *Psycho* and had met Hitchcock for the first time. And that's how it all began and she ended up in Hitchcock's shower.

The rough cut screening of *Psycho* was held on April 26, 1960, just for the director, screenwriter, Hilton Green, George Tomasini, Peggy Robertson, George Milo, Jack Russell, Rita Riggs, Helen Colvig, Jack Barron, Robert Clatworthy, and a handful of studio executives. The press was not invited, nor was Marli, who had to be kept a secret. But when Hitchcock excluded the reviewers, this would come back to bite him in the form of hostile reviews. When Stefano saw the rough cut, he thought it was "a truly terrible movie" but couldn't say this to Hitch. "He was sitting beside me," he said, "and he looked at me and he went to pat my knee and said, 'It's just a rough cut, Joseph.' And I thought 'Well, okay.' He's the master, and it's in his hands." Hitch's relationship to his writers was always that of students sitting at the feet of the master.

But though he put on a brave front, Hitch also had doubts about *Psycho* after watching the rough cut. It wouldn't work and couldn't be fixed. Hitch began to despair. He decided he didn't like it and began to speak about cutting it down to an hour and using it on television. He was planning on expanding *Alfred Hitchcock Presents* to an hour in a year or so and it could go there. It was all a disaster and a financial bloodbath.

In Chicago Marli was working at the Playboy Club, appearing on the *Playboy Penthouse* program, and wondering if such people as Norman Bates actually existed. It did not seem possible. It was an innocent time, and yet, yet . . . *Psycho* was based on a real case, Hitch had told her that much, and his film was a case of art imitating life. When *Psycho* was finally released, Marli would find that life could also imitate art.

In Los Angeles the Bouncing Ball Strangler was on the prowl and no woman, young or old, was safe. He was a relatively unknown killer but that was how he did his work undetected by Thad Brown's detectives and how the public had been lulled into a false sense of security. There were monsters on the prowl who could be anyone, including the neighbor next door or the shy, innocent-faced boy in glasses down the street whose mother owned a restaurant.

Hitch didn't shoot as much coverage as other directors. Some directors shoot ten times as much as needed, but he could fit all his leftover film into a small box. There was no way a producer could come in and reedit his film. For the second screening in late spring, Hitch added sound effects—shower noise, water coursing down the drain, and overdubbed screams. For the sound of the stabbing knife Hitch selected a knife being plunged into a melon. He tried a watermelon, cantaloupe, and honeydew, but settled for a casaba, very pleased with his choice.

Hitch wanted visual, not musical, impact for the Shower Sequence and told composer Bernard Herrmann to keep the scene silent. For the first time Bennie went against Hitch's wishes and added a discordant, nerve jangling violin and cello score. Written in black ink on Ricordi music paper, the all-strings piece would become the most recognizable musical sequence in cinematic history. Composer Danny Elfman couldn't find a false note in the entire score. "The strings' taut, internal shrieking expressed the stifled nonstop scream one would feel at a moment like that," he said. "The narrative of the story was always expressed in the music." The parsimonious director would give Herrmann a bonus, something he had never done before with anyone.

With cutting and scoring completed, Hitchcock felt confident when he invited Robert Bloch, Lew Wasserman, Janet Leigh, Tony Curtis, Hilton Green, and some of the technical crew and their wives to a drab little screening room to see the lean, mean 111-minute answer print for *Psycho.*

Marshall Schlom sat in the back row with his wife next to the Hitchcocks. Bloch, who sat in the front row, was puzzled by the screeching of the Shower Sequence. Stefano felt he was seeing a totally different movie now, compact, paced, exquisitely put together. When he saw it with music, it wowed him so much he nearly fell out of his seat.

"Even though I knew what was going to come," Janet Leigh said, "I screamed. And even though I knew I was sitting there in that screening quite alive and well, it was a very emotional thing to see your own demise."

"What do you think of it, my dear?" Hitchcock asked her afterward.

"I believed that *knife* went into me on the screen. It was that real, that horrifying. I could feel it!"

"My dear, the knife never went into *you*," said Hitchcock. Janet thought he meant actual penetration, but Hitch was thinking of Marli and how he himself had pushed it just below her navel and then withdrawn it quickly.

Janet Leigh realized that "all the violence in it is really more what one brings to it as an audience, rather than what is actually on the screen." She thought the Shower Sequence was chaste and discreet, the scene's violence implied by artful cutting. "He allowed the audience to create what they thought they saw," she wrote. "And when the audience becomes part of the creative process, they're not going to forget that."

The severe restrictions placed on Hitchcock were similar to the restrictions placed on neophyte art students in keeping them to a limited palette of three colors and asking them to create the illusion of a full color painting. Janet would receive an Oscar nomination for her superb performance as Marion.

Outside the screen room, Bloch told Hitch *Psycho* was either going to be his biggest success or his biggest flop. He didn't know which, and considering how he had been screwed out of a potential fortune share, he didn't care. In fact he was going to go on the radio and tell everyone within earshot the secrets of *Psycho*.

Chapter Thirteen
The Bouncing Ball Strangler

A round noon on May 1, Mother threw Sonny out of the house. His expression puzzled her—stunned, yet joyful at the same time as the door slammed behind him. Mother watched him carry his single bag down the stairs and onto the street. All morning long, Sonny had been wringing his hands and pacing the living room on his long legs, wiping his glasses and biting his lip. Lately he had been more nervous than usual and had taken to losing himself in films at the local theater on Hollywood Boulevard. It was just over a month before the limited release of *Psycho*, a film he eagerly anticipated, in three cities—New York, LA, and Chicago. But Sonny would have to wait to see the film that was creating so much buzz and he had so much interest in. He had other things to do. He was going to murder someone just like Mother.

Mother thought she had figured out the reason for Sonny's anxiety, or at least what had set it off. That didn't excuse his frenzied activity, which had reached its zenith this morning. Sonny was distraught over Caryl Chessman's impending execution at San Quentin. Over the last few months he had gotten to be a bug about it. Even last year, she had been concerned that he followed the case so avidly and with such vehemence. Now Chessman's execution was only hours away and Sonny's anger was accelerating as it became obvious that the condemned man's delaying maneuvers had finally run out. Mother was growing afraid of Sonny, and with Chessman's execution she didn't know what to expect.

Earlier that morning, Mother had seen him perusing one of the true detective magazines so popular in 1960. His favorite, which had a color photo of a steel-jawed detective on the cover, had elicited comments about Chessman from readers. Sonny read her one comment aloud: "Everybody talks about Caryl Chessman and everybody forgets about the victims of his many horrible crimes. Americans are funny that way. I suppose it is because we are softhearted. There is nothing wrong with a soft heart. I just worry that we are becoming softheaded."

A second letter was more in-line with Sonny's own feelings. This reader felt that Chessman had been kept on Death Row for so many years that it had become dangerously near cruel and unusual punishment. "I agree that Chessman deserved to die," he wrote. "But he should die *once*—not once a year for twelve years."

Sonny's outrage was understandable. The entire world was outraged over the execution. In Japan, Tachikawa Air Force Base had restricted all personnel to base until after Chessman was dead and the State Department had canceled President Dwight D. "Ike" Eisenhower's trip to Tokyo because of fears of violent protests. Earlier, California Governor Edmund "Pat" Brown had called for a stay of execution for Chessman to ensure Ike's safe tour of South America. Now Sonny and Chessman could only wait.

When Mother expelled Sonny, it happened fast. Sonny, finding himself suddenly outside 5623 Virginia Avenue, dusted himself off, picked up his brown leather bag, and tried to make sense of the situation he had created. Yet he was offended.

Mother, so much older than him, so gregarious and well-liked, should know better. What was he to do next? He had lived with Mother the last three years, and she had finally had enough of his erratic behavior. But that's what he had wanted, wasn't it? Some freedom, a chance to be on his own and bring women home anytime he wanted and not have to tiptoe out at night. He had created the situation to force himself out.

Sonny admitted he liked older women (like Mother) and probably had a deep-seated mother fixation, but there was nothing he could do about that either. Those impulses were too ingrained. He wasn't too worried—he could find a new place before noon, and Mother had actually suggested a modest apartment house at 1522 North Mariposa Avenue in his familiar Olive Hill section. It was an easy move—only a block away from the family restaurant. Mother, who he knew was softhearted, owned that building and several apartment houses and properties in the area. There would always be a place there for him if that didn't work out no matter how Mother felt.

At the Mariposa property, the landlady, Mrs. Elynore Riley, a slender brunet woman in glasses, showed him to a second-floor bachelor apartment in the rear. It was neat and clean. He closed the door in her face, unpacked, and set to brooding in the overstuffed chair. He put his small radio on the kitchen table, plugged it in, and spent the afternoon listening and following news about Chessman. The convicted rapist and red-light bandit had gotten last-minute reprieves before. He might just get one this time, though as the hands of the clock advanced such an outcome began to look doubtful to Sonny.

Throughout the afternoon, all night, and into the next morning Sonny continued to fret, angry at Mother and furious over Chessman's imminent execution. To the north of San Francisco on the far point of Tiburon peninsula mainland crowds were holding vigil before a long, low, peach-colored building—San Quentin prison. Night and day protesters paced with white placards, proclaiming the condemned man's innocence. Chessman said he was innocent. Sonny had figured out why he was sympathetic toward Chessman—he had himself been a wrongfully accused murder suspect in August 1956 when he was picked up on suspicion of killing pretty red-haired Eudice Erenberg. He was still angry that his friend Steven Ernest Shaffer, the restaurant bartender, had tipped the cops that Sonny had purchased a .32 revolver from him. The police had put the screws to him until Robert Lee Nichols, a petty crook, confessed that he had shot the girl in a failed stickup.

But Sonny was still on the hook because of the unsolved murders of Helen Jerome, Ruth Goldsmith, Esther Greenwald, Barbara Jean Jepsen, and Linda Martin. All but Martin, a USC coed, were older women; all were Sonny's type. It was fine to be punished for something you did, he thought, but to be wrongly accused was unacceptable. One might as well have done it.

Twelve years ago, Chessman, out on parole from Folsom Prison, had been wounded in a high-speed chase and arrested as the infamous "Red Light Bandit" who targeted lovers' lanes, surprising couples, robbing the men, and raping the women. Chessman was charged with eighteen separate crimes, including robbery and the kidnapping and sexual mistreatment and attempted rape of two women. The kidnapping consisted of transferring the women from their own car to his own, a matter of a few feet, but sufficient to qualify as kidnapping under California law. Kidnapping carried a mandatory death sentence.

Chessman had been found guilty after a two-week trial in which he acted as his own lawyer. He was sentenced to eight five-year sentences for the robberies and two death penalties for the kidnappings. Jack Webb had produced two *Dragnet* episodes based on Chessman called "The Big Badge." So far Chessman, through his own efforts, notoriety, legal appeals, and the publication of an exceptional autobiography and a few other books, had received eight stays of execution over the nearly twelve years he had occupied cell 2455 on San Quentin's death row.

As the minutes ticked away, Sonny was praying that Chessman would cheat death a ninth time. He was right to be hopeful. It had happened so many times before. In fact, behind the scenes, Judge Goodman, a federal judge, had just agreed on a one-hour stay of execution. He had his secretary call the prison to give them the information. But in attempting to reach the prison, his secretary misdialed the phone number on her first attempt and had to redial.

Just before Chessman entered the gas chamber, he told the sixty invited witnesses: "I specifically state I was not the Red Light Bandit." The executioner dropped three pellets of potassium cyanide into the bucket beneath the chair. Chessman smiled as he inhaled the hydrocyanic gas. Whether those few wasted seconds caused by the telephone misdial would have saved Chessman is open to question. The emergency phone rang and the secretary relayed Goodman's message to Assistant Warden Reed Nelson. "It's too late," he said. "The doors are sealed. The execution has started." Nelson couldn't open the door and rescue Chessman without the deadly fumes escaping and killing others. Eight minutes and fifteen seconds later, at 10:12 A.M., May 2, Caryl Chessman was pronounced dead. The news came over Sonny's radio almost immediately and he began to cry. He heard static in his head and thought it came from the radio. It rose in intensity.

Distraught, he walked over to see Mother and commiserate but then stayed on the street outside, unable to summon the courage to enter. Finally, he decided to visit Mrs. Elmyra Miller, a friend of his mother, instead to see if she would spend some time with him. Elmyra had always been a willing listener, and Sonny was not only tortured, but lonely. The seventy-two-year-old widow lived in a tiny bungalow just around the corner at 1450 Normandie Avenue. Sonny, who had known her all his life, used to drop in and see the "old lady all the time." She had not been well and was under a doctor's care, so they didn't go out, but sat on her couch and talked. She was in her housecoat. When Miller got up to get them both something to drink, Sonny's bottled-up rage rose to the surface.

"I went to see her," Sonny said later. "We sat talking for a while and then this urge came over me." All the pent-up emotions from the execution bubbled up inside him, an overwhelming impulse that galvanized him and made his hands go rigid. "That screaming sound in my head from the war came back," Sonny said later. "I had fought it off for a long time." He dared not confront Mrs. Miller directly but waited until she had her back to him at the sink and he could not see those sorrowful eyes. He took several steps forward, reached out, and gripped her by her neck. "I kept fighting it, even after that." His strong fingers tightened. Her frail body stiffened. She didn't say a word.

"I strangled her," Sonny said later, "then I pulled up her housecoat to make it look like a sex crime and throw the police off my trail." It seemed strange to him that though his mind was aflame, a portion of his brain was working methodically and coolly enough to think of laying a false trail and avert suspicion from himself. He needn't have bothered. It would be a botched investigation.

In the morning, when Miller missed her medical appointment at the clinic for a heart exam, the doctor drove to her house. He parked and walked up the flagstone steps to see if there was a problem. Elmyra Miller had never missed an appointment before. He found the door to the little bungalow open an inch. Gingerly, he pushed it open just enough to see into the room: Miller was lying on the floor, her thin blue housecoat disarrayed and pulled up over her hips. The doctor rushed to her, felt for a pulse, and found none. Then he studied her body cursorily and, finding no marks of violence, straightened her housecoat for her. Because of her cardiac condition the doctor ruled her death as heart failure. The coroner arrived, his attendants conveyed the body to the morgue, and that was that. Sonny followed the press and saw no mention of his crime. Had he imagined it all?

This wasn't the first time he had killed someone. Later, when asked if he had, he replied: "Yes, I did, now that I think of it. It was with the First Cavalry in Korea in 1952, at a POW stockade outside Inchon. There was a Chinese prisoner there limping around. He'd been shot in the leg. That was when the urge came over me for the first time. I stuck him good with my bayonet. There were already so many bodies lying around, no one knew what I had done. But that was my first killing— outside of regular combat, I mean. Old Mrs. Miller was my second. I fought down the urge until then." Was it his second though? He just didn't know. Sonny vowed from now on he would fight any impulse to murder with all his might.

Things continued to go well for Sonny. The coroner agreed with the doctor's finding that Elmyra Miller had died from a heart attack. Later, during the autopsy, he saw some things that didn't fit. He examined the free-floating hyoid bone in the throat and realized the old woman had actually been strangled. He contacted the LAPD and Ray Pinker of the crime lab responded, dispirited as he climbed the steps, moving in as if his feet were lead. Pinker, a slim, balding man with a retiring manner, trod to the door, slowly wiped his feet on the mat—back and forth, back and forth—and sighed. He was in no hurry. So much time had elapsed he didn't expect much of a crime scene to be left.

Finally, he entered. Motes of dust were caught in shafts of morning light. He was alone. In a normal, timely investigation, two detectives' cars would have pulled up in front of the Miller house and another two uniformed cops and himself would have jumped out, taken the stairs at full gallop, roped off the scene, and secured any evidence. After a search of the neighborhood for witnesses, they would have detained any suspicious characters in the vicinity. Now it was too late to do that, unless the killer had been a neighbor, which was unlikely but sometimes happened.

Inside, Pinker placed his hands in his pockets and began to poke around. Probably the top criminalist in the nation, he had joined the LAPD Crime Lab in 1929 after two years of chemical engineering study at UCLA and a bachelor of sciences degree in pharmacy from USC. His former crime lab partner, Lieutenant Lee Jones—a big white-haired man with the calm demeanor of an insurance executive—had pioneered the Scientific Investigation Division (SID) when it had only one little lab and a few microscopes. Jones had retired about two years earlier, and now Pinker had a new partner and the SID took up an entire floor in the new LAPD Administration Building. The new lab was filled with state-of-the-art centrifuges, autoclaves, and electronic measuring devices, and an entire section was taken up with furnaces, steam baths, and ovens for processing evidence.

Everyone knew Jones and Pinker from Jack Webb's juggernaut of a radio and television program, *Dragnet*. A stickler for accuracy, Webb used many authentic touches such as the LAPD's actual radio call sign (KMA-367) and the names of real department officials, such as Pinker and Jones, and their boss, Thad Brown. On the dramatic radio version from mid-1949 until 1957, Herb Butterfield and later Olan Soule played Pinker. Webb adapted the same scripts to the *Dragnet* television program. Each morning Chief Parker delivered LAPD badges for the actors by special courier and had them returned to police headquarters each night. On *Dragnet*, Webb tried to show the police officer as he really was. "I think we really dispelled a lot of myths in our day," he said.

Pinker and his "hard facts men," the mobile units of detectives, criminologists, latent fingerprint specialists, and photographers, wondered if they could link Miller's strangling to a series of similar attacks on elderly women around UCLA. For some time, a tall man in his late twenties had been killing elderly women and had Hollywood and Central Homicide officers worn to a frazzle. Pinker suspected Mrs. Miller was a victim of the same fiend because her home, just off Sunset Boulevard, was a part of the killer's regular stomping grounds. Her strangling had all the other earmarks of the others. A copycat? But that was as unusual as the murders and rapes of older women.

At headquarters Thad Brown was more anxious than ever to capture the strangler. Thad's practice of loaning ex-cons money and finding them rooms or getting them jobs, provided him extensive contacts with the underworld. These snitches brought him invaluable leads. "There are few cities in the United States where I can't pick up a phone and get some policeman on a person-to-person basis," Brown said. But so far no new leads on the strangler–rapist. That made him suspect they were dealing with a loner who probably lived with his mother.

Pinker would love to clear those cases along with Miller's. They shouldn't be related, yet it was so unusual for so many old women to be murdered in sex crimes that they had to be. The LAPD's latent print ace, Sergeant Jay Allen McLaughlin, lean, dark, tough looking, dusted Mrs. Miller's door and other surfaces. He used a camel hair brush to dust for prints with one of two types of light- and dark-colored powders for different surfaces. He didn't find anything of use.

From the sidewalk, Sonny gauged Pinker's activity inside the house and wondered if he had left behind a clue that might lead to him. He had made one mistake already by confiding in Ernie Shaffer, the restaurant bartender, that he had strangled somebody. Like Mother, he suspected at first that Sonny was making up stories. Then when Miller's death was ruled a homicide, he decided Sonny had really done it. Shaffer decided to say nothing to the police because of a prison conviction in his past. He was in no hurry to involve himself with the police in any way.

Sonny lived only two weeks at the Mariposa Apartments before another tenant, a woman, warned Mrs. Riley that Sonny was a "Psycho."

Riley did nothing, but privately admitted Sonny was quiet and weird and told her she would keep her eye on him. Sonny was taking no chances. He wasn't that crazy. He went out and bought a police scanner. Back in his room the lens maker listened to the transmissions far into the night, until his nosy neighbor complained of all the squawks and squeals. Sonny went out and purchased some earphones. The phones kept the scanner noise down, but failed to stifle the static Sonny heard buzzing inside his head. Above the noise he heard the voice of Mother.

For the soon-to-be-christened Bouncing Ball Strangler, all the publicity surrounding Mrs. Miller's death and the linking of it in the papers to his campus murders must have thrown him into a frenzy. Immediately after the news announcement the long-sought strangler committed three more murders in rapid succession in the Southside University district. One of them was Mrs. Mercedes Langeron, seventy-two years old. She had been strangled and raped in her apartment on West Twenty-third Street and South Vermont Avenue just to the north of USC and Exposition Park on June 26, ten days after the second of the three new killings. Her home lay in an absolutely straight line south from Sonny's doorstep, a drive of only 4.9 miles and sixteen minutes.

Thad Brown asked for his men to come to the briefing room where he could put the fear of God into them if they didn't catch this monster soon. He straightened the picture on his desk as he waited. For long minutes his eyes never left the face in the photo in the silver frame. Then he got up and went out to raise hell with his men and get something done. His rule of thumb was: "If a detective isn't doing his best, get rid of him."

Chapter Fourteen
Topanga Canyon

O ver the Memorial Day weekend, as uncontrollable urges swept over Sonny, hordes of free spirits were attending the Topanga Day's Fair and Parade. Celebrants and free spirits held it every year at this time on the grounds of the Topanga Community House. The fair was a feast for the stomach, eye, nose, and ear and this weekend was no exception. A hundred craft vendors were serving fairgoers dishes ranging from Cajun to hot tamales to sausages. There were imaginative costumes and two stages packed with nonstop music and belly dancing. In the brilliant light, Marli's friend model Diane Webber, who taught belly dancing at Every Woman's Village in Van Nuys, was shimmying on stage, hips moving, stomach muscles undulating. The wind caught her hip scarf and veils; the jangle of her coin jewelry and zills rose above the music.

"Diane was in my nudist club," Marli said. "She and her husband Joe Webber, a bodybuilder, were members of the Sundial Traveling Club and we went down to a real pretty camp in the San Diego foothills, someplace around El Cajon." A spiritually based nudist, Diane later became a television spokesman for the nudist life and was formally crowned

"Queen of the Nudists." "The life of naturism—being active in the nudist movement—has given me a capacity for enjoyment I would not otherwise have had," Diane said.

Marli was dating a fellow nudist at the time, a real cute guy. "It's a lot," she said of the number of men in her life. "I had a lot of fun and sure enjoyed myself." When Marli could, she loved to pack her suntan lotion, bathing cap, striped towel, sun mat, sandals, dark sunglasses, and wide white sun hat and get away with Diane, Joe, and her Sundial boyfriend. Joe had first interested Diane in nudism, but Marli hadn't been really drawn to the naturalist lifestyle until she filmed a commercial at Lake Mojave Ranchos.

"They flew everybody up there in a couple of planes along with a film crew," Marli said. "The director on that shoot, William Brown, was a director on Channel 11 in LA. My dad advertised heavy, heavy on that station. We started talking and Bill remembered me from being on the set. He and his wife, Jeri, were nudists and they got me into going to the camps." It turned out to be a nice mix of pleasure and business for Marli. "He got me a lot of work with a lot of photographers who worked with people from Sundial, really helped me get started. Later, Bill wrote a book on the nuts and bolts of film editing for people who are making their own movies."

In 1960 local nudist camps were springing up all over southern California—the Acacia Club, Air-a-Thons, and Solar Bears in LA, the Swallows of El Cajon, the Lazy K Ranch, Oakdale Guest Ranch, and Olive Dell Ranch in San Bernardino. "Bill and Jeri belonged to the Pacificans [listed only as a Burbank post office box]," said Marli. "Basically it was a family-oriented club. My involvement with it was that it was a good-natured place with a lot of sports. I played volleyball constantly. Lots of volleyball." The clubs all had one thing in common: Their lifestyles were dedicated to fresh air, exercise, sunshine, dynamic living, and the "tingling freedom of nude living."

Recently a group of northern California naturalists promoting nudist outings had leased a private Santa Cruz beach with three large cabins and accepted reservations from thirty nudist families. To allow the pioneer sunbathers to enjoy the sun and water, the sheriff's office patrolled the nearby roads to keep gawkers out. But for Marli, the remote, un-improved beaches of Baja California, Mexico, offered an exciting chal-lenge for sun worshiping and for fishing. In the future, she longed to spend as much time as she could in Baja. She loved the people.

As free and open as Sundial was, there were still strict rules. Any club member photographing bathers had to have the prior permission of the subject, and any photos for publication required a written release from the subject. Married couples had to apply, join, and visit together. Marli didn't know of a single nudist park that admitted a "married single." No swimming suits were permitted in the pool, though women could wear bathing caps to keep their long hair from clogging the drains. Alcohol was forbidden, but there were no restrictions on diet or smoking and—Thank God!—no compulsory calisthenics. Clothing was even allowed for protection against sunburn, extreme heat, and cold.

Marli and Diane had more in common than just nudism—both were gorgeous women who had been photographed by the same pinup artists; both had been *Playboy* models, and both had connections with Hitch-cock. In May, Diane would play "The Other Woman" in an episode of *Alfred Hitchcock Presents* titled "The Pearl Necklace." As the most pho-tographed pinup model of the 1950s (as Marguerite Diane Empey), she had been Miss May 1955 and Miss February 1956, the first-ever two-time *Playboy* Centerfold. Though Marilyn Waltz had been Miss April two years in a row, it was Diane who had inspired Hef to develop the concept of his Playmates as the ideal girl next door. He even directed a feature on her called "Preparing to Be a Playmate."

"Everyone expects the final pose to be [a] pretty and provocative one," he wrote, "but when the model is as attractive as Marguerite Empey, even the preparations are a pleasure to behold." Hef noted that this was Maguerite's second *Playboy* appearance and that the photographer was Russ Meyer (aka, E. E. Meyer and B. Callum), *Playboy's* most success-ful and reliable lensman. The crewcut, bull-nosed ex-GI had discovered more beautiful women than all the staff and freelancers combined and had photographed half the *Playboy* Centerfolds during the magazine's first year, but none like Diane. Meyer was the first to photograph this astonishingly beautiful woman. His underwater photo of her in 1956 distinctly showed her pubic hair—another *Playboy* first. "It has been more than fifteen years since I took my first set of glamor pictures," Meyer wrote at the beginning of May 1960 for an upcoming article in *Nugget*. "I used my wife [Eve] as the model and I highly admired the results." Since then approximately a thousand girls of varying beauty, temperament, and fame had passed before his camera. "Out of this kaleidoscope of pulchritude and personality, one face and figure comes back to me as the best (my wife excepted) I ever saw in my view finder. She was Diane Webber, a girl of classic beauty and consummate poise whose pictures appeared during the early and mid-50s in all the leading magazines. She must have appeared in more than fifty glamor sets, of which I took at least a half dozen. Scores of photographers used Diane as a model."

For Hef's Playmate article Meyer posed Diane in the bathroom before the makeup mirror and took a flurry of shots of her clad in only a striped pajama top while on a couch. Diane's natural grace emanated from her ballet training, so Meyer posed her in ballet togs and dance poses. Ballet came naturally to her. Diane's mother had been a ballet dancer, and in the late 1920s, when she won a beauty contest, she journeyed from Montana to Hollywood to appear in films. Diane was born in 1932. Her father was screenwriter Arthur Guy Empey, author of a bestseller that sold a million copies. Her parents divorced when Diane was five years old. When she was eighteen, Diane became a San Francisco nightclub chorus dancer earning $80 a week for three shows, six nights a week. She wore a costume on stage, but when she quickly changed backstage with the other women, she didn't wear a stitch. For the first time, Diane realized how favorably her nude body compared to those of her fellow dancers. One of them, noting her astonishing curves, suggested Diane could make $20 an hour modeling for a professor at UCLA. She sat for art classes for a while and, when she returned to LA, posed for Russ Meyer, Keith Bernard, Peter Gowland, and fashion photographer Ed Lange (who was into nudism).

"I enjoy being photographed in the nude because I have an acting talent and professional pride as a model," Diane said. "But when I am modeling there is no confusion in my mind about sexuality. I project what I feel I am, but I am not thinking what effect the pictures will have on the viewer. I try and look my best which may or may not be 'sexy' according to the eye of the beholder. On another level is the sexpot, which I am not." When Hugh Hefner was shown a series of her color photos he liked them and that was the beginning of Diane's long association with *Playboy*.

Diane was only twenty-one when she became the myopic "nudie cutie" who revolutionized pinup modeling in the 1950s. Her full-busted form (thirty-nine-D bust, twenty-three-inch waist, and thirty-seven-inch hips) inspired Gay Talese to write of her: "Her curves, her tantalizing erect nipples, her exciting belly, and half-revealed pubis launched uncontrollable masturbation fantasies for men all over the country." Diane Webber was "a breath of fresh air in the uptight fifties." Throughout the 1950s Diane's face and figure were on practically every cover.[1] She appeared with Joe Webber in George Von Rosen's *Sunshine & Health*. Von Rosen, a lively, lean, green-eyed Midwesterner, offered the only U.S. magazine showing pubic hair. In October 1959, *Modern Sunbathing*, another Von Rosen magazine, printed Diane as a full-frontal nude, but airbrushed, obscuring her pubic hair, a practice all nudist magazines followed, even Von Rosen's own *American Sunbather, Sun*, and *Art Photography*, which depicted statue-like nudes in classic poses.

"Diane had all the qualities of a great model," Meyer wrote, "—marvelous facial contours, lovely long hair to frame them, a beautiful and profoundly feminine form, and, above all, a great pride and self-confidence about her charms that enabled her to feel completely at ease in every situation, whether she was clad from clavicle to metacarpus in

[1] A December 1955 *Escapade* depicted Santa delivering Diane wrapped in a clear plastic wrapper tied with a red bow, and in April 1956 *Show* spotlighted her in "Private Photos of Nudist Queen." That same month *People Today* cover-featured her in a mink stole as the "Queen of the Nudists." *Peter Gowland's Glamour Camera* used her on the cover behind a scale, and the August 1956 *Escapade* showed her in a white polka-dot bikini. As one fan wrote: "Oh those wonderful buns and curves." *Dude* featured her in May 1957. In 1958, *Mermaid* had her as the first Mermaid of the Month (Diane had just played a mermaid on *Voyage to the Bottom of the Sea* and would soon play one again in *Mermaids of Tiburon* with wild man Timothy Carey).

flowing robes for a housecoat commercial or, barefoot, up to the chin, for some figure studies."

In spring 1960, Meyer was going through his file cabinets when he discovered a set of Diane's photos he had held back for several years because she had been so overexposed during her peak years. Now he was poring over the contact sheets for publication in Nugget. "Nugget, you know," noir writer Charles Willeford once remarked, "is one of those half-assed Playboy things with a lot of nude women. But not first rate. These are older women. Twenty-eight. Thirty. You know."

"They are my favorite shots of my favorite model," Meyer wrote, "Diane is now married and a mother and doing very well in both her roles. They came, as everything else, quite naturally to her."

In 1958, Meyer invented a new genre of film that would alter his life completely and provide Marli Renfro with her second motion picture role and Francis Ford Coppola with his first, though he would later be ashamed of it.

Chapter Fifteen
The Strip

A ll through May 1960 Marli continued to work in Chicago at the Playboy Club, each day anxiously awaiting the release of *Psycho*. Hitchcock was really keeping the wraps on this one. For now, the twist ending and the identity of the girl in Hitchcock's shower were still the best-kept secrets in Hollywood. Hitch continued to fervently deny that anyone else but Janet Leigh had been in the *Psycho* shower. So did Janet. Unfortunately, the director's confidentiality was making it tough on the critics by not allowing them to preview the picture. "They were pissed off," Stefano told Stephen Rebello. "They wanted to see it in a screening room as they always did, all by themselves."

After all Hitch's work—buying up Bloch's paperback reprints, insisting on sworn oaths, and misdirecting the press to believe there really was a Mrs. Bates—he had no intention of giving away the secrets of *Psycho*. But in the process, he had inadvertently engendered a lot of bad blood, which would reveal itself in predominantly negative reviews. Used to a string of great reviews (excluding a few misfires) as far back as *Rebecca*,

Hitch loved critical acclaim. He wasn't making *Psycho* for them, but for the audience and for Alma—the one critic he listened to.

A review in *Playboy* could make or break a film. With its circulation growing monthly (and the club even more successful) Hef's magazine wielded tremendous influence and it didn't hurt that Marli Renfro, the girl in Alfred Hitchcock's shower, would be *Playboy's* cover girl the same month the movie opened, and that issue would contain their review of *Psycho*, which was already written.

Marli, who possessed little vanity, didn't care that people would not know that was she in the shower. But was she missing a chance to advance her career? A great number of *Playboy's* Centerfolds and cover models had gone on to become movie stars, mostly in 1950s science fiction movies, Westerns, and B pictures. Marla English, an impish, brunet *Playboy* Centerfold, appeared in the noir classic *Shield for Murder* and in Hitchcock's *Rear Window* in 1954. Raven-haired and statuesque Mara Corday had done it in reverse. The Santa Monica native had been a showgirl at the Earl Carroll Theatre on Sunset Boulevard while still in her teens, a pinup girl in dozens of men's magazines, and by the early 1950s a Universal International Pictures contract player. Universal gave her bit parts in various second-bill films and sci-fi classics and in 1955 cast her opposite John Agar in Jack Arnold's *Tarantula*, which provided her friend Clint Eastwood with a bit part as the jet pilot who slays the giant spider. It wasn't until October 1958 that Mara became the first double centerfold in *Playboy's* history (along with blond Pat Sheehan).

Was such a career in Marli's future? Did she even want such a life? Perhaps she would go through life boating, fishing with Dr. Ralph and playing volleyball in the sun and meeting exciting men, a fantasy woman living a real life of fun and adventure. Still *Playboy* opened many doors if she could stay interested long enough to enter them. Marli kept telling herself it would be wise to take advantage of the possibilities *Psycho* and her *Playboy* cover offered.

Marli had worked on the Vegas Strip, a four-and-a-half-mile stretch of Clark County in the unincorporated towns of Paradise and Winchester, where so many *Playboy* Playmates had been discovered. Hef's photographers, like Bruno Bernard, constantly mined the Strip for pulchritude, all to considerable profit to *Playboy* and the American male libido.

Marli had just turned eighteen in early May 1956, when she auditioned for a job as a chorus dancer in Vegas. "I was doing beauty pageants and I was at this one in Venice, Muscle Beach, where I came in second. The girl who took first, Barbara Johnson, later married Mickey Rooney. This older man, Niles T. Garland, he went by the initials N. T. G., gave me some tips. Shortly before I went to Vegas I got a job through one at the El Mirador Hotel in Palm Springs. I modeled for sports cars and posed around the pool for the El Mirador's postcards and brochures."

N. T. G. told Marli about an interview they were having for dancers in Las Vegas. "They're not really looking for experienced dancers," he said. "They're just looking for pretty girls."

Well, thought Marli, that's me. "So I went to get the job. And that's it. That's how it happened. I didn't know anybody there and got to talking to Laurie Summers and some of her friends. 'You want to ride up with me?' Laurie asked. And I said, 'Sure.' And we became fast friends as we tooled along US-91 hoping for the best." Laurie was headed to the audition knowing she already had the job. Earlier, a photographer had stopped her as she left her West Hollywood apartment on Cory Avenue behind the Jaguar agency. Andy Anderson had mistaken her for Marilyn Monroe, which happened often because of Laurie's platinum hair. Anderson, who worked with Bernard of Hollywood, the man who discovered Monroe, thought Laurie would look great on the cover of *Playboy*. "He flew me up to Vegas to do a series of pictures," Laurie said. While lounging around the pool in a black one-piece swimsuit cut high on the sides, she got a severe sunburn which left her pale and burned in stripes. "I've probably decided to go with Tina Louise," Anderson said as he studied the photos he had taken of her, "but come with me."

Anderson drove Laurie out to the El Rancho Vegas and introduced her to the owner, Beldon Katleman. Beldon's eyes were so deep and glaring she thought he looked like a hawk. "He scared me to death," she said. Beldon looked her up and down and said, "Can you come back in two weeks and appear at the auditions? Just go through the motions. You've already got the job."

The El Rancho Vegas, the first casino-resort and template for all future hotels on the Strip, had opened on April 3, 1941, Marli Renfro's third birthday.[2] Because the redhead had a thing for numbers, the date held significance for her. It just had to symbolize the El Rancho job was meant for her too. In the beginning, the site had been just a gritty patch amid the endless sand hills, creosote bushes, jackrabbits, and howling winds of the Sonoran desert.

In 1940, developer Tom Hull was already managing hotels in California when Vegas businessmen James Cashman and Robert Griffith ambled into his office. They were eager. "You've recently opened El Rancho motels in Fresno, Bakersfield and Sacramento," Cashman said. "What do you think about opening one in our neck of the woods?"

Hull said he would scout for a suitable location. As he and a friend were driving east from LA along Highway 91 they had a flat tire. Hull got out feeling the temperature. Curtains of wavering heat swept over him and he wiped his brow. The desert was like a furnace. He estimated they were stranded two miles south of downtown Vegas. Hull, who had battled Pancho Villa in Mexico and walked six hundred miles back to the United States, let his friend hitchhike for help while he waited. Hull studied the vast desert and ragged scrub all around him and saw a mirage shimmering before his eyes like a cool lake.

"How refreshing it would be take a dive into a swimming pool right about now," he thought and leaned back against the hot surface of his auto. He watched car after car with out-of-state plates whiz down the dusty road past him. As more and more whipped past, he began to imagine these motorists too were searching for a cool oasis and the mirage began to take the shape of a low-rise Spanish Mission-style hacienda encircled by cottages and bungalows with red tile roofs. Hull began to count the autos, so many he lost track. With so much through traffic, this undeveloped area would be the perfect spot for a modern hotel, especially if there were a swimming pool fifty yards from the highway mo-

---

[2] The first Las Vegas resort was Tony Cornero's Meadows Club and Casino, which opened in 1931 just beyond the city line and burned to the ground that same year. The Vegas fire department wouldn't respond to fires outside the city limits.

torists could see as they passed. When Hull's friend returned and they got into town, Hull surprised Cashman and Griffith by telling them he had decided not to build downtown on Fremont Street.

"Instead," Hull told them, "I'm going to put my next El Rancho along the highway outside the city limits." He purchased a large corner parcel on Sahara Avenue at the southwest corner of Las Vegas Boulevard South and Sahara in Clark County. Because it was just over the line from Vegas, he got the land cheap and would save on taxes. Hull hired Wayne Mc-Allister of McAllister and McAllister, an architectural firm, and described to him a Hollywood Western set in the center of a flowered sixty-six-acre watershed. He gave his landscapers $500,000 to plant towering palms, wide green lawns, and flower gardens so that motorists, at the end of a long, choking journey, could swim in a long pool by the white hacienda, and sip cool drinks on chaise lounges under colorful canopies.

Atop the El Rancho, Hull had erected a high tower and atop that a white windmill with neon-lit blades that dominated the desert landscape. As he intended, the giant neon sign was the first thing weary night travelers saw as they jounced along the potholes of Highway 91: "Stop at the sign of the windmill!" it screamed above red neon script, drawn like the curves of a cowboy's lariat, declaring: EL RANCHO VEGAS. Across the four-lane highway, Hull's men erected an illuminated sign that declared the "El Rancho Presents . . ." followed by a list: comedians Chico Marx, Joe E. Lewis, and Jackie Gleason and singers Rudy Vallee, Sophie Tucker, and Dorothy Dandridge. Neon circled the sign counterclockwise before exiting as a huge arrow pointing toward the El Rancho Vegas.

Hull had personally designed the main building, a rustic-style, brown-shingled hacienda. In front, authentic Western wagon wheels served as hitching posts. The Western motif continued inside the Stage Door Steak House, the Wagon Wheel Tavern, and the Chuck Wagon Buffet. In the Round Up Room, where headliners performed, wagon wheels hung from wooden ceiling beams, the dining tables had hurricane lamps with stitched-leather lampshades, and the chairs had a stitched-leather design. Dead center beneath the huge windmill lay the tiny Casino, which held only three hundred patrons, seventy slots that paid trifling jackpots, two blackjack tables, a roulette wheel, and one craps table.

The casino-resort was an immediate success, but there was a constant turnover in its management: Stanford Adler, later barred from Nevada gaming, ran it. Charlie Resnik, who had suspected affiliations with Detroit's Purple Gang, ran it. Hull, who could be demanding, went through thirteen managers before selling the resort at the beginning of 1943. Joe Drown owned it, then Joe Kind and even Wilbur Clark before he started the Desert Inn. In 1946, Clark sold his share of the El Rancho Vegas to Maurice "Jake" Katleman. When Jake was killed in a traffic accident in 1947, his quirky twenty-nine-year-old nephew Beldon Katleman, a UCLA mathematics professor and math prodigy, was drafted to manage it. Beldon swiftly acquired his aunt's 49 percent of the stock and by 1950 had easily bought out the remaining shareholders. Beldon wasn't the type of guy you wanted as a partner. Writer Steve Fischer described Beldon Katleman as a great businessman but "just an absolute unpleasant personality . . . a miserable character." And wrote, " 'Crazy' and 'psycho' were the most common descriptions of him." Conventional wisdom on the Strip was "Never turn your back on Katleman or ever let him get something on you."

On October 7, 1952, Milton Prell's ritzy Moroccan-themed "Jewel in the Desert," the Sahara, opened up across the highway from the El Rancho with twelve hundred slots and sixty-two game tables. Panicked, Beldon invested $750,000 to replace the El Rancho's outmoded interior with a French Provincial design, increased its 180 hotel rooms to 220, and expanded its casino to eighteen thousand square feet, making it the largest in Nevada. He had the interior painted a garish blue and gold (Beldon was colorblind, Laurie Summers explained). Above the egg yolk–colored front awning he had painted yellow lettering on two blue scrolls announcing the new OPERA HOUSE THEATRE. This brick-walled showroom was where the stars and dancers performed. Four feet down from the stage was the dance floor, which sometimes doubled as a second stage and the dining room. He added a second raised tier at the back so that additional diners could see over the front tables and invented the complimentary breakfast from 4:15 to 6:30 A.M., his greatest contribution to the Strip.

Beldon hired impresario Tom Douglas to design the Windmill Revue, his little theater idea, and contracted Dick Rice and the El Rancho Vegas Orchestra to play and signed the Renee Molnar Dancers to replace the El Rancho Starlets. Bandleader Harry James made the Opera House his venue and brought along his wife, gorgeous film star Betty Grable, who would also perform. Finally, Beldon hired the greatest casino manager of them all, a pro gambler and stand-up guy, Big Carl Cohen, who famously knocked out Frank Sinatra's bridgework in a legendary fight. A casino is only as good as its manager, and no one was better than Cohen. Business picked up immediately. Cohen liked the job, but disliked Beldon, so when Joey Adonis approached Cohen in 1953 he easily enticed him over to the Sands.

In 1956, the El Rancho took a leaf out of the short-lived Moulin Rouge's book and began recruiting the most beautiful women in California to be chorus dancers. That's when Marli and Laurie arrived.[3] "I didn't have any formal training dancing," Marli said, "though my mom sent me to Meglan Kiddies in Hollywood, where Shirley Temple once studied dancing and I learned a lot there." Laurie was well trained. She had attended dance school in Westwood and taken gymnastics lessons. Marli tried out for Renee Molnar, who was brunet, toothy, and friendly, and she was hired. She and Laurie immediately began to rehearse for that night's show.

"There were six of us dancers and the principal dancer, Renee," Marli said. "Dancing on stage was just so easy. I'm just a fast learner anyway. My parents belonged to a club that held dances at least once a month." They always took Marli and her older brother, Barry, along so they could learn all the dance steps. "My parents had a lot of old records so I learned how to do the Charleston and the Fox Trot. Dancing just comes so easy and natural to me. I could do the Cha Cha and the Tango, just whatever was popular at the time. The one dance I had a hard time with was the Twist cause your body went the same way. It was like pitching with your right hand and your right foot is out." Those numbers lasted ten or fifteen minutes. "The numbers in Vegas we were

[3]In 1954, the Moulin Rouge Hotel and Casino on Bonanza Street, the first integrated hotel on the Strip, held nationwide auditions for black chorus dancers.

on for maybe seven minutes [once at 8:00 P.M. and again at midnight] and we didn't do the really hard work. Rene Molnar was the one who danced—tap and so on. We just walked around and looked pretty." All the lookers in Vegas were dancers or showgirls. There was one fast rule: You could call a showgirl a dancer, but *never* call a dancer a showgirl. They were artists. It was as big a difference as between a movie stand-in and a body double."

"The dressing room was probably eight feet wide and it wasn't very long at all, fifteen, twenty feet long," Marli said. A shelf came out maybe two feet with angle braces every few feet to support it. The entire wall was mirrors, bulbs all around the long mirror and close-up mirrors and fluorescent lighting around the ceiling. "You had the long counter coming out and little white chairs all around it. They had all of our makeup on the long counter in front." There were dozens of makeup bottles, cans of hairspray, and bottles of nail polish. "Each girl had a drawer for makeup. You had to wear a lot because they have pink lights on you and it takes all of your rose colors out of you."

"We applied Max Factor pancake makeup with a sponge," Laurie Summers said. "We used lots of eye makeup, so much so it irritated our eyes and made them burn, so much tears ran down our cheeks and streaked our makeup. To get the lashes to stick we had to use glue which was painful." Soon they began using hot wax instead to apply the lashes. "They had lots of places right behind us to hang costumes and street clothes and a recess under the makeup counter where you could hook your shoes by their heels." In such close quarters it was difficult to dress.

"Marli had the most perfect breasts," Laurie Summers recalled. "None of the girls in the dressing room could take their eyes off them when she was nude. 'Aren't they gorgeous,' 'Aren't they beautiful.' They all said that."

The costumes they wore were simple. "You just had your one outfit that you wore the night. Cocktail dresses," Marli said. "That's every girl's dream—dressing up every night. It was not a large stage and to the people in the audience it was probably chest high." Surrounded by a huge gilt frame, they danced before satin curtains and painted proscenium arches. The stage floor was polished, and musical notes were painted on the soundproofed white ceiling. Marli danced in front of a full orchestra but never wore the feathers, sequins, spangles, ostrich plume headdresses, and feathered pompoms now associated with Sin City. Renee and her dancers had breakaway skirts and performed in white pumps and gloves in what was really only a modest two piece swimsuit, though studded here and there with a few rhinestone sunbursts.

"In the beginning we just did two shows a night," Marli said. "One Saturday night all the Renee Molnar Dancers [one redhead, two blond, and four brunets] went to see Sinatra's third show at the Sands." Sinatra owned a piece of the Sands and later featured it in *Ocean's 11*. "Then we went to a party afterward. Sammy Davis, Jr. was there, Eddie Fisher and his wife, Debbie Reynolds too. I remember her standing there so stiff and she had a little mink stole she was clutching so tight around herself." Laurie was quite a fan of Sammy's. "He was a sweetheart," she said. "When we went to one of his parties, he had everyone put on terry cloth jumpsuits designed by Sy Devore. Sammy wanted everyone to be dressed the same."

They upped the number of their shows to three on Friday and Saturday nights, [at 8:00 P.M., midnight, and 2:00 A.M.]. "I am a morning person," Marli said, "which was hard on me in Vegas. We worked six weeks without a break, and then they finally got a floater dancer to relieve us. Joey Lawrence was there performing three or four times a year and he was there for quite a while—four to six weeks. He would always have two or three drinks down at the footlights and he would say, 'Post time!' and reach down and get a drink. By the third show he was reeling. Just a sweetheart."

When there weren't many customers in the casino, the dancing girls still had to stay until 2:00 A.M., so they got free cocktails at the bar as they socialized with the customers. Otherwise they had to buy their own drinks. "We'd sit up at the bar and order all these different drinks—brandy Alexandre, grasshopper, whatever was different," Marli said. They got to wear gorgeous fur coats the management provided as they mixed. "We just had a lot of fun." After the shows, the girls went anywhere to eat but the El Rancho Vegas. "Laurie and I went on a binge for a while of cherry pie à la mode. We had that for a few days at this little drive-in."

Marli personally worked with Milton Berle, Sophie Tucker, Joe E. Lewis, Gloria De Haven, stripper Lily St. Cyr (who brought her own bathtub onstage), Jane Russell (a Howard Hughes discovery), Henny Youngman, and a score of old-time comedians and new singers, including Shirley Bassey, whose first job in the United States (eight years before her *Goldfinger* hit) was at the El Rancho Vegas. Because she and Marli were the same age, they became fast friends. "Shirley was really far out," Marli said. "With her tight-fitting silver lame dresses that looked as if they were sprayed on. In those days everyone else had flouncy skirts. In her short spiked hair she was a decade before her time." Shirley gave Marli her teddy bear to keep for her, and Marli hung onto it for years. Later, when the singer was *Dame* Shirley Bassey, she told NPR that her closest friends were those from the early days of her career at the El Rancho but lamented she had failed to keep in touch with them. She had heard many had died. "Now I am only a lonely, old woman," Bassey said and pretended to cry, before breaking into wild laughter.

Casino expansion became so wild that "Glitter Gulch" comedian Joe E. Lewis joked that, "I just met a man who isn't building a hotel." He was a tragic figure. A favorite of Capone's, Lewis had been playing at "Machine Gun" Jack McGurn's Green Mill Gardens Club in the 1920s when he jumped ship for a better-paying venue. McGurn evened the score by having his thugs slash Lewis's face from ear to throat and administer a brain-damaging gun butt beating. He recovered but became an obsessive gambler and alcoholic who "drank to forget he drank." Lewis was working for free. Each week, forty-eight weeks a year, at Friday noon, he showed up in Beldon Katleman's office and signed over his $6,500 paycheck to him. "I owe that son of a bitch Katleman $1.2 million," Lewis said. He owed more to other casinos. "I'll never get out from under." Beldon did let Lewis live on the grounds in Bungalow 422 for free.

"When singer Janice Paige was playing at the New Frontier," Marli said, "people would come up to me and because we looked so much alike ask me for her autograph. Once we were on a float for the Hell Dorado

Celebration. It was a water scene, and Laurie and I were mermaids and Eddie Gomez was King Neptune. We had the fins and were down on the lower level flipping our tails." She and Laurie had a contest to see who could flip their tail the highest, and Marli won. "We had a thermos of drinks and by the end of the parade were feeling no pain," she said.

"One Friday I went to Gene Shacove's hair salon in Beverly Hills (I had gone to them quite a few times)." He was the hottest women's hairstylist in LA right after Jay Sebring, his friend and mentor. "I dated Gene Shacove and as I understand it, the movie *Shampoo* was based on him." The Luau restaurant next door to the salon was where Shacove first pointed out Sharon Tate to Jay Sebring. As Marli sat down, she told Shacove she wanted to be a blond. "I had three or four bleachings, but I had so much red in my hair the shade turned out light orange and just kept getting lighter and lighter orange. They just couldn't get that out. So they put a beige tint in my hair and that dye, hitting my scalp made raw by all those bleachings, the pain was horrendous! It turned my head into just one great big scab.

"Monday, Gene just cut my hair real short and dyed it pink, real pale pink with a little silver in it, real short. My first night back to work, I'm walking in with Laurie and a couple of other girls and Beldon Katleman looks over our way and does a double take on my short pink hair. This scowl came over his face and he just looked fierce. Beldon always scared me. He was tall, very tanned, and wore his dark hair combed straight back. He had those two lines going up from your nose up into his forehead. So I went into the dressing room and brushed my hair around in a circle. One side it fluffed my face and the other side went straight back. In back up at the top, it had a little circle and looked like a twist. Then that was acceptable. It didn't stay pink very long."

Marli got away from Beldon and the stage show whenever she could. During the time she was dancing on the Strip, there was only one nudist camp in all Nevada, in Vegas out on Route 1 in section B246 and within easy driving distance, but she didn't recall ever getting to it. There were too many exciting things going on.

"I witnessed some cattle rustling outside of Jackson Hole, Wyoming, in 1957 while I was fishing with a friend," Marli said. "We stayed at a beautiful downtown hotel and we were down in the bar. We're feeling no pain, this guy about nineteen asks us, 'Wanna go rustle some cattle?' "

"Sure," Marli laughed.

"Well, meet me down here at 2:00 A.M.," he said.

"So we did," Marli said, "and we drove out to some holding pen. They were loading cattle up into semi-trucks. They gave me a cattle prod to move the cattle along. We could have been hung. The guy says, 'Why don't you stop off at my parents' ranch on the way back to Denver.' So we did and the Old Man—ohhhh . . . was asking all these questions. I thought, 'I don't think he knows what his son is doing.' "

When Beldon signed Zsa Zsa Gabor, a former Miss Hungary 1936, for a two-week appearance she refused to work with the beautiful girls. Beldon had to give the dancers two weeks off, so Marli and Laurie flew to New York, where they stayed with Jeffie Boyd, who got them third-row center tickets to Broadway shows. Bob Evans the producer invited the two beauties to his Central Park West place to attend a cocktail brunch of mimosas and bagels in their honor. All his friends were there, including a few big recording producers and record industry mobster Morris Levy, who owned the Birdland jazz club. Everyone wanted to meet the "girls from Vegas."

Another time Marli and several of the El Rancho line dancers were flown to LA where they boarded a train filled with Shriners and rode with them back to Vegas. When they arrived, everyone went inside the El Rancho where photographer Dottie Gunn shot photos of them and the dancers and the headliner together on stage. Then she took Marli outside and snapped candids of her. "I'm in Bermuda shorts in front of the windmill with my little poodle," Marli said. In March 1957 another of Marli's photos shared the cover of *Night and Day* with Sophia Loren.

In October, as Marli was preparing to leave the Strip for good, she realized how much the shows had changed during her time there—more glamorous, expensive, and very revealing. Taking advantage of a Vegas city ordinance that allowed nudity as long as the girl didn't move, Lisa Medford became the first nude on the Strip. When the Stardust opened at the north end, the Lido de Paris's international cast of sixty Bluebell girls (singers and dancers) performed on a huge six-part stage, and the Ça C'est l'Amour's live nudes descended from the showroom ceiling. A bellman would even drive you to your Stardust room in an electric go-cart. Over at the Thunderbird they had aesthetics. Icecubettes producer Marty Hicks, a "sub-zero Minsky," preferred size thirty-sevens. "I've looked over a few 42s," he said, "but they're just too big for the hottest thing on ice."

One of the new dancers in these lavish reviews was Felicia Atkins, a twenty-six-year-old Australian model and swimmer who had quit the Australian swim tour in New York City. While her roommate, Carla, was out job hunting a man called their apartment with an offer for Carla. Since she wasn't there he asked Felicia, "What do you look like?" "Like Carla." Within hours Felicia was on a plane to Vegas to dance at the Y-shaped, three-hundred-room Tropicana Resort and Casino as a show-girl in the Folies Bergère. The sophisticated Parisian cancan spectacular would become the longest continuous running production in Vegas, and Felicia the showgirl with the longest tenure. The ever vigilant *Playboy* photogs, Bruno Bernard and Bill Bridges, documented Felicia's "finely fabricated five-foot, seven and a half-inches" as she posed by a sixty-foot-high, tulip-shaped fountain in front and by the Tropicana pool. Hef made her the centerfold for the April 1958 *Playboy*, which had a Vegas theme.

On January 29, 1958, actors Joanne Woodward and Paul Newman were privately married in Beldon Katleman's bungalow on the El Rancho grounds. They had been Tony Perkins's first friends when he arrived in Hollywood. In November, Laurie and her husband bought a home in Laurel Canyon and offered it as a rental. Paul Newman and Joanne Woodward showed up at their door, took off their shoes, and walked around looking. It was a little too small for their taste, so they put on their shoes and left. When Beldon Katleman bought a Bel-Air mansion, Gary Cooper's former "House of Flowers," he invited Laurie to his parties. "It was near Hugh Hefner's place," she said.

Betty Blue, a self-described nudist and *Playboy*'s Miss November 1956, also worked as a Vegas showgirl. Her new husband, film producer-director Harold Lime, wrote a featured part for her in his nudie comedy *Not Tonight, Henry.* Hank Henry, a Vegas crony of Frank Sinatra's, played the frustrated husband, Henry, who yearns for romantic escapades with history's sirens Josephine, Cleopatra, and Delilah. He casts himself in a dream as Napoleon, Marc Antony, and Samson. Lime's was only the second of a new kind of film that was raking in millions. He hadn't invented the genre, only copied it. This modern skin-flick, one with satire, irony, and humor to get around the censors, had been created by one of Hef's favorite *Playboy* photographers, who now had become a director like none before, not even Hitchcock.

Chapter Sixteen
The Old Vegas Dies

On June 16, *Psycho* premiered in a very limited prerelease engage-ment at the Baronet and DeMille Theatres in New York. There were no other screenings or previews, owing to Hitchcock's strat-egy to keep the ending secret. In spite of the embargo and limited seating, mobs circled the block waiting to get inside and braving the elements. Of course it rained. Hitch had the theater managers hand out umbrellas.

The day after *Psycho* played in New York, Marli was working as a Bunny at the Playboy Club, vaguely excited about her one and only motion picture. Did she want to do another? Was she that ambitious? Marli was a naturally optimistic individual, and it seemed to her that those who strove to succeed had some interior emptiness that needed to be filled by fame, praise, and achievement. She best described herself as not happy, but cheerful. Laurie Summers described her with one word: "enthusiastic." Yet doing another film might not be so bad, she decided by the end of her shift. She had enjoyed the experience, and Hitch had been charming and attentive. She had really liked Tony Perkins. Now she was berating herself for not insisting that Hitch give her a credit. It was a decision that would cost her.

The rest of the night passed uneventfully, and Marli went to bed barely able to sleep with the excitement of her movie (and secret part) on everyone's lips, as if she were the only one in the world who knew. But others did know. The guys at *Playboy* knew. Their review of *Psycho* in her forthcoming cover issue had to be more than coincidence. Her very pose on the cover imitated the look of the Shower Sequence. Hef knew. A few of her fellow dancers and Bunnies knew, Tony Curtis knew, and so did Janet Leigh, but Marli was still "The Mystery Girl" to everyone else.

Perhaps there was something to the phrase that redheads were hot tempered and fiery. Fire seemed to follow Marli. Several freakish blazes and inexplicable fires had involved her. Two of her cars had caught fire for no reason.

"One time I had a slumber party," she recalled, "and we all piled in my mom's model A Ford, dressed in our jammies, and she took us to the drive-in theater and left us there to pick us up after the movies. Well, we're sitting in the car, watching the movie when we noticed smoke coming from the engine compartment. We got scared and had to get out of the car. The smoke attracted a lot of attention from nearby cars and someone found the source (an electric wire) and fixed it, but I think we attracted more attention in our PJs than that model A smokin'."

Another time, Marli and Norma Shoberg were "toolin' around town" after dinner in Norma's brother's car, when a car pulled alongside them. "The couple inside were waving at us," said Marli, "and we waved back, but they insisted and finally signaled us to roll down the window to inform us the car was on fire. Yikes!" Norma pulled to the side of the road, and while she and Marli jumped out and got away from the burning car, the couple leaped out and put out the flames.

On June 17, Marli's ringing phone awakened her. The voice on the phone said something about a big fire. Marli rubbed her eyes. The last (and first) of Old Vegas was burning.

"When the El Rancho went up in flames," Marli said, "my closest female friend, Laurie Summers, called to tell me all about it." The Las

Vegas fire marshal wrote: "Probable cause of fire: intentional setting of fire in area behind kitchen storage. Accelerant probably used." It was a fortuitous fire for Beldon Katleman. The El Rancho's bills were going unpaid, and when the March *Playboy* printed an exhaustive review of the Vegas hotspots, the editors gave short shrift to the former Queen of the Desert by focusing only on her past glory days.

The reason some thought Beldon had set the fire was because the fire insurance was paid up for only twelve more days. But when Laurie described Beldon in the cashier's cage with a couple of people gathering up the money, Marli decided he hadn't done it. "If he had, they would have been prepared and gotten most of the money out beforehand," she said. Beldon still filed an insurance claim for $500,000 he said he had in his office safe. This wasn't the first big fire he had had at the El Rancho. In August 1955, a mysterious blaze ignited in the kitchen and spread to the attic, causing $250,000 in damages. But, if not Beldon, then who was behind the arson?

Laurie's husband was cognizant of all the intricacies of the Vegas gambling world, from craps to twenty-one to the races, and was well informed of the Chicago mob's involvement in schemes to gain control of various casinos on the Strip. He said, "The boys did it." "Laurie and her husband who had stayed at the El Rancho a year or so after they got married," said Marli, "believed the mob wanted to buy the El Rancho since it was about the only hotel on the Strip that wasn't mob-owned. Beldon kept refusing to sell so they finally set fire to it."

Three weeks before the fire, Marshall Caifano, enforcer for the Chicago mob in Vegas, had gotten drunk at the El Rancho. Beldon had his security guards take him outside and throw him into the parking lot. Caifano, "a dangerous man with a hair-trigger temper," didn't take that from anyone. He was the same "supposed gangster" who had taken Marli out in March at the Playboy Club. Caifano, born Marcello Giuseppe Caifano, a graduate of Chicago's notorious Forty-two Gang, also used the aliases Joseph Rinaldi, John Marshall, John Michael Marshall, and Marshall Califano.

After his brother, "Fat Lennie" Caifano died in 1951, Marshall became the prime suspect in ten unsolved murders. Before Sam Giancana

sent Caifano to the Strip in the late 1950s to be the omnipotent over-
seer of the Chicago mob–controlled casinos, he first admonished him
to "Lay low in Vegas. No one gets hurt without clearing it with us."
Caifano, flashy and loud, with brightly colored suits and ropes of gold
chains, did everything but that.

Allegedly, Caifano had gotten even with Katleman for his beating
by torching the El Rancho. Within a month, Chicago Tony Accardi and
Paul Ricca would dispatch Johnny Roselli to replace Caifano who, once
he was placed on the Nevada Gaming Commission and State Gaming
Control Board Exclusion/Ejection List, was useless to the outfit on the
Strip.[4]

On the night of the blaze, the El Rancho headliners were movie
star Betty Grable, singer Pearl Bailey, and the comedy lounge act of Phil
Ford and his toothsome wife, Mimi Hines. At 4:40 A.M. Clark County
sheriff's detectives Conrad Simmons and Robert Metler were at the El
Rancho when they smelled smoke. Unalarmed, they walked backstage
of the Opera House Theatre where they saw a fire just beginning. "The
place went up awfully fast," Simmons said. "Too fast. That fire is especially hot." While Metler tried to extinguish the out-of-control blaze in
the showroom, Simmons rushed into the casino to warn the patrons.
Few were gambling at this time of morning, and the evacuation was
orderly as cashiers began grabbing up cash before it burned.

By radio, the officers alerted the fire department and their partners
at the Sheriff's Department. The first all-out alarm came in three minutes later, summoning firemen from neighboring counties. At the rear
of the El Rancho at Channel 13 where the Opera House stars did live
television interviews, Pearl Bailey was just leaving the studio after a taping. She offered Phil Ford and Mimi Hines a ride, and as they got into

[4]Some conspiracy theorists suggest Caifano was personally involved in President John
F. Kennedy's assassination in November 1963. In March 1980, he was arrested in West
Palm Beach for transporting $2 million in stolen securities over state lines and sentenced
to two concurrent terms of twenty years each. Released in 1990, he died September 6,
2003, of natural causes in Fort Lauderdale, Florida. The enforcer who replaced him on
the Vegas Strip, Johnny Roselli, was found in 1976 off Miami Beach cut to pieces inside
a fifty-five-gallon drum.

her car, blue-tipped flames suddenly burst through the back wall of the Casino. Thick black smoke rolled over the auto. Bailey, blinded and panicked, floored the gas pedal and backed into a tree just as the fire leaped toward them. The auto stalled, one wheel slightly off the ground, and trapped them. Luckily, Ford kept his head, fought his way out of the rear seat, and, crouching low, grabbed both women's hands and led them through the smoke to safety.

At 4:50 A.M. three engine companies—a ladder truck, a new aircraft crash truck, and two veteran pumpers—wheeled round the corner and ground to a halt as pulsing black smoke obscured their vision. By the time the other fire engines arrived, the main building was almost completely engulfed in flames, and what intact window glass that still existed was crazed with cracks. The smoke eaters began pumping the first of thirty thousand gallons of water onto the blaze.

El Rancho employees, who had escaped, were fighting off flames leaping to the surrounding bungalows and cottages. Some of the guests had their luggage out on the lawns and were helping beat down the fire with their blankets.

As Marli listened to Laurie, she remembered the people who lived on the El Rancho grounds and hoped they were all right. "Sam, the father of a good friend of mine, David Kantowitz, lived in one of the cottages," she said. "He was an old guy, real neat and lived there all the time." Sam's son, David, hated Beldon Katleman.

"Just for starters," he alleged, "Beldon tried to drown my father. He stole a bunch of TVs when Magnavox held its convention at the El Rancho and he caused some lady to kill herself after he told her he was having a relationship with her girlfriend. Women would come to his house and he would steal from their purses. A guy who worked for Guicci came over, left his briefcase on the table, went to the bathroom and BK stole six watches while the guy was in the head. And he was a card cheat."[5]

When Sheriff W. E. "Butch" Leypoldt and Undersheriff Lloyd Bell

---

[5]In 1966 Beldon admitted to an FBI agent that he had installed a Vegas-type eye in the sky in the ceiling of his Bel-Air card room, which allowed him to fleece his Hollywood friends at cards.

arrived at the blaze, Butch got a crowbar from the trunk of the cruiser and broke in the door. The inrush of air created a twister effect in the smoke. They made their way to the huge walk-in vault where the casino kept their money. Gaining entrance, they formed a bucket brigade and with the help of employees, including Beldon Katleman, passed out scorched boxes of cash from the cage until forced to abandon the building. Within half an hour, pounds of silver dollars, over $400,000 worth, had melted into slag.

Outside, crowds of people—the chorus dancers in their short nighties among them—stood silently watching the blue flames consume their workplace. Comedian Red Skelton, who had been headlining nearby, was in front of the crowd snapping pictures of the inferno. Betty Grable (who, with her husband Harry James, was suing Beldon over wages) was pale and weeping uncontrollably. Over $10,000 worth of exotic costumes from her lavish revue were turned to ashes as she watched helplessly. The giant windmill was going now. Grable turned away, but Red Skelton moved even closer, his camera clicking and red hair illuminated. He got a great shot of the fire eating at the windmill's base. With one great bite, the flames sent the tower tilting so far to one side it could never be righted. The windmill trembled as if in a hurricane, then flailing its mock wind vanes in a last, futile gesture for help fell farther. The burning beams gave a great hiss and expelling of breath.

The great windmill was in its death throes. Electrical sparks and shattering neon lit up the night. A crash and whoosh of sparks, and in seconds the great symbol of Vegas gaming was a blackened skeleton. Finally, the frame toppled over into ash, which the desert winds scattered until nothing was left. The fire had lasted only an hour, and with it the flames took what for almost twenty years had stood as the symbol of the Las Vegas gambling and resort industry.[6]

[6]After the ashes had cooled some of the other hotel owners paid a visit to Beldon and told him to take his money and get out of Vegas. Katleman took his fat insurance settlement and moved to Bel-Air ten months later. He was involved in litigation with Howard Hughes over the El Rancho property for ten years. Hughes hated Beldon too. The El Rancho was never rebuilt and is a vacant lot today.

It was hard to believe that the El Rancho was gone.

At that moment fifty-three miles away from the blaze in a small mining town, plans were being laid for a film, Marli's second film, one quite different from *Psycho* but involving the luckiest man in Nevada, the seventh son of a seventh son, and a fledgling director just as great as Hitchcock, perhaps even more high-minded. His first film could almost be called an experimental film, at least that's the way Marli explained it later, when it was all over. But it was really a sex comedy, one of a new genre.

Chapter Seventeen

Psycho

On June 22, *Psycho* opened in Boston at the Paramount (three people fainted), at the Arcadia in Philadelphia (people screamed aloud at the Shower Sequence), and at the Woods during a thunderstorm in Chicago (managers handed out umbrellas to the waiting throng, imitating the same ploy Hitchcock had recommended to New York theater managers). Even in the rain, enthusiastic crowds snaked down the block, anxiously crowding forward and nudging their neighbors in anticipation. Hitch's highly effective advertising campaign is still copied to this day. When the film went into wide release, everyone in America would be talking about Hitchcock's shocker.

In Los Angeles, Sonny anticipated seeing the film. He knew *Psycho* had something to do with the leading character's mother though he did not know the ending to Bloch's novel. He had had trouble finding a copy. Daily, Sonny grew more anxious in another, darker quest that had nothing to do with Caryl Chessman. At night he cruised the bars and by day scanned the surrounding parks and wooded areas looking for something. Perhaps he was only scouting Griffith Park because of its lofty remoteness. A body could get lost up there forever. At night he studied, determined to be prepared for any of those unplanned accidents that could trip a man up and get him arrested or killed.

Ten days later, on June 26, Mrs. Mercedes Langeron, seventy-two, was strangled and raped in her West Twenty-third Street apartment at South Vermont Avenue about nine blocks from USC. Thad Brown added this latest crime to his list of strangulation murders. The LAPD had been lucky this time. They had a witness, Mrs. Langeron's roommate, who walked in seconds after the attack. Outside Mrs. Langeron's apartment door, she observed a tall, swarthy twenty-nine-year-old bouncing a red rubber ball. The stranger saw her approaching, forcefully threw the red ball down and leaped through Mrs. Langeron's door, which he had left ajar. Through the open door the roommate saw him effortlessly vault the backyard fence and bound away on his long legs. Behind him in the hall, the red ball, losing momentum, continued to bounce more and more slowly. Finally it stopped altogether. Motionless, it was more menacing though it was one of the most common objects one could imagine.

From that moment on, the campus-area killer was known as the Bouncing Ball Strangler. With this strangling, the killer had brought his total of known murders to six. If Brown and his men included Mrs. Miller, that would make seven and in his mind, Thad had already done that. He visualized that red ball still bouncing with an energy and life of its own. That the killer had left the red rubber ball behind meant nothing. It was like millions that could be purchased anywhere. Lee Jones was unable to lift prints from the ball since the strangler had worn gloves. Thad was visibly upset over Langeron's assault. Any criminal who injured his elderly victim infuriated Brown. He kept suppressed a deadly temper that he reserved for brutal rapists and smash-and-grab robbers.

"I'm strongly in favor of stakeouts on those cases to kill those clowns," Brown said bitterly of a gang led by a six-foot-four gunman who had been robbing liquor stores and clubbing clerks' heads to avoid being identified. "We had five guys in the hospital with depressed skull fractures," Brown said, "so I staked out forty-six detectives with shotguns backed up by forty-six armed rookies. We killed ten holdup men in three weeks and didn't have another liquor store robbery for three months."

As the Bouncing Ball Strangler stalked Hollywood and put a fright into older women and college girls, Sonny took to concealing lethal weapons on his person as if afraid for his own safety. In his jacket he carried a razor box opener, a blade box cutter, and a thin, eight-inch-long sawtooth steak knife. He really didn't need weapons. All he needed were his big strong hands. Besides, his victims were pretty helpless to begin with.

Yes, Sonny was anxious to see *Psycho* but couldn't concentrate on it because his mind was in a whirl, filled with thoughts that would occupy him throughout the blazing summer of 1960. Thus he delayed seeing *Psycho*, a film that would have a profound effect on him and one that he was longing to view, but did not want to go see alone. When Hitchcock's movie opened and he found time, he would bring Mother. Or someone just like her. And after they saw the film—who knew?

Chapter Eighteen
Russ Meyer's Brilliant Idea

On a June afternoon, Russ Meyer stood by the sparkling sea by a Malibu beach. He rolled up his trouser legs, removed his loafers and socks, then lit a cigarette, and got down to work. Meyer wore a wine-colored short-sleeved shirt with white buttons, an expensive Timex strapped to his left wrist and, around his neck, three small cameras. He smiled. "The Bosom," completely nude, was stretched out on a striped blanket he had spread out on the sand in front of a blue wall, to which someone had nailed three huge starfish. In the blinding sun, the white of the model's tan lines sharply contrasted with the copper of her body.

The Bosom's five-foot six-inch height and 128-pound body were pretty consistent, but her voluptuous dimensions were constantly changing. Or at least the press thought so. They gave her statistics variously as forty-three DD/twenty-two/thirty-six, or forty-four/twenty/thirty-six, or forty-five/twenty/thirty-six, or forty-five/twenty-two/thirty-five. "I'm still growing," she said. In answer to her most frequently asked question she replied, "Forty-three D, sir, and that is that!"

Artist Violet Parkhurst considered June "The Bosom" Wilkinson to have the *"most beautiful"* figure she had ever seen. "She is so full-breasted it is almost *unbelievable,*" she said. "Yet, she combines this with a tiny waist and well-proportioned hips." June appeared first in *Playboy* in September 1958 in a spread titled "The Bosom," which suggested she had "the kind of figure that can be better imagined than observed." The nation had a breast fetish; one had only to look at the movie queens of the time—Sophia Loren, Jayne Mansfield, and Marilyn Monroe—huge breasts to be seen but not touched.

One had only to look at Russ Meyer's models to see he loved his work and how well he knew his audience. That audience of immature, repressed men wanted what Meyer wanted—the most gigantic mammaries possible. Meyer had the biggest breast fetish of them all. That was what made him a king in his field. Like Mickey Spillane, he might not be a fine artist ("That's not writing, that's typing," critics said of the hard-boiled writer), but everything Spillane wrote was filled with pulse-pounding energy, a certain honesty, and a lack of pretense. And wasn't being dull the greatest sin of any artist? Meyer was the most successful freelance photographer at *Playboy*. He had photographed all the biggest names and breasts of the fifties: Liz Taylor, Anita Ekberg, Jayne Mansfield, Barbara Nichols, Vikki "The Bottom" Dougan, Gina Lollobrigida and Mamie Van Doren, and, of course, The Bosom, who was a force to be reckoned with and one of a kind.

A natural brunet, The Bosom was able to break through as the era's photo model sensation only after she became a blond. Last August, Meyer had photographed her second *Playboy* appearance, "The Bosom in Hollywood." She would eventually do seven spreads for Hef and appear in over fifty men's magazines. For that reason, though, she could never be a *Playboy* Centerfold, though she was obviously Hef's favorite, second only to Diane Webber. The centerfolds were supposed to be the obtainable girl next door, and seeing them in *Modern Man, Adam,* and a score of other girlie magazines would shatter the illusion Hef was trying to create. The Bosom was also under contract to Seven Arts, which made a centerfold appearance doubly impossible. "I know being a girl with a big bust has done all this for me," she said, thrusting her chest out as far as it would go. "I realized some time ago that as long as there were men in the world I'd make good."

The busty, statuesque eighteen-year-old had discovered herself. Born March 27, 1940, in Essex, England, June Wilkinson attended professional school at three years old, danced as a child as Red Riding Hood in *Babes in the Woods*, and had a part in *Cinderella*. When she was fifteen she joined the Donna Maresca Ballet Company, and at sixteen danced topless and created a nightclub act. She was a fan dancer at London's famed Windmill Theater, the youngest ever, and performed at London's Blue Angel before coming to the United States. She brought her mother along as her chaperone, but when June's contract to promote a plastics company ran out, both were stranded in Chicago and running out of money. Her mother wanted to go back to England, but June had other ideas. She had Mom call *Playboy* and tell Hef that "June is the prettiest girl on earth." He took one look at her in person, decided Mom was right, and personally staged every scene of her first photo shoot with Art Paul at the Playboy Building.

Russ Meyer, his back to the surf, pressed his V-strut tripod deeply into the sand, steadied it, and hung a heavy thirty-five-millimeter camera from one of its legs. He squinted through the lens and saw the brown scrub of Malibu Beach climbing the dunes and flights of green and white stairs vanishing somewhere above. He could hear the drone of passing traffic in the distance and surfers calling to each other. A warm wind swept in from the sea. To his left, photographer Ken Parker, Meyer's long-time friend, set up his own equipment and began snapping pictures of Meyer at work, part of a documentary he was preparing.

The thirty-eight-year-old Meyer, the son of a policeman and a nurse, was fourteen when his mother pawned her engagement ring to buy him his first movie camera, an eight-millimeter Orthochromatic Univex. He had found his passion. Russ grew up shooting movies around Oakland and during World War II studied at the MGM School of Motion Picture Photography.

Meyer got closer to The Bosom, dropped down on his left knee, and narrowed his eyes as if they were camera lenses. Stretching out his left hand, fingers stiffly extended, he directed June's pose like an orchestra conductor. The Bosom raised her right arm toward a starfish nailed above her head—reached—reached, gave up, and then leaned on her left side and tucked her legs beneath her. The white of her huge breasts, sparkling with beads of sweat, shone brilliantly in the sun. They jiggled so it was impossible for Meyer to draw his eyes away from them. Soon sand clung to every crevice of her body and lay along the flat of her belly.

June had never felt typed because of her nude modeling. "Definitely not," she said. "This modeling was initially started to build me up as a sex symbol. I can't see myself as a Marilyn Monroe or Jayne Mansfield [When Jayne and June compared breasts she bested Jayne by a full inch]. Some people think so, but our looks, personalities, and abilities are so different."

June rose, drawing the towel around her body, and walked with Meyer down to the water. At the tide line she posed in white fur muffs and mink hat, even dipping a toe in the foam. "Hold it," said Meyer. With a tube of flesh-colored lipstick he retouched a discoloration on June's right hip. Now she moved into the raging surf and Meyer came right in with her, *click-click-click*, waves crashing around his rolled up gabardine trousers, which were soon drenched up to the thigh and spotted with encrusted salt. Meyer didn't care. He loved shooting film. It was thrilling. He loved big-bosomed women. *They* were thrilling. He wasn't quite the luckiest man on earth. Hugh Hefner was.

Meyer slid into the glamor business by the side door. One day his old army buddy, Don Ornitz, the son of one of the blacklisted "Hollywood Ten," Sam Ornitz, and one of the 1950s fan press, which included Hymie Fink of *Photoplay*, Bob Beerman of *Modern Screen*, and Don's partner at Globe, Larry Barbier, called him.

Don suggested Meyer make some extra money shooting girlie calendars and magazine pinups. Ornitz did a lot of work for *Playboy*, but Meyer soon surpassed him with his shots of Mansfield and Ekberg and fledgling starlets for George von Rosen's brainchild, *Modern Man*, which had preceded *Playboy* by two years. Von Rosen's first cover girl was Jane Russell; Hef's first cover girl was Marilyn Monroe.

In surf up to her knees The Bosom posed in the white mink, lifting the fur high above the water to keep it dry. She was fully nude under-neath. The contrast was too erotic for Meyer to use in print but he shot anyway. After ten minutes, June waded ashore, tossed the coat to him and lay down in the water. She raised one leg high above her head and imitated a pair of scissors. Finally, the voluptuous girl emerged, wrapped herself in a towel and, shivering, trudged up the sand to a freestanding pipe with a head and a faucet mounted on a latticed deck. The crude outdoor shower had been set up so she could wash the sand away before she left the beach.

The Bosom took a long shower, having discarded the towel she had been coyly holding in front of her and luxuriating in the spray. A tan sailor's cap was tilted rakishly over one eye as she stood on tiptoe so Meyer could hose her back down. He directed the stream of water with his right hand, all the while patting his pockets with his left. He lo-cated a pack of Luckys, shook one out, put it to his lips, and lit it. Water beaded on June's considerable flesh like white diamonds. As a brisk wind wafted in from the Pacific, her nipples hardened. Her blond hair caught the sun. It was glorious. And Meyer was filled with inexpressible joy.

Meyer had the ability to see a finished layout in his mind, even ar-ranged against the type on a printed page. In his early days with Hef, Meyer often sketched out his pictorials before he photographed them as if they were movie scenes—*two* wineglasses, a disordered bed, the shadow of a lover cast on the sheets. He used props to advance the story. And Meyer was a great storyteller. It was while shooting a fantasy lay-out for *Playboy* two years earlier that he had gotten his $3-million idea. Not so long before that Meyer had still been working out of Oakland, California, doing projection stills for major motion pictures, acting as a cameraman for Gene Walker Productions; shooting industrial films for the SP Railroad; and moonlighting as a movie projectionist for Pete DeCenzie, the crew-cut owner of the fifteen-hundred-seat classic El Rey Burlesque Theater in downtown Oakland.

Meyer regarded his buddy's showplace as the last great striptease show in the nation. "Peter DeCenzie was a very serious guy when it came to putting on these shows," said Meyer. Every show had an orches-tra, a top stripper, eight beautiful co-stars, and innumerable burlesque veterans performing classic comedy sketches as interludes between the acts—"How do I get to Floogle Street?" asks a visitor. "Floogle Street?" anyone he asks replies in horror, "Why, my husband died on Floogle Street!" or some such, and beats him up.

Candy butchers, working their way up and down the aisles during intermission, sold snacks and "sexy" pictures to an audience of uniformed sailors from the Alameda Naval Station and shy guys in raincoats. "Hold this little camera up to the light later, and you will see a startling picture," they spieled, but it was a con.

Out of sentimentality, DeCenzie had kept old-time burlesque star Tempest Storm's (Annie Blanche Banks) name emblazoned across the marquee for years. In 1950, she had appeared in DeCenzie and Meyer's first movie, *French Peep Show*, a filmed record of one of her striptease acts at the El Rey. Meyer shot it in sixteen millimeter, then enlarged it up to thirty-five as a "wet-gate blowup" (one of his innovations) so it could be shown on the big screen.

In 1958, DeCenzie dialed Diamond 8-6317 from Oakland, reached Meyer at his new Hatillo Avenue studio in Canoga Park, and got right to the point. He wanted his buddy to make a second film with him, a nudist film this time. Meyer turned him down flat—"Are you kidding?" One hundred and fifty black-and-white nudist camp films had already been made, he explained, naturalist films portrayed as deathly serious documentaries to sneak past the censors. Meyer considered them a glut on the market and dull as lead with their endless games of volleyball and "paunchy, sunburned" nudists standing awkwardly to hide their genitals. Nudist documentaries were moderately successful because in such a repressed nation it was all the little boy-men had. In the late 1950s, it was all about getting a glimpse of female flesh—any female. It was the same curious desire that had driven Ed Gein, the real-life model for the original Norman Bates, to dig up female graves and for the Norman character to install a peephole in the Bates Motel.

Meyer thought about DeCenzie's request the next morning and remembered a shoot he had just completed of *Playboy* models in imagined nude fashions of the future such as Marli had posed for. The layout's premise—a man fantasizes he can see through women's clothing—gave

Meyer an idea that he hurriedly jotted down on the back of a laundry ticket. Ticket in hand, he rushed to the phone to call DeCenzie.

"The public is waiting for something new," Meyer excitedly told him. Their film would be lovingly photographed for a more upscale audience, college students and the middle class, and could play in the art houses specializing in sexy European imports. When the imports weren't sexy enough, distributors added sex scenes with American actors. Theirs would already be sexy enough. "Ours will be the first film to be done with humor, tongue in cheek," Meyer continued to DeCenzie, "a live-action cartoon of funny vignettes, as ribald as *Playboy* . . . a comedy about a man who is afraid of women but who undresses them with his eyes. We'll even use *Playboy* models . . . a moving cheesecake calendar." Meyer had just invented the nudie cutie, the first sexploitation skin-flick.

"No one had gotten into that kind of thing at all," Meyer said later. In the guise of humor, the *Playboy* photographer intended to take advantage of recently liberalized obscenity laws to put naked breasts and buttocks on the big screen. It would be the first mainstream film to unashamedly depict women as glorified sex objects, but disguised as a comedy about an old man afraid of women. Meyer's only real worry was that the puritanical Eastman Kodak company might not process their film because of the nudity. Meyer's way around that involved some personal finesse. He hired one of the Kodak tech representatives, an old pal, to work as a photographer from the onset and thus sway him to convince Kodak to be more cooperative. Meyer would even advertise his nudie as "Filmed in Revealing Eastman Color."

Meyer and DeCenzi each ponied up $12,000 for a one-hour-plus film using a four-man crew and a four-day shooting schedule. Meyer planned to shoot their full-color nudie on sixteen-millimeter film and make a thirty-five-millimeter wet-gate blowup. They would shoot silent (sound was expensive) and add an ironic soundtrack narration to divert the censors who might still have to be bought off with something as simple as a good meal in a fancy restaurant.

Meyer and co-screenwriter Edward J. Lakso (who wrote the narration voiced by Irving Blum and composed the simple musical score) refined the plot. Instead of an old man who is terrified of women, their hero would be a middle-aged denture delivery man in a straw hat, a dirty old man for an audience of dirty old men, who is terrified of women. He would never touch them, only look—that was vital to their target audience. Lakso wrote cameos for Pete DeCenzie as "Burlesque Announcer" and Meyer as an "Audience Member." The plot was simple. Meyer's protagonist visits his dentist and, under the influence of Novocain, imagines the dental assistant nude. As he goes about his rounds on a Schwinn two-wheeler, he observes "well-developed nude women" everywhere. Meyer was the northern California rep for "W. Ellis Teas—Associated Photographs, 137 Harkin Place, San Francisco" and thought he would be perfect for the lead. A World War II army buddy of Meyer's from the 166th Signal Photographic Corps, "Bill" Teas, far from being afraid of women, was an aggressive girl chaser. He agreed to the titular role of "Mr. Teas." Casting the female costars would be much more difficult.

"We need four, maybe five well-stacked nude chicks," Meyer said, his eyes gleaming with the possibilities of so much firm flesh. It was surprising that none of his regular cheesecake pinups were interested, nor were DeCenzie's seasoned strippers who balked at full-color, live-action nakedness on a giant screen. None wanted their flaws exposed on such a grand scale. The strippers DeCenzie could get were un-toned by today's standards—earth mother, child bearing-types, who photographed poorly.

Inexplicably, it didn't occur to Meyer to ask his gorgeous *Playboy* Centerfold wife, Eve Flores, a famous pinup model with a startling thirty-nine-D bust, twenty-three-inch waist, and thirty-seven-inch hips, to star. She had been *Playboy* Miss June 1955 and appeared again in March in a layout that Hef personally storyboarded. Eve was not only an able producer but was a film actress (her unbilled film debut had been in 1955 in *Artists and Models*).

To solve his casting problem, Meyer enlisted another girlie photographer pal, Earl Leaf. Goateed and bald, Leaf was the lustiest of a wild and eccentric breed and the most unpredictable of the two-fisted cheesecake artists. He shared a camaraderie with Meyer equal only to that of his old World War II buddies like Bill Teas. Leaf, in love with snapping tantalizing photos of beauties in little or no attire, had photographed the famous and about-to-be-famous over the last eight years. He advised budding starlets to take it all off. "Nothing risqué, nothing gained," he would leer and add he had never met a successful actress who had been ashamed of her cheesecake past.

Leaf didn't begin his "real" education until he quit school in the seventh grade and began to travel. Over the years, he kept books in San Francisco, sailed with the navy, reported for the United Press and while traveling the Orient taught Mao Tse-Tung to rhumba. Back in New York, Leaf spotted a sign offering nude model classes for amateur photographers, bought a camera at the corner drugstore, and rushed into class. "Then and there I decided to become a photographer," he recalled. "I began to hire my own models to come to my house at night. Pretty soon, I was selling some of the figure studies. Then I went as far as to put a few clothes on the girls and started with cheesecake. After a while I was earning as much money with my girl pictures as I was at my regular newspaper job."

Leaf didn't let Meyer down. He sweet-talked Ann Peters into playing a waitress (as Nan Peters). She was the best-endowed of any girl that Meyer had ever photographed, save one and she was his biggest discovery. More than any other, Meyer wanted The Bosom in his revolutionary nudie comedy. He begged her, but her Seven Arts contract prevented her from appearing in any films but theirs. Meyer thought of a way around this legal impediment. Nude body *part* doubles are used to shoot inserts. A common one is the butt double or stunt butt. Why couldn't June be a stunt boob? The Bosom went for that. As a personal favor, she would appear in Meyer's film as an uncredited body part. Though she would be an anonymous pair of breasts framed in a window billed only as "Uncredited Torso," June was confident everyone would know they were her breasts. "Breasts are like fingerprints," she said, "No two are alike." June Wilkinson had reached the pinnacle in sexual objectification—a pair of breasts thrust through an open window.

Meanwhile Paul Morton Smith, another girlie photographer Meyer knew, recruited Michele Roberts to play a secretary (as Mischele Roberts). DeCenzie convinced Marilyn Wesley to play the dental assistant and Mikki France to portray the psychologist. Meyer himself spotted the last girl, Dawn Danielle, "bouncing down Sunset Boulevard" and enticed her to play a beach beauty. He assured them all they would just be animated pinups who would sit, stretch, or walk and maybe speak a word or two, but that would be all. "It's not really a sex film," he explained, "but a sex comedy." Comedy was the loophole that would get them past the censors. No theatrical film in history had ever had this much daring nudity.

Meyer shot *The Immoral Mr. Teas* at a secluded lake in the Malibu mountains, El Namez Beach, a Westwood ice-cream parlor, and his own home. As he was filming a scene at his dentist's office, Eve busted in, furious he hadn't given her a part and ran out after ruining the shot. Meyer chased after her, promising, "Honey, I'll use you in the next one!"

After a police bust on opening night, Meyer's nudie cutie didn't get another showing for eight months. "Once the goddamn picture caught on [in Seattle]," he said, "it was booked all over the country in these art houses." *Mr. Teas* returned more than $1 million and by the time Meyer stood on a Malibu beach photographing June Wilkinson, it had earned $3 million. As Hitchcock's *Psycho* had reinvented the horror film in black and white, "King Leer" had reinvented the stag movie by effectively adding comedy, beautifully photographed nudes in color, and sound effects—without moralizing. *Mr. Teas* was simply about beautiful women and the men who are afraid to touch them. It was an odd time with even odder men who could only watch and never participate.

Mr. Teas's vacuousness stumped critics. "There was no passion, no flesh touching flesh, no consummation shown or suggested," wrote critic Leslie Fielder. "For pornography the woman's angle of vision is necessary, but there were no women outside of Bill Teas's head . . . he could touch no one—not in lust or love or in the press of movement along the street." Just like Sonny, just like Norman Bates, a living body was sacrosanct, but a lifeless body, that was different.

Meyer said his nude starlets "performed with a minimum of complaints and rebounded at night when we had dinner and enjoyed the evening, then got a good night's sleep and got out of bed at five o'clock in the morning and they're putting on body makeup, you know." When

Meyer starred his wife in his 1961 nudie, *Eve and the Handyman*, "She broke her ass," he said. "She just said 'Look, whatever you want to do, let's do it, okay? I'm here, I'll get up early in the morning, and I'll look right.' With her I could do it, you know."

The nudie cuties bailed out hundreds of failing theaters threatened by TV. "Nudie cuties became the grindhouse rage in the late 1950s," Eddie Muller and Daniel Faris wrote, "once the U.S. Supreme Court ruled that nudity, per se, was not obscene. Unlike earlier Adults Only movies, which were obligated to show the shameful degradation that followed sex, nudie cuties presented women as glorified sex goddesses, and the men who ogled them as bumbling dolts."

Meyer had stretched the limits of censorship, revolutionized mainstream films, single-handedly created the adult film industry, and helped usher in the Sexual Revolution. His nudie cutie also launched an entirely new career for the *Playboy* photographer.

The success of *Mr. Teas* gave Francis Ford Coppola, a young filmmaker at UCLA, an idea on how to make some money and get his name on a film, any film, something he wanted more than life itself. As for Marli, she had been taking film classes at UCLA though their paths didn't cross right away.

Chapter Nineteen
Robert Graysmith

n 1960, we didn't have nude pinups at Tachikawa, and it looked like we weren't going to have *Psycho* either. You could say I sailed all the way from Japan to San Francisco to see *Psycho*. Colonel Burton K. Sams, the base commander of the 2710th Air Base Wing and its subbases for Northern Air Material Area, Pacific, would never have allowed Hitchcock's controversial film to be shown uncut on Tachikawa, the U.S. Air Force Base where I lived with my parents. Which was a shame, since Tachi had one of the most unusual movie theaters in the world. Before World War II, the Japanese Army had erected a huge research-and-development facility there and constructed the biggest wind tunnel in Asia to test the strength and maneuverability of the aircraft built there. The U.S. Occupation turned the tunnel into the hangar-size Tachi West movie theater, surely a spectacular setting to see films with snow-covered Mt. Fuji looming in the background as one entered.

The circular base was so large, it had an east and west side and a north-south runway handling over four thousand landings and takeoffs a month. The largest, most complete air force installation in the Far

East was a great place to live if you weren't an airman. We got our medical care from the 6407th U.S. Air Force Hospital. As the dependent of an air force officer I lived in dependent housing on and off base while I attended seventh and eighth grades in Green Park Dependent School, a long, lonely bus ride. At age twelve, I worked in building 1470 on the *Tachikawa Marauder*, a slick weekly in English with a circulation of seven thousand and a Japanese edition of ten thousand. I drew a comic strip and a few sports cartoons and wrote a column for the *Maurader* during the summer and got the newspaper bug. When I was seventeen, I spent my senior year at Yamato High School just outside the base and about twenty-five miles from metropolitan Tokyo. At Yamato High I was taught by teachers too rebellious to get work in the United States but who had started our school.

My mother, Jane, worked at the library and ran a thrift store, the joy of her life. My lieutenant colonel father, Robert Gray Smith, ran the Tachikawa Commissary and later the Post Exchange, both the biggest in the Far East. The TAB Commissary had all the main features of a modern U.S. supermarket, frozen food flown in by the Mobile Air Transport Service and an assortment of locally produced foodstuffs. At the East and West Base Exchanges, retail items, shoes, watches, and jewelry at discount rates; snack bar; and a magazine stand where *Playboy* wasn't sold. They did stock a heavily abridged serialization of *Psycho* in a black-and-white men's adventure magazine. I had always been a huge fan of Hitch's work and was anxious to see what he had done with Bloch's novel. It apparently was going to be a new kind of film, one with nudity and other shocking elements.

I sailed back to the States in August 1960 to attend college on full scholarship in the Bay Area. The term started in September, but the big MATS ship got me to San Francisco two weeks too early. For a while I was the only one in the two-story dorm on the hill above wooded paths and a goldfish pond. Some nights I walked the narrow steps under the heavy trees down to feed the fish. Later, in the winter, the pond would freeze over with a thin sheet of ice. The goldfish shining through the ice looked huge then, but that was just magnification. I waited for the semester to start and others to arrive. There was no power in the dorm yet, so I spent nights walking the Oakland and Berkeley streets. Behind the school was an old rock quarry, and uphill of that was a posh district of shops and homes. It was pretty lonely, but I figured that just before my eighteenth birthday I would finally get to see *Psycho* because it was going to play downtown.

After my freshman year began in September, when my classmates at the university were partying (we had the first coed dorm in the nation and were first with very long hair), I often made my way down to Oakland's skid row. Under the neon lights I studied the interesting faces and postures of the downtrodden; heard their tragic stories; and wandered black streets that were trash-littered and seedy, with even seedier theaters. Those theaters showed triple bills, Italian sword and sorcery movies, Randolph Scott Westerns, Hercules and Hammer films for little money. I went as often as I could. Instead of watching the films, I watched the audience and sketched them.

In a pool hall, one flight down on Sixteenth Street, overhead lights, as mustard-colored as Van Gogh's painting of a pool table, shone down on hopeless men, mostly former boxers. On the west side of Twelfth Street a pawnshop window displayed cowboy great Tom Mix's wallet. Mix had survived dynamite and bullets only to have his neck broken by a flying aluminum suitcase thrown forward when he suddenly braked his station wagon for a deer.

This tawdry landscape was Russ Meyer territory too, where he cut his nudie teeth, worked with DeCenzie, and came up with *The Immoral Mr. Teas*, which was still playing. I studied the marquee with Tempest Storm's name in huge letters. I wouldn't have been surprised if the huge-busted burlesque queen, dressed in pasties and spangles, passed me in the evening light. Having grown up on a repressed air force base, I was curious to see Meyer's film. *Mr. Teas* was lively, professional, and well photographed. Mostly it was funny.

On Tuesday the September *Playboy* hit the stands at DeLaur's News-stand below the *Tribune* Tower. Publishers dated their magazines as late as they could and got them on the stands as early as possible. *Playboy* had a review of *Psycho*, the movie I had come so far to see. I turned to the review.

The Hitchcock jolter for *Playboy* contributor Robert Bloch's same-name novel starts slow but builds to shocks that make the most blasé of moviegoers clutch their partners and let out full-throated shrieks of horror in the best tradition. The plot, which wild horses won't drag out of us, involves . . . full-bosomed Janet Leigh (who spends most the picture in her bra or nude in the shower) . . . and Anthony Perkins as a young motel operator. There is also a Mrs. Bates, who is not at all handsome. Which one's the psycho of the title? Go see . . . this is expert Guignol entertainment that recalls no other U.S. film, but, rather, the goose-fleshy French *Diabolique*. . . . It is such stuff as bad dreams are made on.

I closed the magazine and studied the cover, which featured a stunning redhead in what looked like a shower. The very warm cover was made up of puzzle pieces with one piece missing. That missing piece had to make you wonder who she was.

In Chicago, Marli Renfro put down her September *Playboy* and left it faceup to show off to her roommate. She had been astounded at how well received *Psycho* was and how notorious, especially her scene. She was famous and yet not famous, unable to reveal that it was she on the screen. Marli, like the rest of the cast, had given her word to Hitch and could not break it.

Later a girlfriend asked her, "Did you know *Psycho* was based on a real case?"

"It had never entered my mind before Hitch brought it up," Marli said. *Psycho*'s embittered author, Robert Bloch, was speaking out in the press and on the radio. Marli heard what he had to say about *Psycho* and the inspiration for it, and the facts were even scarier than Hitch had intimated. "I know evil is out there. I know that now," Marli said. She didn't sleep that night.

Chapter Twenty
Bloch's Revelation

All over the country, viewers of *Psycho* speculated whether that really was a nude Janet Leigh in the shower. Or was it someone else? No, it must be her. Impossible! "After *Psycho* came out, all the press wanted to talk about was the murder scene," Tony Curtis wrote in his autobiography. "Janet had never enjoyed media attention and when the pressure of this new celebrity began to get to her, she started to drink a lot. And when Janet had a few drinks in her, she became a different person: belligerent, accusatory, and downright nasty. I didn't want to provoke her rages, so I started staying away more and more." Could Hitch's movie have been responsible for destroying Janet's marriage?

The success of *Psycho* continued to rock the nation. The lines around the block were undiminished and people were remarkable in cooperating with Hitch by not giving away the ending. *Psycho* was tripling his investment of less than $1 million. And he got to keep it all. There was one unsettling aspect. *Psycho* author Robert Bloch had been stiffed financially. Unlike Marli, he was under no vow of secrecy and talked as much as he wished.

Like so many who had worked with Hitch, Bloch discovered the director had taken most of the credit for the film's success. Bloch hadn't been invited to the screening or the red carpet opening. Hitch had treated his soul mate in the world of suspense no differently than he had Cornell Woolrich, the author of the novella *It Had to Be Murder* (as William Irish) that *Rear Window* was based on. Woolrich, who lived in Manhattan's Sheraton Russell residential hotel with his mother, was not invited to the August 4, 1954, New York premiere at the Rivoli Theatre. He spent most of his adult years in that hotel locked in a love–hate relationship with his domineering mother. In a decade, he would die there alone from a gangrene infection caused by a protruding nail in one of the cheap shoes he wore though he had made millions for others.

Bloch, who had no percentage of the movie profits, hadn't even received "a thank-you bonus," which is common when a movie is a hit. Tony Perkins had gotten one—$2000, which he used to buy a new nose for a lifelong friend. But at no time had there been any attempt to cut Bloch in on the profits, ever. He not only had received no bonus but had signed away his characters forever, as he discovered when he tried to sell a sequel to *Psycho*.

The idea for *Psycho* had come to Bloch as if a gift from the blue. In late November in 1957, on an exceptionally frigid day, he was sitting in his kitchen in Weyauwega, Wisconsin, "a town so small that if you sneezed on the north side somebody on the south side said 'Gesundheit.'" He shook open his bed-sheet-size paper and read that thirty-five miles away to the west, in an even smaller town called Plainfield by State Highway 73, someone had walked into Ed Gein's shed on a Saturday morning and discovered a woman hung in the rafters dressed like a slaughtered deer.

Until now Ed Gein (rhymes with *fine*) had seemed harmless enough to the folks of Plainfield. The perpetually grinning fifty-one-year-old handyman and part-time babysitter kept to himself on the 160 acres his parents, George and Augusta, and alcoholic brother had left him. The brother had died in a mysterious fire. The town, made up mainly of German immigrants, now discovered Gein was really a monster.

Police had been looking for Mrs. Bernice Worden, a local hardware store merchant, ever since she vanished from her blood-spattered general store. Her pickup truck and $41 were gone too. Worden's son, a deputy sheriff, discovered Gein's name on a partially completed receipt for "1/2 gall. antifreeze" in the store entry book and recalled seeing Gein lurking around the store a week earlier. Worden led police to Ed's farm.

"Did you kill Mrs. Worden?" police asked Gein.

"Maybe," he said. "I've been in a kind of daze."

So, Gein was subject to amnesiac necrophiliac fugues, as was Sonny.

In 1954, he shot fifty-one-old Mary Hogan in her Pine Grove bar with a .32 rifle, piled her body on a sled, towed her home, and strung her up in the summer shed where he slaughtered pigs. He made stockings out of her legs and a topcoat of her skin, and tanned and hardened her abdomen until he could slip it on like a girdle. Mary had reminded him of Mother, who would get on her knees and pray her husband would die. Like Sonny, Gein had a thing for older women, in Ed's case, mother-substitutes for his hellfire-and-brimstone-spouting mother. Gein slept next to the corpses, just as the LA *Psycho* killer of older women would.

"After my mother died [of a cerebral hemorrhage in 1946]," Gein confessed, "I began to have strange visions. I developed an uncontrollable desire to see a woman's body. I began to visit cemeteries at night when the moon was full." With the help of an elderly crony, a mentally slow farmer named Gus, he dug up the graves of females around his mother's burial site over forty times. The pair stole corpses from graves in Plainfield and snatched a few from Hancock and Spiritsfields cemeteries. When Gus was committed to an old age home, Gein gathered some bodies on his own but found it too difficult to lift dead weight on his own. Finally he realized it was easier to murder fresh victims. He liked taxidermy but mainly liked to take things apart to see how they worked. Donning the women's skins, he danced in the moonlight.

That Saturday night, police, searching by flashlight (there was no electricity), discovered ten or eleven bodies in Gein's rundown farmhouse. The corpses were so decomposed that the authorities could hardly tell they had once been people. Gein had scattered them—a human nose in a frying pan, a cupful of noses on the counter, human lips strung like popcorn on a string, and a skull made into a soup bowl. He had cut the mouths away from four women's faces and made cutouts for eyes so he could wear them as Halloween masks. When the flashlights gave out, the police worked by the light of a kerosene lantern that illuminated a belt of nipples hanging from a doorknob, and ten skulls grinning down on them from a high shelf.

In the desolate summer shed, cops came to the nude, headless torso of Bernice Worden hanging upside down from pulleys attached to block and tackle and hoisted to the ceiling. Scattered around the farmhouse were Bloch's stories in *Marvel Tales* and *Unknown Worlds*, anatomy books, and catalogs of embalming supplies. Upstairs, the sickened investigators located five dusty, unused rooms. Gein's deceased mother's bedroom door was nailed shut and when they broke it down, they found the only clean room in the house unchanged from the day she died.

Bloch put down his newspaper and considered what he had read. His hands were shaking a little. The article suggested to him that even the reclusive loner down the road might really be a killer, something he might use in a book. He tried to figure out how such an ineffectual man could get away with murder for so long. He was really intrigued when he read Gein's comment that he had had a thing about his mother ever since he had lost her. "I decided to write a novel based on the notion that the man next door may be a monster," Bloch wrote, "unsuspected even in the gossip-ridden microcosm of small-town life."

In a week he had completed a first draft, shipped it to Harry Altshuler, his New York literary agent, who sent it to Harper & Brothers, who rejected it, and to Simon & Schuster editor Clayton Altshuler, who did not. Clayton acquired *Psycho* for their Inner Sanctum Mystery Book series for a $750 advance on a run of sixty thousand copies.

Hitchcock, finished with shooting *North by Northwest* and preparing for postproduction, wasn't particularly searching for his next project. As his production assistant Peggy Robertson recalled, "Hitchy would read the *New York Times Book Review* over the weekend and bring it into the office on Monday." On April 19, 1959, Peggy was scanning Anthony Boucher's crime fiction column, "Criminals At Large," in the

Book Review when her ears pricked up. She circled the article in pencil. "Boucher is raving about *Psycho*," Robertson said, passing Hitch the paper: "More chillingly effective than any writer might reasonably be expected to be . . . a believable story of mental illness that can be more icily terrifying than all the arcane horrors summoned by a collaboration of Poe and Lovecraft."

Hitch knew Bloch, who had written several teleplays for *Alfred Hitchcock Presents*. Hitch finished the review, put the paper down, and smiled. "It's excellent. I think we better get it right away," he told Peggy. "Call Paramount and get coverage." On his way to London, Hitch called her from the airport after buying a copy of *Psycho*. "Haven't you got coverage yet?" he asked. Paramount hadn't covered it, but he read the book on the way over and called Peggy again when he landed: "I think I've found our next subject," he said with delight.

Hitch never bought a literary property himself, but secured the movie rights clandestinely through a second party to avoid paying a high fee. On his behalf, MCA agent Ned Brown, who was also Stefano's agent, made a blind bid of $7,500 for the *Psycho* screen rights. "We've got to get more than $7,500," said Bloch. "Why don't you try $10,000?"

On May 5, Altshuler countered with $9,000, a still "shockingly low price." He advised Bloch to accept. "I can't get them any further."

"All right," said Bloch. After Uncle Sam and everybody else got their cut, Bloch cleared $5,000 on the deal. "It was then I learned that *Psycho* had been bought by Mr. Alfred Hitchcock," said a stunned Bloch.

Marli was shaken too when she heard Bloch's remarks on the Plainfield horror. Now the fun-loving redhead believed such dark creatures as Norman Bates existed in this world. She was relieved that Ed Gein was locked inside the Central Hospital for the Criminally Insane in Mendota, Wisconsin.

Not too many miles away from the smoking ruins of the El Rancho Casino in Las Vegas was a small mining town called Searchlight. There plans were being laid for the third nudie cutie film (which would be long delayed) inspired by Meyer's blockbuster film *The Immoral Mr. Teas*. And farther away, in LA, a young budding director on the campus of UCLA was deciding that he would like to try his hand at one too. There were riches there. And fame. The nudie cutie might be deemed sordid and cheap by his classmates, but the genre would allow him to make enough money to make a film of substance. His movie too would involve Marli Renfro only ten months after she first stepped into Alfred Hitchcock's shower.

Chapter Twenty-one

The Cover

I n September 1960, I taped Marli Renfro's *Playboy* cover up in my studio, a chilly redwood-planked cabin high in the Lafayette Hills. I had begun working as a gardener for a wealthy French family in exchange for the space and planned on moving out of the dorm and up here at the end of the semester. The thick-necked landlady could have stepped out of a Daumier lithograph: arms like a blacksmith's, legs like redwood trees, and white hair in a tight bun. Occasionally, she had me lift her frail mother back into bed from the floor where she had fallen. Deadweight was immensely heavy, I discovered to my surprise. The first evening I made some sketches of the redhead's pose and stashed them in my portfolio to take to anatomy class. Just before dawn I cut across a golf course to get to school, just about the time the sprinklers were activated. I dodged among them.

The sun was coming up as I approached the old marble quarry, a jumble of blocks and huge gaps where stones had been cut out. I stopped and studied the gray water far below where some people had drowned. At the campus I climbed the steps to the anatomy room for Life Class.

There was a rectangular skylight at the top where you could see into the studio from outside. Looking up, I saw a nude woman flash past the window, then fly backward in a second only to reappear again. The instructor sometimes put a model on a rope swing and had the class try to draw her in motion as she swung back and forth.

Each figure drawing class lasted three hours, three classes a day at three units each and then evening classes. I tacked my sketches to my easel and as my classmates sketched and painted nude models, I tried to make a painting of the redhead. She projected warmth and that *Playboy* cover was extremely warm. I used a limited palette, mostly warm, reds and yellows, just like the cover.

I also worked part-time as a sports copyboy at the *Oakland Tribune* in the *Tribune* Tower. On the ground floor was DeLaur's, the oldest newsstand in the West, which offered the largest selection of current magazines and newspapers in the world. Row after row climbed the walls. The redhead was there and there and there in a dozen covers all over the high wall in an overwhelming panorama of her image. A nudist magazine identified her as Marli Renfro, which I took to be a professional name and not her real name.

One Wednesday I brought the original *Playboy* cover into class along with a scrapbook I had begun to assemble of Marli's photo layouts. Renee S., our figure model, commented on the photo. Our anatomy professor, Ralph Borges, a realist painter, commented on the poses. Professor Harry Krell, art historian, found the classicism of Ancient Greece in Marli's poised figure. In each picture, the pose was natural, the model as relaxed in the nude before a male photographer as she would be with a gaggle of her female friends.

Alone in the cabin, I woke each morning to that cover—its warm tones, haunting face, and puzzle motif. Who was this redhead? She had an indefinable quality that made her unique, unforgettable. She was able to project her personality through her photos, and her all-encompassing gaze compelled you not to look away. That she rarely smiled only added to the enigma. Around this time I had begun to write and wondered if there was a story in that cover about image as a captivating force and obsession. By God, the redhead had something. Whatever it was got under my skin. I laid down two inflexible rules for any book I would write: The subjects must never have been treated in a book before, and if I started a project I would finish it. Yes, someday I would write a book about this unknown woman. Then I began to hear rumors from Hollywood that she was actually the girl in Alfred Hitchcock's shower, and I wanted to write that story more than ever. I was crazy about Hitchcock and *Psycho* in particular. And now I felt the same way about the beautiful redhead.

Chapter Twenty-two
No One Admitted After the Start

"I was in Chicago when *Psycho* came out," said Marli. "It came out in September and I went to see it with a girlfriend." Marli always liked to read the book before she saw the movie adaptation to have a strong visual sense of the characters. "When I see a movie and *then* read the book it changes it for me completely. But for some reason there were no copies of the source material available." Then she remembered that Hitch had snapped up every remaining copy of Fawcett's *Psycho* paperback run of nine printings that summer. Just past the ticket booth Marli saw the *Psycho* poster, which depicted a stern Hitchcock pointing to his wristwatch and admonishing: "NO ONE . . . BUT NO ONE . . . WILL BE ADMITTED TO THE THEATRE AFTER THE START OF EACH PERFORMANCE."

Hitch informed distributors that his advertising strategy "was a vital step in creating an aura of mysterious importance this picture so richly deserves." He stationed Pinkerton guards at the Chicago showing (just as there were in New York and Los Angeles) to enforce the rule.

"Beforehand I thought, 'How boring,'" Marli told her friend, "'I saw a lot of it being shot.' But then it scared me half to death. I couldn't believe it."

Janet Leigh felt the same, possibly more intensely when she saw *Psycho* edited and scored. She wrote she had "perpetual screaming memies . . . felt every thrust of that knife, screamed with every lunge . . . felt completely terrorized." As Janet watched Hitch's trailer for the film, she observed a wicked little smile "skulking behind that angelic, innocent face as he personally conducted a leisurely tour of the Bates Motel and the family's Victorian house, hinting dryly at the gruesome mayhem audiences could expect from his latest opus."

Tony Perkins sneaked into an early showing of *Psycho* with some friends and stood in back quietly watching. He had never seen an audience react like that. "They just screamed and yelled and went crazy!" he wrote. "It was just the most exciting experience of my life just to stand there and watch them go wild." He told his friends as they left, "Face it gang. I *am* Norman Bates." They had already suspected it. "There are a lot of crossed wires in there," one remarked of Tony's inner self, "and I wouldn't want to tangle with them." Another, Mario Busoni, said, "That wasn't acting, that was Tony." The more people who saw *Psycho*, the less the public was able to differentiate between the Tony seen slashing Janet Leigh in the shower and the real-life Tony. As Charles Winecoff wrote, "What had seemed a career boon now became a Hitchcockian nightmare of mistaken identity." When Tony and a female friend went to the supermarket, a group of giggling teenagers screamed out, "That's Tony Perkins and *that's* his mother!"

While Tony was performing in *Damn Yankees!* at the Carousel Theatre in Framingham, Massachusetts, the entire cast drove down to Boston to see his performance in *Psycho*. That night, the musical's producer, Richard Earle, noticed the performance was off-kilter and asked the kids in the cast why? They replied: "That film is so weird, we can't look at him." It was a subtle change, but Earle caught it. "It was palpable," he said. "It was almost at the moment his career did a turnaround."

"The sight of Tony Perkins," *Boston Globe* reporter Joseph P. Kahn wrote later, "hair cut Norman Bates-short and shoulders as boney as a turkey vulture's freely swinging a 9-iron, was usually enough to send terrified tourists scurrying . . . in search of a safe haven."

No matter what happened next, working with Hitchcock had been the happiest experience with a production in Tony's life, and he never forgot it or achieved such dizzying heights again. When *Psycho* opened in Paris in direct competition with Anatole Litvak's *La Verite* with Brigitte Bardot it created a big stir. Tony was awarded France's Victoire de Cinema for creating Norman Bates.

Hitchcock's fierce rivalry with "the French Hitchcock," Henri-Georges Clouzot, had helped inspire him to make *Psycho*. The French Hitchcock had achieved critical and financial success with his low-budget black-and-white suspense thriller *Les Diaboliques*, which had a surprise ending and a murder in a white-tiled bathroom. In 1955, Clouzot snapped up the rights to Pierre Boileau and Thomas Narcejac's *Celle Qui N'Etait Plus* (*The Woman Who Was No More*), which Hitchcock had coveted. In retaliation, he optioned a second of their books, *D'Entre les Morts* (*From Among the Dead*), and in 1958 made *Vertigo*, a lavish color film. It failed critically and financially.

But with *Psycho,* Hitch had tapped into the black-and-white horror market with blazing success, shown up Clouzot, outperformed B-movie suspense kings William Castle (*House on Haunted Hill*) and Roger Corman (*Bucket of Blood*), and regained his crown as the Master of Suspense. And Hitch had done it with a television crew and for peanuts. With *Psycho,* he demonstrated his basic tenet of suspense: "Tell the audience that something awful is going to happen—in the bathroom, say—then let them work themselves into a lather anticipating the pay-off—I'm playing a game with the public—trying to outwit them."

After seeing *Psycho,* Marli, excited by the roller coaster of events, decided to leave the Playboy Club and return to LA to do more photo modeling, television commercials, and maybe another movie. "When I came back from Chicago," Marli said, "I lived at my parents' for a while."

While in Chicago, Marli had dated Steve McQueen's manager, Hilliard Elkins. "And of course I saw Steve a few times," she recalled. "The last time I saw him he lived up in the Hollywood Hills in Nichols Canyon and I had a VW. I was washing my car in my bikini and he came driving up on his motorcycle. We lived in a cul-de-sac and there were three houses on this one driveway, we were the middle one, and Steve was interested in the house on the end as a rental." He and Marli talked for about ten minutes and then the owner showed up and escorted him around the house. He had recently starred on *Alfred Hitchcock Presents* in the classic Roald Dahl story, "Man from the South."

"Steve was filming a television movie directed by Dickie Donner on the beach around Malibu," Marli said, "and so during a break we garnered a couple of horses and rode on the beach." In his third season as Josh Randall on the series *Wanted: Dead or Alive*, Steve had just completed "The Twain Shall Meet," the first of five episodes Donner would direct. Today's filmed episode would run on October 11.

Marli rode her horse down through a dune area toward the beach in a relaxed, upright position. Her strong back enabled her to perfectly balance herself, usually a problem for a female rider. From years of bareback riding she had developed the arm strength necessary to maintain control with just the reins. As she and Steve McQueen thundered along, Marli leaned forward and slightly shifted her weight. They rode silently, but as they neared the beach, the sound of pounding waves thundered in their ears and salt air filled their nostrils. Marli headed toward the surf, directing her mount and shifting her body back in the saddle to slow as they approached the water and then back onto the hard packed sand. Steve, always reckless, went from a canter with a three-beat gait to a full gallop along the waterline sending up a wall of water. Marli kept up, though she was breathing fast now.

Her auburn hair, made redder by the falling sun, spilled over her shoulders. Now it was flying out behind her. McQueen's much shorter hair gleamed golden in the flickering light. Darting in and out of the surf, both horses kicked up a mixture of foam and sand. The two beautiful people felt the ocean breezes rush over them.

Marli thought to herself how much LA had changed while she was in Chicago. It was a dangerous place these days. A new breed of man, like Ed Gein, cloaked in his ordinariness, was walking the streets and, unknown to Marli, haunting the theaters where Psycho was still playing to turn-away crowds.

"There is this brilliant, wonderful, exciting moment with this incredible guy," she said, "and yet there is an undercurrent in LA as the sun is going down." There were people out there like Sonny whom she and Chief of Detectives Thad Brown alike did not know existed, and there was Ed Gein, the perpetually grinning, wide-toothed handyman who loved to babysit and stuff animals and people.

Marli looked to the bluffs as the day waned. Darkness was drifting down over the mounded dunes, and soon all she could perceive was the pounding of the horses' hooves on the sand and the rush of water sounding behind her.

Chapter Twenty-three
The Peeper

A few days later, Marli Renfro was rolling along Sunset Boulevard in the curvy part of Beverly Hills blasting her radio and letting her long red hair fly out behind. She loved all styles of music, whatever suited her fancy at the moment—classical and country Western, jazz, pop, piano renditions: Sinatra, Steve Lawrence and Eydie Gormé, even Celtic of Nova Scotia. This September afternoon, she had an opera rocking and was singing along and completely absorbed in an aria.

"I naturally have a lead foot," she said, "and was speeding when a motorcycle cop overtook me and pulled me over. He wants to know, 'Where's the fire?' I told him, 'I'm on the way to UCLA to register for a film class.' Well, he looks at me like I'm crazy as I'm too far west to be going to UCLA campus, then I explain that the offices are downtown.' He says he's going to give me a ticket anyway because I almost ran him over when I was going from lane to lane. He goes back to write the ticket and I turn up the volume on the radio and turn my back to the window which makes him really have to get my attention to hand me the ticket."

That was the first of only three tickets she would receive in her entire driving career—all for speeding.

At the UCLA Extension she enrolled in a documentary film class. "We had to do a synopsis of a film we'd make," she said, "and I chose 'Man's Inhumanity,' as it isn't always directed to man alone. One scene I played out was on obesity starting with a slender person taking a bite of food and the scenes getting quicker and shorter. It ends with a bang of a 500-600 pound person gorging. Then I described a few ideas of inhumanity toward the Earth, animals, and children." The instructor liked what she did. She wasn't just a pretty face.

In the autumn of 1960 Francis Ford Coppola was a UCLA film student looking to get his toe in the door of the motion picture industry. It wasn't going well. First, they kept the Theater Department in the woods behind the university as if they were ashamed of it. Francis also didn't have much film equipment to work with—three Moviolas, a tiny sound stage, and an old Mitchell BNC #87 camera on wooden legs that the university had bought a decade ago. The Mitchell came with a huge gear head, motor, thousand-foot mags, four lenses, follow focus, matte box, and a side finder with flip-up focus. Manufactured in nearby Glendale, it had been the camera of choice for major motion picture production throughout the 1950s.

His first impression of the class was that it was "dry, gray, and full of talk." It irritated him that the students talked a lot, but never seemed to make anything happen. Not so with Francis who was a real production guy and always chomping at the bit. Every aspect of moviemaking thrilled him. "I was ready to build the scenery," he wrote. "I had this overwhelming urge to make films; not to read about them or see them, just to make them. All I lacked was the opportunity." All he wanted was the chance to work behind the camera and get his name on the screen.

Coppola's grad work included making shorts, and they were all well made and expertly done (even a young Francis Ford Coppola is still Francis Ford Coppola), but these shorts weren't going to bring him the money he needed for future projects. He studied the market and realized that Russ Meyer's recent sexploitation film *The Immoral Mr. Teas,* which had been made for thousands, had earned Meyer and his partner millions. Not only that, Meyer had used full nudity and hadn't been busted by the cops. He had gambled on the new Supreme Court ruling saying nudity wasn't pornographic in itself and won. Screen nudity was now legal. The surprising thing to Coppola was that it had taken this long for Hollywood to take advantage of the new freedom. Before long everyone would want to make such low-budget films, which returned enormous profits. Film school students were the logical candidates for such work—they worked cheap and needed an opportunity to work on production. Some of Francis's brother's friends approached Francis and suggested that he follow suit and make one of the new nudie cuties.

"Could you produce a script like Mr. *Teas*," they asked. He could and did. He realized intuitively that Meyer, by using no dialogue, few sets, and making the film a comedy, had made Mr. *Teas* economically feasible and bulletproof to censorship. Coppola would do the same.

Coppola may have been inspired by Jacques Tati's recent Oscar-winning comedy *Mon Oncle*. Tati, a tall French mime, had written, directed, and starred as the title character in that film and its prequel, *Mr. Hulot's Holiday*. Both films were essentially silent films (with music and sound effects) in the tradition of Chaplin and Keaton and featured a stork-legged, rain-coated, pipe-smoking man who sets off a series of catastrophes wherever he goes.

What if Coppola created a similar type, a cartoon-like figure who is the exact opposite of Mr. Hulot? He could be a hypocrite, desiring nude women, but outwardly condemning them. And instead of affecting those around him disastrously, the little man himself would end up the battered and bruised victim after each unsuccessful encounter. Coppola would call his little man The Peeper.

The investors liked Coppola's script and wanted to buy it—with one catch. They didn't want him to direct. "Directing the picture was the only thing I was interested in," he said. Instead, he showed the script to other potential investors and raised $2,000 to produce and shoot *The Peeper* himself as director.

His fellow classmates disdained these new skin-flicks and condemned them as "objectifying women as no art form in history had ever done." But Francis Ford Coppola was far from salacious and would never be

Four unpublished poses from Marli's first modeling portfolio. *Marli Renfro collection.*

LEFT AND BELOW: Portraits of Marli.
Marli Renfro collection.

Laura-like portrait of Marli
by her mother, Louise.
Marli Renfro collection.

The El Rancho Vegas, 1959.
Courtesy www.lasvegasmikey.com.

Renee Moldar (far right) and the dancers on stage. *Courtesy Laurie Summers.*

RIGHT: Marli adjusting Laurie's costume in the dressing room.
Courtesy Laurie Summers.

BELOW: Marli (sitting extreme right on bumper) with the El Rancho Vegas dancers.
Photograph by Dorothy Gunn, courtesy Laurie Summers.

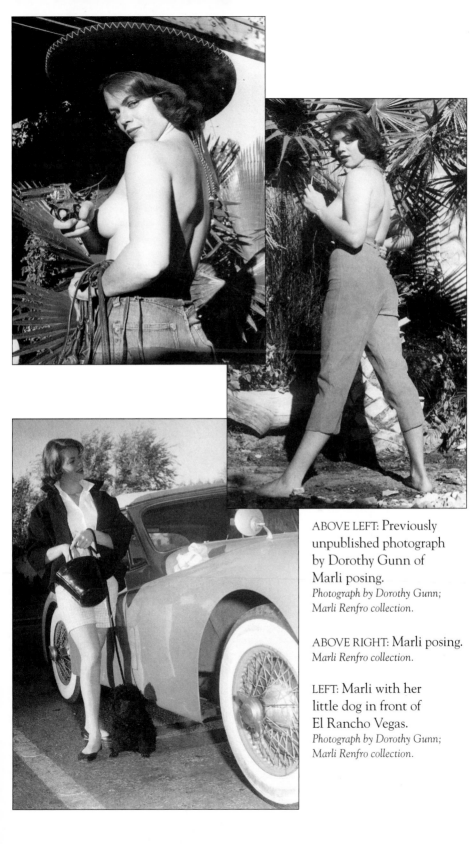

ABOVE LEFT: Previously unpublished photograph by Dorothy Gunn of Marli posing.
Photograph by Dorothy Gunn; Marli Renfro collection.

ABOVE RIGHT: Marli posing.
Marli Renfro collection.

LEFT: Marli with her little dog in front of El Rancho Vegas.
Photograph by Dorothy Gunn; Marli Renfro collection.

Previously unpublished glamour shot of Marli. *Marli Renfro collection.*

Marli on the cover of *Adam*.
Author's collection.

The cover of *Modern Man* with Marli Renfro. This magazine contained a lengthy article on her and *Tonight for Sure! Author's collection.*

LEFT: Alfred Hitchcock publicity still. *Author's collection.*

BELOW: Publicity photo of Janet Leigh. *Author's collection.*

The *Psycho* movie set, 1960. *Author's collection, courtesy Universal Studios.*

Tony Perkins, *Psycho II*, 1983.
Courtesy Universal-Oak Pictures/Universal Pictures Corporation.

Candid black-and-white promotional still; *Psycho* press kit photo.
Author's collection.

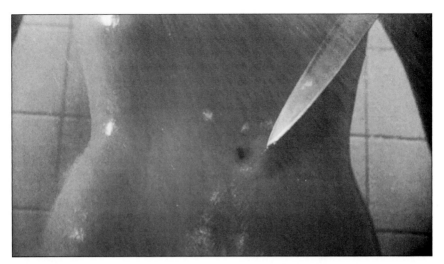

Marli in shower sequence for *Psycho* as body double for Janet Leigh.
Courtesy Universal Studios.

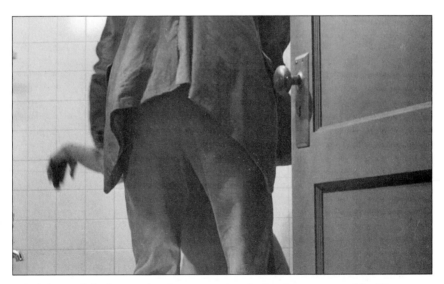

Marli being lifted onto the shower curtain before being carried by Tony
Perkins to the trunk of the car. *Courtesy Universal Studios.*

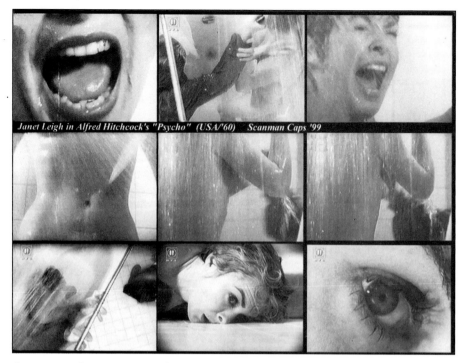

Important photo sequence showing Marli as body double for Janet Leigh in five out of nine frames in *Psycho*. If you can't see Janet's face, it's Marli.
Universal/Scanman Caps '99.

Psycho lobby card. *Author's collection.*

Marli Renfro shooting skeet in Chicago. *Marli Renfro collection.*

TOP LEFT: Sonny and Mother lived at 5623 Virginia Avenue.
TOP RIGHT: Aunt Margaret Briggs lived next door at 5617 ½ Virginia Avenue.
BOTTOM LEFT: Site of Sonny's new apartment at 1522 North Mariposa Avenue.
BOTTOM RIGHT: Mrs. Elmyra Miller's residence at 1450 Normandie Avenue.
Author's photographs.

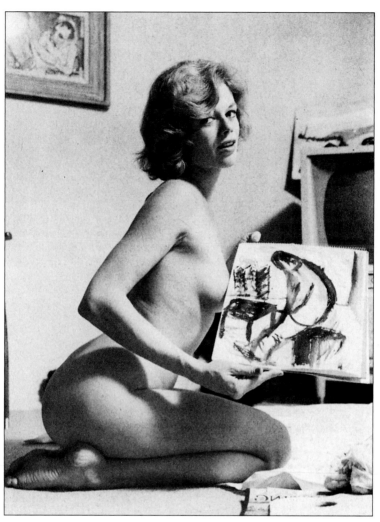

Marli posing with painting. *Marli Renfro collection.*

Detectives arrest Sonny Busch (in glasses) at Briggs crime scene.
Author's collection.

LAPD radio officers Baker and McGowan examine Shirley Payne wrapped
in sleeping bag. *Author's collection.*

The El Rey Casino in Searchlight, Nevada. *Courtesy Andy Martello.*

Jerry Schafer, stuntman, producer, and filmmaker.
Courtesy Jerry Schafer.

Tonight for Sure! cast: (Top) Marli and Willie Martello; (Middle, left to right) Marli, Virginia Gordon, Ginger Gibson, Sandi Silver, and Patti Brooks; (Bottom) The Casino set. *Author's collection.*

comfortable directing nude scenes. "I have great trepidations about approaching erotic scenes in movies," he wrote. "My mother was sort of a fanatic about having to respect women, and I was brought up believing that if you like a girl, if you make some kind of little pass at her, you'll be disrespecting her. So if the actress said, 'Oh, I'm going to do it,' that's okay, but if I have to ask her, I feel like I'm some dirty old man or something." In the early 1960s, few were comfortable with nudity. America was a repressed nation with legions of dirty old men who were at heart fearful peepers.

As uncomfortable as Francis was with naked women, especially filming them, he told himself a credit was a credit. In spite of his reservations, Coppola knew one thing for certain: He would actually be "working as a filmmaker," not just studying about it in school. In the bargain *The Peeper* would provide money for his future projects, projects of a loftier and more artistic value.

As far as Francis was concerned his plot was simply a series of comic scenes depicting the Peeper's futile efforts to see naked women. "I just wanted to make a film," he said, "so we shot *The Peeper* about a little man who finds that pinup sessions are being photographed near his house." Karl Schanzer played the Peeper, Benjamin Jabowski. The first woman chosen for *The Peeper* was Marli Renfro, who was on the cover of almost every men's magazine on the stands in 1960.

"Francis lived in Topanga Canyon when he shot *The Peeper*," Marli said. "He's at UCLA after I get back from Chicago and the Playboy Clubs and start studying film, so it's October, 1960 and Francis is shooting *The Peeper* in and around LA." It seemed odd to Marli to have a wardrobe for her second film appearance. She hadn't worn a stitch in *Psycho*. "I had purchased a suit, a mustard-colored knit, in Denver on my way back to LA from Chicago at the beginning of fall," she said, "and decided to wear that in *The Peeper*." She got her hair cut short; put on black leather gloves to her elbow, added dark glasses, a white round makeup case, and black pumps; and began her first scene of Francis's sexploitation comedy.

"Francis has me walking down the street and going into a building. I think I'm just very relaxed and I'm just being myself. When I see it, I think to myself, 'I look so stilted.' I just couldn't believe it." Upon watching the scene once more, Marli changed her mind. "I didn't look stilted after all, but natural. That scene was shot downtown with the little guy following me." When I saw that same scene years later, I didn't recognize Marli for a moment. Then I realized I had never seen her dressed before.

In the movie, Marli strolls into an abandoned Venice department store, its picture windows soaped over with white "X"s, but suitable for Francis's needs as a cheap set. He shows The Peeper trying to watch a mannequin in the window being undressed. Back in his apartment, the little man, who openly derides pinups, has a number of girlie photos taped to the backs of framed pictures on his wall. One by one he turns them over to ogle the girls. One particular lady has seized his fancy. "A pleasant looking red-haired cutie," he says in voice-over. It is Marli.

"Francis had a photo taken of me and it was like fourteen-by-twenty-inches big," she said. "I thought it was gorgeous and Francis fell in love with it too. He used it in the movie when the older guy puts it on the bed and is looking at it. In the film you can just barely recognize it. It had beautiful rose coloring in the background. They used dry ice to create a mist around me and water swirling around me." As in most of Marli's most successful poses, she is peering coyly back at the camera over her shoulder. "Francis asked if he could take it home and I said yes. Later I talked him into giving it to me. It cost him quite a bit of money to give me that. It wasn't cheap. He gave me directions to his house and told me I could come by and get it. We made plans for me to pick it up after the film was done."

Marli has a scene with her bathing in a tub, glistening with soapsuds and flirting with the camera. While Marli always grows indignant when folks call her a stripper, for Francis she did a very professional strip. His film is packed with glamor girls (it would become a common practice to use burlesque dancers in the early nudie cuties) such as Electra, Exotica, Linda Lightfoot, Laura Cornell, Karla Lee, Sue Martin, Marcelino Espinosa, and Anita Danchick.

So far neither of the first two nudie cuties released had failed to make buckets of money. And nudie cuties had longevity too. *The Im-*

moral Mr. Teas had a hundred-day run in one northern California venue and played so long in Washington it might as well have been called *The Immortal Mr. Teas*. *Not Tonight, Henry*, made for $75,000, would become a lucrative standby at drive-ins. Why couldn't Francis's *The Peeper* join them?

"The whole movie is the equivalent of a *Tom and Jerry* cartoon," he said, "with this guy trying to see what's happening. He peeks through a telescope [which is so powerful he can see only square inches of the women] but sees only a bellybutton, or he hoists himself up with a block-and-tackle [to get himself into a better viewing position to see a nude woman], fumbles around, and then falls down . . ."

In *Psycho*, Robert Bloch had drawn Norman Bates as a peeper, though his actions ended not in a pratfall but in murder and madness. Norman, surrounded by birds he stuffed himself, removes a painting of a classical rape so he can spy on Marion Crane undressing in front of her open bathroom door.

```
NORMAN'S VIEWPOINT
Through the hole we look into Mary's cabin, see Mary
undressing. She is in her bra and halfslip. She stoops
over a bit, places her hands behind her upper back,
begins to unhook her bra.
NORMAN—ECU
He watches as Mary removes her bra. We see his eye run
up and down the unseen figure of Mary.
```

Hitch's voyeuristic film made peepers of the audience. He had chosen the painting *Susanna and the Elders* carefully. Its biblical story held meaning for Renaissance artists who most often portrayed Susanna as a woman overtaken in her bath by voyeurs whose passions were aroused as they spied on her from concealment. It gave them an excuse to paint female nudity. Susanna's story in Daniel 13 tells of the wife of a wealthy Jew who was secretly desired by two elders who hatch a plot to possess her. They knew that each evening Susanna routinely went into her garden to bathe, so they hid themselves to watch. The moment her maids left, they sprang out and confronted the nude girl. They threatened that unless she gave herself to them, they would publicly swear they had observed her give herself to a young man—a capital offense. Instead, Susanna called for help and the two old men carried out their threat. She was brought before the court on the false charge, convicted, and sentenced to death. But Daniel cross-examined the elders separately and elicited conflicting testimony that cleared Susanna.

Coppola, being Coppola, added his artistic and moral qualities to his well-lit film, including pacing, style, and top-notch photography, all elements of his later films. But when he attempted to distribute the completed short, no one wanted to buy it or, if they did, they wanted to make the film longer but didn't want Coppola to direct the new material. It was no soap. Being a director to Francis was the whole point.

Marli knew he was worried his work had been just so much wasted effort, and it broke her heart that he was so hungry to have his name up on the big screen and nothing had come of his first movie, which she called an "experimental film," not a nudie cutie. "When he shot *The Peeper*," Marli said, "Francis, as I mentioned, lived in Topanga Canyon in the Santa Monica Mountains. After watching his movie I was amazed that I am in it so much. He gave me directions to his house and left that big photo of me where I would find it if no one was home. All I could think of was that I wish he had showed a better view of it in the film as it was really stunning." It might have been the best photograph ever taken of her.

Marli started from the Sunset Strip and via the Ventura Freeway headed toward the unincorporated area of West LA at her usual meteoric rate. Topanga, bounded by the Pacific Ocean, the vastness of conservatory lands, and a tiny strip of Malibu, sits high above Malibu Beach. The Tongva tribe named this western border of Topanga "a place above," but the Chumash tribe, who occupied the coast from Malibu northward, called it something less charming and unprintable.

Topanga Creek drains the canyon into Santa Monica Bay. Its coastal outlet is Topanga State Beach (Marli heard this might be a nudist beach). She loved the mountains and the smell of pine, and since the canyon was filled with steep terrain and thick vegetation, she drank it all in. A fabulous place, she thought, as she roared along in her car. She had heard it was a hotbed of revolutionary thought, creativity, and commonplace nudity in the outdoors, just her cup of tea. Topanga began as a weekend getaway for Hollywood stars. In the 1950s blacklisted actor Will Geer sold his Santa Monica home and moved his family there to live off the land alongside Woody Guthrie, who already had a shack in the canyon. A dozen others—Dennis Hopper, Teri Garr, Keith Carradine, and Lynn Redgrave—would come too.

It took Marli about a half hour to reach Coppola's place. She parked and went up to the door. He wasn't home, so Marli picked up her photo just where he said it would be. She was sure Francis would have liked to keep it and had second thoughts. Was he sweet on her? She didn't know. Finally, she started back, the huge photo of herself under her arm. Later the beautiful picture, along with most of the others, would be lost in what Marli called "the fire."

It seemed like paradise in the canyon, but all around was danger, danger, danger. Often dried to inflammability by the hot Santa Ana winds, the canyon lay in constant threat of sweeping wildfires. In the canyon, all ideas were acceptable, life was free and pure, but it was the perfect spot for a malignancy to take root because its freedoms and high-profile residents attracted odd hanger-ons and drifters such as Charlie Manson.

Charlie had first befriended Neil Young, who was living there with his producer, David Briggs. Then Manson and his growing band of misfits attached themselves to Dennis Wilson of The Beach Boys and music teacher Gary Hinman, a good-hearted soul who opened his home to anyone in need of shelter and food. Manson's goons murdered Hinman for his kindness and trust, then went looking for new victims and eventually settled on Jay Sebring, who lived in Topanga Canyon. Marli had dated the famous hairstylist.

"Jay Sebring took me to my first ballet at the Greek Theatre in LA," Marli said. "I was at my hairdresser Bob Beaumont's salon when I met him. It was Bob who put Jay into a men's hairdressing salon—the first of its kind. Before that they were all barbers. Sebring was the name of it and it was in Hollywood or Beverly Hills." Sebring had taken his new name from his middle initial and his last name from the famous Florida car race. "Jay was personable, shy, quiet," Marli continued. She knew a lot of hairdressers, Gene Shacove for one, because she was continually having her red tresses done as part of her work. Gene's friend Jay Sebring was the best though, and world famous.

Born in Birmingham, Alabama, Sebring grew up in Detroit, then joined the navy and served in the Korean War before moving to LA. During his navy stint Jay developed new techniques in cutting hair, and upon his discharge became the premier stylist in the country and a major force in the development of men's hair products and toiletries. Jay lived a playboy lifestyle, counting among his high-profile clients such stars as Frank Sinatra, Peter Lawford, Warren Beatty, Paul Newman, and Steve McQueen.

Within four years, Sebring would meet actress Sharon Tate again at a party at the Whisky a Go Go and begin a relationship. After his divorce a year later, they became engaged. Sebring bought Jean Harlow's old house in Benedict Canyon, and Sharon spent much of her time there. But in London in early 1966 she fell for her director Roman Polanski, and Jay gracefully accepted the turn of events. On August 8, 1969, Charlie Manson's followers entered Polanski's residence on Cielo Drive and killed Sebring, Tate, Polanski's friend Wojciech Frykowski, and San Francisco coffee heiress Abigail Folger, an investor in Sebring's empire. No one knows just how many victims Charlie and his monstrous family actually murdered. Many were killed on a whim and buried somewhere in the desert.

But in fall 1960, other things were going on in the beautiful wilderness of Topanga Canyon besides murder. Americans trying to throw off the shackles of sexual repression and discover themselves sexually came together there. Seven acres were taken up by the Elysium Institute, a nudist growth center hidden behind high fences and tall trees. The free love institute offered stables for horseback riding, pools, tennis courts, saunas, and massages—all devoted to the pursuit of pleasure and physical awareness.

Elysium's founder and president was Ed Lange, a tall, well-built former *Vogue* and *Bazaar* fashion photographer with a neatly trimmed beard. He had moved to LA in 1940, worked as a Hollywood set de-signer and freelance photographer, and with his wife, June, become the publisher and editor of *Nude Living* and *Sundial*. Lange, a friend of Marli Renfro at the Sundial Traveling Nudist Club, often featured her in his magazines. He was also active in the Western Sunbathing Association, vice-president of the International Naturist Federation, and author of a number of nudist pictorial books, including *"N" Is for Nudist* and *Fun in Sun*. Ed espoused free love ideals at his Malibu nudist colony Elysium Fields and did nude photography only, including children (which got him in hot water with his critics). As one of Diane Webber's earliest photographers he had shot some of her most famous figure studies.

Diane Webber and her body-builder husband, Joe, often visited Ed with their infant son, John. "The life of naturism—being active in the nudist movement—has given me a capacity for enjoyment I would not otherwise have had," Diane told journalist Gay Talese who, in his book *Thy Neighbor's Wife*, wrote about a man who was obsessed by Diane's photo for decades. As part of his preparations for writing his book, Gay lived for several months at another nearby clothing-optional, open-sexuality resort. Sandstone Retreat was located at Sandstone Ranch, a fifteen-acre estate high in the hills in the Santa Monica Mountains overlooking Malibu and the Pacific. The Retreat, founded by John and Barbara Williamson and managed by a residential community of about twenty persons, was later the subject of a documentary. Sandstone of-fered members and guests over the age of eighteen the resources of a spa, communal bathrooms, and several large open indoor and outdoor com-munal sleeping areas. Prospective members were intensively interviewed to determine suitability.

Marli was aware of the new sexuality blossoming all around her. Hef, Hitch, and Russ Meyer had opened new doors and allowed print and film new freedoms. It might be for the better, she thought and recalled how the men dribbling chocolate syrup at her feet during the filming of the *Psycho* Shower Sequence were afraid to get close to her. One had been trembling at the feet of a nude woman. There had to be better, healthier attitudes toward sex.

Coppola's *Peeper* and Hitchcock's *Psycho* are about guys afraid to get close to women—voyeurs. In *Psycho* Norman's eye fills the screen as he watches Marion strip naked, slip on her robe, and walk out of view into the bathroom. In *Psycho*, he had been the peeper. In *Mr. Teas*, the hero is watching, but afraid to touch. Talese saw something there, a theme about the inhibited, immature American male at the end of the 1950s trying to throw off his shackles. Women in the new films tended to be striking out, accomplishing great things and being rebellious in their nudity and sexual freedom, but in every case the guys in films are repressed.

Ed Gein, the monster who had inspired *Psycho*, had never caressed the flesh of a woman, at least not a living woman. Hitchcock had turned that real case into art. Now, in LA, another repressed boy next door, an Anthony Perkins kind of guy, Sonny, was about to turn art into real life by imitating *Psycho*. It was hard not to marvel at that kind of mimicking and all the different personalities being reflected back and forth like a hall of mirrors. Art imitating life; life imitating art—full circle, circles within circles.

Just down Sunset Boulevard, Marli was approaching a photo shoot as Sonny was driving just blocks away and thinking nasty thoughts about women who reminded him of Mother and of all the mothers in his life whom he wanted to possess and could not, but only obliterate with all the power in his hands or with the knives in his pockets.

Chapter Twenty-four
The *Psycho* Killer

Throughout summer 1960, Sonny had been up to something. The police would never be sure exactly what. They did learn later he had traveled to New York State during July and August. It's possible Sonny believed the authorities were about to catch up to him for the murder he had committed and tried to blame on the Bouncing Ball Strangler. Sonny felt their eyes everywhere. Once when he was pulled over for a traffic violation, he thought the two cops who stopped him were the same pair who had arrested him on suspicion of killing the little redhead all those years ago.

He was too terrified of Mother to share the details of his clandestine activities with her or with his bartender friend who had already betrayed him once and would do so again. Sonny was too frightened of the implications of those missing hours that he dared not admit even to himself . . . frightened faces, groping, cries before he ran into the night. Sonny plunged on, blotting out as much as he could and feeling his way as if in a fog. If he had a split personality the schism was as wide as that between Norman Bates and his Mother persona.

As his other self, Sonny could never be certain what he had done. Imagine if people told you about things you had done that seemed unlike you, events of which you had no memory or very little at all. There were those odd bruises and the rips in your clothing. The mileage on your car never matched up—unaccounted-for miles. All of us have days when we are not quite ourselves, but Sonny carried these to ridiculous extremes. His worst fear was that there might not be any way back for him the next time, and he might become "the other" permanently. The medical explanation as to why Sonny was in the dark over his actions was because one ego state had no contact with the other fully integrated personality, yet had memories and relationships of its own. Two different modes of being, acting, and existing independently of the other in the same body could have only one explosive ending. Just how aware was Sonny of his alternate state of being within himself? How much did he pretend not to know? He took in a movie, and there was Alfred Hitchcock on screen speaking to him, right to him.

Peggy Robertson recalled that Hitch himself had come up with the idea of doing a tour of the Bates house and treating it in a droll fashion. They had shot the trailer in a single day a week after *Psycho* was finished. Sonny watched the screen: "The fabulous Mr. Alfred Hitchcock is about to escort you . . . on a tour of the location of his new motion picture, *PSYCHO*." The scene shows the corpulent Hitch taking his audience on a tour of a quiet little motel. He indicates its adjunct, an old house, and says, "That's where the woman was first seen. Let's go inside." Hitch sets the scene at the top of the stairs. "In a flash there was the knife," he explains, "and in no time the victim tumbled and fell with a horrible crack, I think the back broke immediately as it hit the floor." Hitch shakes his head. "It was, it's difficult to describe . . . well I, it's . . ."

Hitch waves the thought away as if it were too dreadful to contemplate. Next he escorts his audience to the old lady's room (explaining how you had to feel sorry for the young man), then to the parlor in the motel and along to the bathroom next door. "Well, they've cleaned all this up now. . . . You should have seen the blood. . . . Well, the murderer, you see, crept in here very slowly, of course the shower was on, there was no sound, and . . ." Hitch pulls the shower curtain back and a woman inside screams. Instead of Janet Leigh, it is Vera Miles, her costar, in a short wig. Hitch is still leading his audience down the garden path and misdirecting them in every way he can.

On Thursday morning, September 1, shortly after *Psycho* had gone into wide release, Sonny brought in the *LA Times*. Wearily, he sat down at his kitchen table and sullenly scanned the front page: "Citizens Group Asks More Illumination for Crime Prevention." The City Council was considering whether funds would be available in the 1961–1962 budget to bring streetlights up to the ideal standard of illumination around the university areas where there had been a series of rapes. They estimated such an undertaking would cost $165 million. Such lighting would certainly cut into Sonny's recreational evening jaunts and that of the Bouncing Ball Strangler, who remained a constant threat. Sonny folded the paper, had a breakfast of coffee and jelly and dry toast, and drove the three blocks to the optical lab parking lot at Hollywood Boulevard and Vermont Avenue.

He had worked at the lab as a lens polisher for more than two years now. Did he actually mean to go to work at his monotonous job when there was so much to do in his private life, so many thoughts in his brain, such a sense of urgency, and really no recreation to relieve the pain? He hunched over the grinding/polishing machine—soft start, soft stop and stable speed, soft stop. He operated the upper and lower lapping plate, inner gear ring, and pneumatic control system, which calculated the refractive index. Typical glass has a refractive index of 1.5, which means that in glass, light travels at 0.67 ($1 \div 1.5$) times the speed of light in a vacuum. His eye through the instrument and through his own thick lenses was like that of Norman Bates peering at Marion through the crack. It was identical to the close-up of Marion's eye Hitch had filmed as she lay sprawled on the bathroom floor. Sonny spoke to no one at work the entire day, except for Mrs. Magdalena A. Parra, one of the technical inspectors. The attractive, athletic brunet was friendlier to him than most. He ate a sparse lunch alone. At 5:30 P.M., Sonny polished his last pair of lenses, put them in a black case on the rack, pushed back his stool, and went home, where he lay on the couch watching television and slept until morning, overwhelmed with a sense of exhaustion.

He awoke the next day, made coffee, and brought in the paper again. The bold headlines were out of Moscow: Russian premier Khrushchev would head the Soviet delegation to the UN General Assembly on September 20, a meeting dealing with the disarmament debate. Khrushchev was to lay out a five-point Communist bloc program and speak against "The American aggression against the Soviet Union." Such lies. Sonny felt an oppressive weight on his shoulders and trudged to work to begin the grinding process all over again. At least he had the weekend to look forward to. Sonny had picked up the September *Playboy* from a corner newsstand at the beginning of the month and never gotten around to reading it. Without Mother around, he could leave it on the table in plain sight.

He sat down by the window where the light was good to read the review of *Psycho*. First, though, he studied the beautiful redhead on the cover, some sort of shower scene, he thought, though it was hard to tell because the image was fractured. He looked closer, and saw that the predominantly red and orange cover was composed of jigsaw pieces with one piece missing—in the shape of the *Playboy* Rabbit. Sonny had no idea that the girl on the cover was actually the girl in Hitchcock's *Psycho* shower, but he found her fascinating all the same. Marli had that effect on everyone. Sonny finished the review, looked at the centerfold and a few cartoons, and then closed the magazine. *Psycho* sounded as good as he had hoped. The movie would lift his spirits, he reasoned, and he had to keep them up. Best of all, it would distract him and silence the static in his head which unabated could grow into what he called "the screaming sound."

In the theater section in the *LA Times*, he saw Hitchcock's movie was playing at the Iris Theatre in Hollywood, the Loyola in Westchester, the El Portal in North Hollywood, the Culver in Culver City, and the Wilshire in Santa Monica—everywhere. "Alfred Hitchcock's Altogether

Different Screen Excitement!" one ad read. It showed a picture of buxom Janet Leigh sitting on the edge of a bed, dressed in white bra and slip. At the bottom was a picture of Tony Perkins, eyes wide and with his hand covering his mouth. Sonny knew exactly how he felt. So far this summer he had gotten control of his anger, except for some trouble in Hawthorne, New York, that was already receding in his memory. He was positive that with a little self-control he would commit no more murders. There were still those blackouts.

On September 3, a hot Saturday afternoon, Sonny felt better. He found it hard to believe that *Psycho* had already been showing in LA for four weeks straight to turn-away crowds and he hadn't seen it. Lines to get into theaters encircled the block everywhere. He read the *Playboy* review again. He had seen the trailers on television and heard a radio commercial Hitch had done tongue-in-cheek. The shocking film had been shaking up America and keeping women out of the shower, including Janet Leigh who claimed that she would never take a shower again. When one husband complained to Hitch that his wife had seen the bathtub murder in *Diabolique* and refused to take a bath after that and after seeing *Psycho* refused to shower, he asked Hitch, "What should I do? She is getting hard to live with." "Send her to the dry cleaners," said Hitch. Sonny didn't want to go to the theater alone so he drove the '56 Oldsmobile convertible over to see Mother at 5623 Virginia Avenue, one of her apartment buildings. He thought he might ask her to go with him. Driving west on Sunset Boulevard, he turned left on North Western, passed Fernwood and Fountain Avenues, then Lexington, and turned right on Virginia. He cruised for another block and parked a few doors down from Mother's under the shade of a tree. It had taken him about four minutes to drive the 1.2 miles. He parked, slumped behind the wheel, and thought for a moment. Did he really want to go with Mother? Of course, she would dislike the film. That was a given. He could hear her shrill voice, shrill to him, in his head: "A mother's boy, that's what you are." Sonny ran through the catalog of acquaintances in his mind, and stopped at Mrs. Shirley B. Payne, a gray-haired, twice-married seventy-two-year-old divorcee who lived across the hall from Mother. He had known Shirley for over three years, and the two used to go out. He should ask her instead. Sonny decided that was the best plan. He locked the car, climbed the steps, and used his key to let himself in the front door. Inside, he worked his way down the hallway on tiptoe hesitantly looking about for Mother. He was so close to her (she was just across the hall and he could hear her television going) that he rapped lightly on Shirley's door.

The older woman opened the door, gave him a big smile, and asked him inside. She was in a robe the color of strawberries. Sonny plumped down on the couch and asked Shirley if she would like to go see *Psycho* at the nearby Hollywood Boulevard theater. The long lines were finally dying down, and they had a good chance of seeing it if they went to an afternoon show, but they would have to go now. Shirley excused herself to get dressed and was done by 3:50 P.M. They went down to his car, and Sonny drove to Hollywood Boulevard. As they passed the theater he saw Hitchcock's name and *Psycho* spelled out in black plastic letters on the marquee. They got a space right away and walked briskly to the ticket window. A sign outside said, "The manager of this theatre has been instructed, at the risk of his life, not to admit to this theatre any persons after the picture starts. Any spurious attempts to enter by side doors, fire escapes or ventilating shafts will be met by force—Alfred Hitchcock."

At 4:32 P.M. Sonny bought two tickets at seventy cents apiece, and he and Shirley went inside the thankfully air-conditioned theater. Sonny was gripped from the first frame—Saul Bass's remarkable designs, the fractured *Psycho* lettering, and the amazing score. The power of the movie immediately swept over him. He watched the plot unfold: An attractive secretary, Marion Crane, runs away after embezzling $40,000 from her employer; lost in a rainstorm, she checks into the deserted twelve-cabin Bates Motel. Norman, the shy young owner of the motel, invites her to have supper with him inside the forbidding Victorian on the hill. When he climbs the hill to ask his mother, Marion hears shouting from the house. Norman returns to apologize to her. "Mother," he stammers, "—what is the phrase? She isn't quite herself today." Neither was Sonny who looked a lot like Tony Perkins and whose mother, from his point of view, was as domineering as Norman's in the film. As Norman and Marion have supper in a parlor behind the office she suggests he put Mother in an institution. Norman becomes furious: "She just goes a little mad sometimes." He speaks several memorable lines, some written by Tony:

> A man should have a hobby. It's more than a hobby. A hobby is supposed to pass the time, not fill it. . . . Do you know what I think? I think we're all in our private traps . . . and none of us can ever get out . . . There's no sense dwelling on our losses. We just keep on lighting the lights and following the formalities.

Once Marion goes to her room next door to the parlor, Norman peeps through a hole behind a picture as she undresses.

In the audience, Sonny ogled body double Marli Renfro, who he thought was Janet Leigh. He became aroused, studied the older woman next to him, and put one arm over her shoulder. As Marion showers in her motel room, she is stabbed to death by a shadowy female figure. Sonny watched as Norman, like a dutiful son, cleaned up the bathroom, wrapped the corpse in the shower curtain, put it in the trunk of the girl's car, and sank the auto in a swamp. Mother's room seemed familiar to Sonny—frescoed vanity, tasseled draperies, turkey-red carpet, Dresden figurines, and a four poster. The deep indentation where Mother had lain, the outline of a body, a wallpaper design of rambler roses, all affected him.

At the end, Sonny learned the killer was actually Norman, crossdressed in his mother's clothing and a wig and wielding a kitchen knife. Apparently, Bates believed he was Mother, avenging "herself" against the woman trying to seduce "her" son. Norman, dominated by his mother while she lived and guilt-ridden for murdering her ten years earlier, has attempted to erase his crime by bringing Mother back to life. He accomplished this by embalming her stolen corpse and burying a weighted coffin in its place. "Nice," said Sonny as they watched the end, "embezzling secretary stabbed to death by a cross-dressing madman." As they left the theater, Sonny was overwhelmed by the same old urge sweeping over him. The film had reignited something inside him. "I took her to see the movie *Psycho*," Sonny said later. "Well, we saw that picture and after the show, I asked her up to my place for some beer, then we went to my apartment." He parked the Olds five doors down so no one would see them and they went upstairs.

"When we got inside I tried to make love to her," he said later. "She refused. Suddenly I found myself on her. I got her down to her slip." He attacked the elderly woman, but he felt no sexual pleasure. "Afterward— we were standing up, fully dressed—she turned her back to me and suddenly this urge came over me to kill her. It was like static on the radio—a pounding, a noise inside my head that just kept pounding up till I couldn't stand it. I had to kill these women to get relief. I didn't want to do it. But I had to. That noise was the loudest I ever heard it. I tried to leave, but my legs wouldn't do it. And then I had her in my hands."

"I told her, 'I'm going to strangle you.' She got down on her knees and prayed to be spared, but her prayers didn't bother me."

Sonny did worse than kill her right away. Sadistically, really on a whim, he decided to draw a sketch of her to prolong the agony. He took out his pad and with a red crayon drew a bikini-clad woman with her limbs bound and a gag tied in her mouth. He didn't know why he did that, but instead of calming him the act of drawing oddly excited him. Now he realized he wanted to extend her agony while she was pleading for mercy in a soft, low voice and kill her slowly. It was common for stranglers to slowly increase the pressure until the victim blacked out, revive them, and begin the process all over again. "She kept praying and praying. So I grabbed her around the throat from behind and strangled her with my hands till she was dead."

Sonny came out of his fog. He was surprised to see that Shirley's blue-and-white polka-dotted dress belt was knotted around her neck, puckering the flesh, though he could have sworn he had used only his hands. "And I strangled her," he admitted later. "I don't know why I did it. Why does anyone strangle anyone? All I know is, every now and then, I get this urge to kill somebody. Most of the time I get rid of it by watching TV or going to the movies. But sometimes . . ." Well, his safety valves hadn't worked this time. A trip to the movies had only made the compulsion worse.

He sat for a while and studied the still form. She seemed to be deflating. Later he took off her clothes and tied her hands and feet [like his drawing] with gilt cord, bound her feet together with her nylon stockings and wrapped her in a sheet just as Tony Perkins had wrapped Marli in a shower curtain in *Psycho*.

"So I arranged her next to me on the bed," Sonny said. He lay down next to the woman's body and sorted his emotions like a deck of cards, but in the end came to the conclusion that he felt no remorse at all, that he felt nothing at all. His eyes grew heavy. Now the body next to him seemed to be swelling and growing heavier. "At least after she was dead," he said later, "I had this picture I had drawn to look at." The roar in his head had gone away for a little while.

Sonny slept soundly until 6:30 the next morning, a Sunday. When he awoke he studied the body. There were knife marks all over it, all made after death. There were knife cuts on his hands too. He didn't remember that part. Now he had added a knife to the equation—like *Psycho* and like the slashing Mother who was also the Son. Sonny moved the corpse to one side, interested in the impression she had left in his bed, so like Mrs. Bates and the rut she left in the bed after lying there for so many years in the spot where Norman had killed her and her lover. The real-life indentation was nowhere as deep as in the film. He rolled away from her and watched a shaft of morning light crawl along the wall. He tried to sleep, but couldn't. He had his fill. Pulling the quilt over his head didn't help because he could still smell her perfume.

Sonny planned on disposing of her body by driving up into the mountains and throwing the corpse over a cliff. Not a swamp? He laughed, recalling Tony Perkins and how the car had almost not sunk, how Hitchcock had gotten the audience rooting for the only character in *Psycho* left to root for. Sonny didn't even know where a swamp was. Finally, he rose, yawned, and bundled up her clothes, undergarments, and purse. Looking around for any early risers, he walked casually down to his car and slipped her dress under the passenger seat and stowed her bra and girdle in the trunk. Sonny recalled a big drugstore on Vermont not far away. He waited patiently in front until it opened then went inside and bought some white plastic clothesline and, since they didn't have shower curtains, a dark green plastic sleeping bag, which he brought back to his apartment. It would have to do.

Inside the apartment, he lifted Shirley's body and could see her imprint on the soft mattress, down pillow, and sheets was deeper now. The corpse was heavier than expected. Much heavier. Dead bodies react differently from the living and he found it difficult to get her inside the bulky sleeping bag. When he had accomplished this, he unwound the clothesline and bound the bag tightly round and round, then cinched it. He intended to put her in the trunk as he had seen in the movie, but with the addition of the bag she was more slippery and so heavy he couldn't lift her. Tony Perkins had made it look so easy in the film. But now Sonny recalled he had slid the body to the car. There was no way Sonny could slide the corpse down two flights of stairs unobserved. He could only get the bag as far as the door. He would need help and thought of the forty-two-year-old bartender he confided in, Ernie Shaffer. Oddly, the original Norman Bates, Ed Gein, had hired an older man, Gus, to help him lift bodies from the graves. When Gein's confederate died and he was unable to lift the corpses from the graves by himself, he turned to living people to get his body parts and skins to wear. Sonny had not expected this complication. He watched TV for a while, which calmed him a little.

Sunday night Sonny drove over to 6124 Hollywood Boulevard to see if Shaffer would help him move the body. Sonny saw the mustached bartender behind the bar across the room. Sonny sat down at the far end of the bar and waited until the single customer left. Then he called Shaffer aside to whisper something.

"What?" Shaffer asked.

"I've done it again!" Sonny whispered again.

"Done what?" Shaffer asked, but knew from past experience what had happened. He saw tears in Sonny's eyes, magnified ten times by his thick lenses. "You, know. I've strangled another woman. If you help me I'll give you this as payment." Sonny fumbled in his jacket pocket, then withdrew his hand and pressed Shirley's three valuable diamond rings into his palm.

"This would be payment for services rendered," Sonny said earnestly.

He grinned crookedly. "So I just left her lying there on the floor arranged as if sleeping and I need some help to move her." Back in May Sonny had told the bartender he had killed Mrs. Miller, but Shaffer hadn't believed him then and didn't believe him now. But Shaffer accepted the jewelry anyway and decided to do nothing because of his forgery conviction. Police were the last thing he needed unless there was a reward in the future.

He told Sonny he would have to wait for help. Sonny returned home and saw that everything was as he had left it, the TV flickering in the darkened room. Now an overwhelming sleepiness came over him. His muscles ached. He lay down, put his arms around the wrapped corpse on the floor, and slept next to it. Sonny slept the night away. The moon, the timeless "Mother of Madmen," dominated the sky and lit up the room with its light, erasing all detail, and making the green mound look like part of the rug.

The next day, Monday, was Labor Day. Sonny got up, rubbed his aching muscles and went out to get the paper. It was impossibly hot outside. Once back home, he saw that the Associated Press announced that 404 had been killed in traffic nationwide on the holiday weekend. California led the nation with thirty-nine traffic deaths and matched those of last year's Labor Day. Sonny saw that Earl Long of Louisiana had died of a heart attack at age sixty-five. Sonny went over and lay down by the corpse in the sleeping bag. Overcome with drowsiness, he stayed home all day again waiting for Shaffer. The weather was so oppressive he didn't want to go out in the blazing sun.

Meanwhile Shaffer had decided he believed Sonny after all. He realized he could be arrested as an accessory to murder on the grounds he knew about two of Sonny's murders and had failed to report either of them. He went to a corner phone booth, dialed the police anonymously and got a duty man on the phone. "But I didn't give them any names," he said later. "I just told them a fellow in a certain car who lives in the area of Nomandie and Sunset, had committed some murders." Shaffer was terrified by what he had done and hung up.

On September 8, there was some smog as the mercury rose to ninety-three by 1:25 P.M., the fifth day the temperature had exceeded the ninety-degree mark at the Civic Center. An odor began to fill Sonny's apartment. This horror was so different from the movies. What was he going to do? Where was Shaffer? He tried again to lift the body.

The next day, September 9, there was light smog in all the western areas of the basin. Scorching weather was due for the next few days for Los Angeles with a high of ninety-five and a hundred before the heat spell would break some time in the next week. Portions of the San Fernando Valley were expected to top a hundred and five. At the beaches, there was relief—a temperature of eighty and the water, a cooling sixty-eight.

As the sun went down, Sonny awoke from his long sleep, barely able to breathe from the decomposing corpse. Soon the neighbors would notice, Mother would hear. He got up filled with energy, ready to do something about his dilemma, though there was that relentless roar of static in his head again. It had to be satisfied. He didn't want to see anybody, didn't want to try to move the body, but couldn't stand staying where he was. Suffering an overwhelming thirst, he was too tired to wash or eat. Leaving the body by the door (still as far as he was able to drag it using a throw rug under it) he circled the corpse and attempted again to move it into the hall. He tried and failed until the sun came up. Because he now realized there was no way to get the corpse to his car, he slipped out of his apartment, found the Olds where he had left it, got in, and headed down Hollywood Boulevard looking for some way out. There had to be an answer. Briefly he considered calling Shaffer, but decided to wait to hear from him. The bartender wouldn't let him down. He was in as much trouble as Sonny.

Chapter Twenty-five
Marli in Men's Mags

arli Renfro raced along Hollywood Boulevard headed for Ron Vogel's photography studio with the radio blaring. As she glimpsed new shops and tall buildings fly by, she realized that the area was in the midst of as much change as Vegas. Just two years earlier, the first star had been placed on Hollywood Boulevard's new Walk of Fame, a section from Gower Street to La Brea Avenue known as Gower Gulch. Back in the 1920s in front of the Columbia Drugstore at the corner of Sunset and Gower, fifty milling cowboy actors saw Blackjack Ward empty his six-gun into Johnny Tyke, punctuating each complaint against him with a bullet—this bullet's for this, this bullet's for this, this, this . . . six complaints. Blackjack never served a day in jail because the shooting was deemed justifiable homicide because Tyke was so much bigger.

Marli roared past the Walk of Stars, in 1960 only a few assorted footprints in concrete at the corner of Hollywood and Fairfax. A lot had happened since she had closed up her affairs and left LA as a model and girl Friday—she had been employed at the Playboy Club, worked as a waitress at the Cloisters' Club and returned to the Playboy Club as a Bunny. She modeled for ads that appeared in the Club magazine, had been on Hef's fledgling television show numerous times, and was still getting offers as a glamor model. And the men—Lenny, Steve, Gary . . .

Marli rented a cozy one-bedroom house built a few decades earlier in the 300 block of Channel Road on the north side of the street in Santa Monica. "I really loved the house," she said, "it had such character—wood floors, fairly large rooms, a front porch, but no garage. I sparsely decorated it in period furniture that I purchased at the local Salvation Army, some really nice things." She bought a four-poster bed and a few rocking chairs; although she didn't have a TV, there was a windup Victrola, which was fun to operate and listen to in the dining room. There was a huge baker's block in the center of the kitchen, the kind that has bins for storing flour and rice. "If I wasn't working I'd walk my two dogs down to the beach [three blocks away], which was practically vacant as it was off-season, and sit and listen to the pebbles and coarse sand being gently moved about as the water receded. You could tell when there was a storm out at sea. That's when the waves would be big and loud. I love the ocean, any body of water, but especially the ocean. It's like a fireplace with its constant motion." She now had some interest in becoming a Realtor. In the meantime, she was still using her parents' place for modeling sessions.

Her *Adam* cover would be out in December and a few days later her *Debonair* Centerfold, with a four-color three-page spread. Marli had so little ego that she often didn't collect her own work. She entered a modest office building and saw Ron Vogel across the room. Movie-star handsome (Vogel had once been an actor), dark with wavy hair, he moved with energy, setting up his lights and backgrounds at high speed. Marli had a soft spot in her heart for him. Vogel had taken the beautiful photo of Marli that Coppola had used in *The Peeper*. He was a high-energy guy. As competitive as his old army buddy, Russ Meyer, and his friend Earl Leaf, Vogel was outpacing both of them in the glamor field.

"Vogel has an amazing talent for constantly finding beautiful new models," said one magazine editor. "I frankly don't know how he does it, but he seems to have located about three times as many new models as the other photogs with whom I do business." Ron had made it his mission to seek out and photograph the most luscious undiscovered feminine talent in Hollywood. He located beautiful models in Los Angeles nightclubs and restaurants, but just as often discovered them in the public library. Several librarians turned out to be gorgeous—once they let their hair down, took off their glasses (just like in the movies), and got out of their clothes. Consequently, some outstanding figure studies had come out of his studio. "I just keep my eyes wide-open," Vogel explained.

His passion for photography had begun as a hobby nine years earlier when Vogel attended a photography school. Four years ago he struck out on his own. Vogel checked his layout sketches. His rush photograph of Marli was also for *Adam*, a men's magazine that actively sought "small, but bustiferous redheaded women that measured thirty-five/twenty-three/thirty-five." *Adam*, a competitor of *Playboy*, offered their own bedside and stag party records and advice to the reader on the swinging life. They blatantly used a typeface and centerfold exactly like *Playboy*'s and had their own version of a Femlin.

In July, Marli had three pages of her poses in *High* magazine and she had an *Escapade* photo shoot after this, for the October issue. Marli was flattered during this election year that they had titled the article: "Marli for President."

She looked around the studio unsurprised at so few props. Vogel scorned props and gimmicks, relying instead on photographing girls so stunning that accouterments wouldn't be needed. He wanted the model's beauty to shine through and carry the picture. But Marli had something more beyond her stunning good looks—something indefinable that always had people asking, "Who is that red-haired woman?"

Vogel always judged a model at the first instant because once he started talking to them, "they all started to look beautiful." So far he had never been wrong about a girl being photogenic. His friend Keith Bernard had. Bernard, who had photographed Marilyn Monroe and Jayne Mansfield, knew exactly the kind of woman that made a great pinup. But the first time Betty Brosmer, a wasp-waisted teenager, walked into his studio she left him cold. As he studied the blond in horn-rimmed glasses, her hair piled up into a bun, and her figure hidden in a loose-fitting dress, he wasn't the least bit impressed. "I told her I couldn't use her. Then she showed me her photography album—and I changed my mind immediately . . . I broke all my appointments for the next day so I could photograph her." Betty Brosmer became the bestselling pinup Bernard had had in his ten-year career and one of the most beautiful girls he had ever captured on film.

Because the glamor business was so competitive, Vogel worked every day, except Sunday. Audrey Vogel (Ron's first model) greeted Marli, poured some coffee, and sat her down at an elaborate makeup table crowded with tins, bottles, spray cans, and brushes. Audrey helped the models prepare, rubbing on cold cream, accenting the eyebrows, delineating the hairline, and putting on lipstick. Marli did her own makeup, but Audrey would have to apply her body makeup.

She stripped and put her arms over her head as Audrey filled a round sponge and began to apply makeup. Body makeup is thin. Only a trained eye can tell if too little or too much has been applied. Ideally, the neck, back, legs, arms, and bosom are worked on slowly and carefully. "It's not until you work closely with the body of a beautiful girl that you realize what really makes her beautiful," said Hollywood makeup artist Ed Craig. "You notice, after a while, that every curve and line of her body has a way of blending—of belonging together—that it is almost unbelievable. She is supple where she should be supple, firm where she should be firm. You come to realize that size has nothing to do with beauty . . . It's all the same when it goes together right."

Marli was uninhibited and comfortable nude, from her weekends at the traveling nudist club. Vogel saw the nude model matter-of-factly executing a series of stretching exercises as if she were the only one in the tidy white room. What was it that Peter Gowland had written? Oh, yes. "A good model has to be a little bit of an extrovert . . . The girl's face is most important, but a good figure is really outstanding." Marli was all of that. Vogel studied her through the lens. Her trim, athletic body was one of the best he had ever seen, and there was a sunny glow to her skin. He began to snap photo after photo, stalking Marli from different angles and shouting encouragement as he whirled and turned. He studied his watch—just time for a final pose: Marli peeking over her left shoulder, her arm thrust through the long sleeves of a persimmon-colored knit, worn backward like a hospital gown. The swell of her left breast and nude back were captivating. The fabric wasn't transparent but it clung so perfectly it gave that effect. This would be the shot he would send and the magazine would use.

Marli had to rush to another studio. She had an appointment to be photographed that same day—by another of the top glamor men. "Sammy Wu was one of my photographers," said Marli. "We rarely worked at his studio, but I came there today. We would shoot the last set at my place. My parents had an apartment in Hollywood and he often came there instead because it was convenient." Her parents' apartment was on the south side of the street in the first block east of Western and a couple of blocks north of Hollywood Boulevard. Busch's Gardens was about an eighth of a mile away and less than a minute's drive from Sonny's apartment.

Marli's posing sessions rarely lasted more than a couple of hours. She preferred the familiar surroundings of her parents' apartment to the polished hardwood floors and klieg lights of Wu's studio. The studio was rather spartan.

Marli parked, entered. She saw Sam Wu waving to her from across his Hollywood studio. Sam was slender, fit, and bespectacled with short black hair. Always calm and at peace, his peers judged him to be "precise as an engineer and as sensitive as an artist." The first time he had read over Marli's file ("Los Angeles-born Marli worked as a dancer in Las Vegas, Manhattan, and Miami . . .") a smile had lit up his expressive face. "I love working with dancers!" Sam exclaimed "You hardly have to pose them. About all you have to do is say 'Go,' and make sure they're in focus. Dancers are excellent at achieving motion poses because they can move their bodies and 'hold' at precisely that point with a sense of action." For this reason Sam constantly searched Vegas for possible models, and it was there he had first seen Marli. There was another line from a layout about her that Sam had read. "Now a full-time model she shares a Malibu apartment with two dachshunds, Phoebe and Nietzche, and paints in her spare time."

"I understand you are a painter," Sam said. "I paint too. Water-color."

"I'm taking a class in pen and ink and watercolor," Marli said. "I just enjoy that work so much."

Like Marli, Sam executed watercolors in the transparent method, or English method (the most difficult and unforgiving medium of all). Though born in Boston, Wu had developed his watercolor painting style in Canton, China, where he spent his youth. Just before Pearl Harbor, he returned to the United States, and during World War II worked as an industrial photographer for Lockheed Aircraft. After the war, he settled in Los Angeles, attended the Art Center School, and expanded into advertising work, then glamor shots. Now in 1960 over half his income was still derived from advertising, but the glamor work was gaining. He used Rolleiflex and Hasselblad cameras, but preferred the Mamiyaflex when he was working in 120-size format. He tended to use a Pentax or Nikon for portrait work in thirty-five millimeter. On his first session with a new model, Wu always photographed her in close-up in at least six different stages along a 180-degree angle—front, two full profiles, and three to four in between. After every session with a model, he made notes and kept them with a set of the contact proofs he had just shot. Next time Wu used a particular model, he had only to look at his records to see what weaknesses she had and what angles to avoid.

Marli undressed and posed in pearls (necklace and bracelet on her left wrist) and thin black panties. She noticed a few props scattered about—apples for her to eat, a phone for her to answer and different-colored socks for her to pull on, but she wasn't asked to use any. Sam had an electric fan that could be used to blow her hair. Photographers were always looking for ways to energize a picture, dressing their models in the fad of the moment. "Bikini bathing suits, now dead as dodoes were the rage among editors a few years ago," advised Earl Leaf, always on the cutting edge. "Next came the shortie nighties as transparent as a lover's lie. This fad was followed by tight Capri pants, with bare bosoms covered by a bit of foliage. All these are now passé, and the photogs are scrounging around for a new gimmick."

Sam Wu posed Marli in front of silkscreened butterfly wallpaper.

That photo would be captioned: Marli likes men who are "more intelligent than most" and "dreams of one day marrying one and retiring to Mexico." "Oh, if only that could come true," she would think when she read it. In a perfect world it would. She would see. They finished up and went out to her car. Wu followed behind in his vehicle carrying his cameras, an armload of aluminum suitcases, and two black boxes.

Chapter Twenty-six
Aunt Margaret

Sonny, still thinking about the deep trouble he was in and looking for relief, wove eastward in his car not certain where he was bound. His head was in a whirl. He still managed to get lost, though he had lived in the area all his life. The street names and numbered streets got all jumbled up in his mind, that's why he liked to keep in a straight line, and in that way he always found his way home. He swung onto a quiet, tree-lined residential street on the other side of the Hollywood Freeway and stopped at the corner to get out his cigarettes. He shook one out, lit it, and took a deep drag. His mind was reeling and his cheeks were hot. He was still thinking about *Psycho*. The Shower Sequence had gotten into his blood and into his dreams. He could still see the woman in the shower flickering on the silver screen and the flash of the knife.

What had drawn him here? The streets were empty and silent. "I got tired of staying home last night," he said later, "and drove over to Virginia Avenue." But was that the real reason? He took a deep drag on his cigarette. Sonny swung the car around the corner and up ahead saw the entrance to a courtyard. Inside, the small cottage at 5617½ Virginia adjoined his Mother's building at 5623. Shirley Payne had lived across the hall from his mother. The site was uncomfortably close to the strong feelings that had gripped him. Once more, he parked down the block in the shadows of trees and walked back, chain-smoking as he walked, a stranger in his own neighborhood. He jumped at every noise and saw the police behind every tree.

Sonny looked down at the brown envelope in his hand and began thinking about Margaret M. Briggs, Mother's fifty-three-year-old sister whom he called "Aunty." A widow, Aunty worked as a restaurant hostess and a confidant to the disturbed youth. "I decided to come over to Aunt Margaret's cottage and bring her some green trading stamps I'd been saving for her." Those stamps would be the key that would get him inside her door.

An attractive brunet woman opened the door, and he pressed the envelope into her hand. "This is for you, Aunty," he said. Sonny gave a crooked grin, wiped his feet, and stepped inside. She opened the envelope and shook out pages of pale green stamps embellished by a red "S&H." Fine print on each stamp read "Value 12/3 mills." When you had enough of them pasted into your Saver Book, they could be redeemed for a toaster or some other small appliance.

"She invited me to stay for a while and we sat and watched the old *Ziegfeld Follies* MGM movie on television." Aunty poured two Cokes into tall glasses filled with ice, and they watched the TV without a word. Sonny recognized some of the big stars in the lavish musical numbers, Fred Astaire, Lucille Ball, Judy Garland, and William Powell. She pointed out Fanny Brice as the only cast member in the movie to have actually starred in the original Ziegfeld Follies on Broadway. Sonny wondered if she had been alive back in those days to see the Follies. Sonny could see that Aunty, perched on the edge of the couch, was having a wonderful time. The black-and-white television lit up the small room and cast blue shadows across Sonny's small, triangular head. His neck, almost wider than his head, pulsed. The two huge arteries on either side throbbed. His head began to hurt, and he felt giddy. Shirley's dead body back in his apartment had been forgotten.

"Finally, I got up to leave," Sonny said later. "We said goodnight."

The two had a few cross words that the woman across the hall over-heard. "It was then, when Aunt Margaret turned her back to me, the urge suddenly came over me again—the urge to kill. I couldn't fight it. So I put my arm around her neck from behind." At first she thought he was being affectionate and trying to make up for the harsh words they had exchanged. Sonny tightened his fingers around her neck, felt the alarm grow in her, then released his grip so that she could breathe, then tightened his fingers again. He was like a cat playing with a mouse. "It was slow torture, but finally it was all over. And I strangled her."

After Aunty was dead he made knife marks again, many inadver-tent, but some he meant this time. He had a reason for them in case he should ever have to explain so that people would understand.

"After I killed her, I tried to cut off her clothes with a pocket knife, but it was too dull. So I took a pair of scissors and cut them off—right up the middle. I cut off her clothes to make it look like a sex crime. Since I didn't have a record for anything like that, I thought it would throw the police off my trail."

But there was no sex this time. At first Sonny couldn't understand why he felt no lust. He stood and looked down at the pitiful nude form. He unzipped his pants, then zipped them up again. He couldn't under-stand why he felt nothing. Sonny lit a cigarette, walked to the window, and looked out. It was dark now and he could see lights on in Mother's room. Then the answer to his indifference came to him.

"After all, she was my aunt." That's why he felt no passion. That had to be the reason.

Then he sat down on the dining room floor next to the body and began to cry uncontrollably. Aunty had always been kind to him, he knew that. How could he have done this? "I just sat there watching television," he said later. "I told myself there was no help for me. I had tried other ways to shut out that sound in my head. I was going to go right on killing." Then, his legs trembling, he made his way into the back bedroom and lay down on one of the twin beds there. He could smell Aunty's perfume on the pillow and hear the clock on the bedside table ticking. Finally he pulled the quilt up under his chin, then over his face and, his feet sticking out from under the covers, fell sound asleep. His last waking thought was that now he had to dispose of *two* bodies.

He awoke at 5:00 A.M. on Tuesday morning, September 10, stretched, and made his way to the living room. The television was still going. Aunty was still face down on the floor. The sight of his aunt's nude body sobered Sonny, and it all came back to him. He could barely stand and leaned back against the wall. Steadying himself, he went into her kitchen and pawed through the cupboards to study the remnants of Aunty's sad little life. She had a few pieces of jewelry, but he had stolen before and it hadn't worked out so he left them where they were. He was not a thief. He was hungry though and made some eggs in a skillet, poured some cereal and milk into a bowl, and sat down at the kitchen table. He stared at the food for a while. He couldn't eat, so he went back into the living room and turned off the television. Then he sat down hard on the couch and buried his face in his hands again. He studied the heavy corpse. He was just not strong enough. Where was Shaffer?

"I realized then there was no way out for me," Sonny said. "I was on this thing and I couldn't get off. I'd killed two women already this week. Their bodies would be found sooner or later. I had to keep on going. There was nothing else to do." He stole ten dollars from Aunty's purse and folded it neatly into his wallet though it pained him to do so. He walked to his Olds down the street and saw it covered with morning dew. Then he had second thoughts. He stood looking at the sleeping houses, and when he was confident that no one was watching, walked to Aunty's 1958 Ford station wagon and opened the rear.

A two-stage latch unlocked both the wide, curved lift gate and tailgate. A new type of hinge allowed the tailgate to open fully flat. With the lift gate up and the tailgate lowered and the center seats folded, he had thirty-four square feet of floor space to work with—more than enough for two bodies or more if need be. Maybe he could move the bodies if he worked at night and dragged them in a blanket when everyone was asleep. It would all depend on luck. He might pull it off.

He decided to leave his own car, and take his victim's Ford station wagon. He went back, got Aunty's keys from her purse, slid onto the tan Silver Tweed woven plastic and vinyl front seat and drove away. Sonny didn't know exactly where he was going, but he did know what he was going to do. "I went out looking for another victim—another woman to kill," he said. He felt no remorse over his most recent murder, only guilt that he had stolen ten dollars from his aunt. The bill burned in his wallet as he drove toward the optical lab where he worked and was liked, or so he thought.

"Aunty's still there—in her apartment inside," he thought as he drove. "Aunty's still there. She'll always be there." He knew he could never lift her without Shaffer. He had been kidding himself. Besides the bartender, there was no one close enough to him to help. He imagined the slight indentation her body had made in the rug and, when he got home tonight, planned to lie down beside her and find some comfort to calm his raging mind.

The sun was coming up, and by 6:30 A.M. the smog was already choking. Sonny could barely breathe, but something felt like it was going to burst from his chest. Whatever it was it had claws.

Chapter Twenty-seven
Marli and Sam Wu

The redhead and the photographer climbed to the top story of the new two-story apartment complex where her parents lived. Light was glinting on the swimming pool in the center. Sam Wu entered and put down his cameras in the entry hall. Marli dropped her model's case next to the dark couch in her parents' apartment, a two-bedroom, one-bath modern. All the furniture was simple, 1950s modern with striped pillows on the couch, tan floor-to-ceiling curtains, and a two-tier coffee table. A soccer ball was just peeking out from under the table, which was covered with magazines. A tan television with stubby legs took out one corner and was valiantly defending its space. Her five-drawer chest of drawers was shoved into an alcove. A number of wide belts with large buckles on hooks hung above it. Arranged on the dresser top were several well-read hard-bound, non-fiction books. The floor was wall-to-wall plush carpet in contrast to her plain chenille spread.

Marli worked with the best men in glamor, good-looking photographers, many of whom had acting experience, which helped in their staging of her poses. Peter Gowland was one. As the son of two actors, he had acted, mostly uncredited, in about a dozen films and even had a small part in *Citizen Kane*. "I worked with Peter Gowland once in 1960," Marli said, "doing some experimental work for Polaroid, not black and white. Polaroid was getting into color." Gowland always gave great tips on posing. "Seated poses with the legs brought up form a more compact composition," he advised. "In standing poses have the model lean over so that her figure fits well into the picture frame. Hips appear smaller when the model is seated and her torso leans forward putting her derriere at a greater distance from the lens. A high angle emphasizes the bosom; a low angle accentuates the legs. Thin legs have more shape when viewed from the back or in front poses with knees pulled up. Heavy legs can be minimized by a seated pose with legs bent and feet behind her."

Wu studied the tall red-haired dancer who exuded such confidence and good humor. He hoped he expressed the same demeanor. A model's confidence in a photographer drops if he seems indecisive or fumbles in the middle of shooting. Wu unloaded his cameras and lit the small room. Any time he shot indoors there were lighting problems. He found less difficulty filming outdoors (he liked placing his model against the motion of a fast-moving stream), though there were some problems there too. He had shot a number of pictures of Marli outdoors (using a 120 Rollei and a Mamiyaflex). "With all her muscles in the proper places (a voluptuous thirty-six/twenty-three/thirty-six)," she was captioned, "Marli has only a few freckles to mark her as a fresh air fan so attuned to the wide-open spaces that even Madison Square Garden gives her claustrophobia." Sunlight can cause harsh shadows, which Wu avoided by shooting in early morning. Under the strong midday sun, he shot from the shadow side, backlighting the girl.

They began to work. Sam preferred placing a curvy model like Marli against geometric patterns or straight edges. In Marli's apartment he posed her on the couch nude from the waist down. "A top garment when worn alone is enough if care is exercised in its arrangement," Wu said and had Marli throw her head back (front and profile), and during each of these attitudes he shot from as many angles as he could— straight on, slightly overhead, from slightly below, and so on. Wu liked to cover himself for any eventuality.

"Sure, this is time-consuming," Sam said, "but in the long run it pays off." *Variety* gave the magazine editor enough to choose from. More important, it gave Wu a chance to know his model. "I'd rather spend an extra half hour experimenting with camera angles, than pass up some great shots and maybe lose a great sale." Sam sold his work through Galaxy and that's the way Marli's *Escapade* cover assignment had come about.

Sam always looked for something special beyond sheer physical beauty. Marli had mystery and exuberance. She reminded him of some of his earlier discoveries—Quinn O'Hara, a Scottish lassie who had been cast in four movies, Yvette Vickers, a hippie-type based in San Francisco and a Playmate, and Wende Wagner, who would co-star on the *Green Hornet* TV show as Miss Case.

Sam Wu, like Ron Vogel, used minimal props to avoid detracting from the model and the story he was telling. A few props go a long way. The ideal procedure was to choose just one tasteful object completely compatible with the setting and personality of the model. She could play with a ball or splash in the water, but his most important props were light and imagination. Sam shot her from behind. Marli's taut round buttocks shone in the strong light.

Sam shot a few more frames as if squeezing the last drop out of a grapefruit. Enjoying her fluid lines and natural grace, he reloaded his camera and took time composing in the lens and setting up his shot. The last thing he was worried about was Marli's expression. Facial expressions are fleeting and few can hold a natural expression longer than two blinks. Sam took a colorful, vertical picture of Marli with a light blue-green background as she lay on her back on her white shag rug. The pose played up her long, nude golden legs. Sam scattered around her a turquoise pillow, blue books, a letter bound in blue ribbon, and an oyster gray phone. Her yellow blouse and bright red lipstick emphasized her red hair. She crossed her right leg, and extended the other leg as high as it would reach. A wonderful picture, Sam thought; it would run as a double-page vertical spread.

Though he disdained props he did make use of her giant stuffed dog (named Stumble for a real pooch Marli had as a child). She used it as a backrest, a brown patch over the dog's eye peeking out. The article was titled "A Dog's Life." What became of Stumble? "I gave it to my mom," Marli said later, "and she had it by her front door—it was huge! It really scared people." Marli's own dogs were no longer with her. "Phoebe and Nietzsche, the two adorable dachshunds I got in Chicago, came back with me to California. Where I was living they didn't allow pets, so I had to find homes for them. Actually it worked out well. The lady who was my Santa Monica lawn mate just loved it when I told her to find them a home. She said, 'Oh, I'll take them.'"

Marli had taken pictures for years. "I enjoy the art of photography," she said, but she also worked in a dozen art disciplines and mediums—life drawing, pottery making, leatherworking, and filmmaking. She drew in pencil, pastel, and pen and ink and painted in watercolor, oil, and the new acrylic paints just developed by Bay City in San Francisco. "The artwork is mine," she told Sam, following his gaze, "but the [predominantly orange and blue] oil portrait of me was painted by my mother, Louise. She's my best friend." While Marli worked on the Strip, Louise had driven up to see her once a month and always gotten a bungalow at the El Rancho Vegas.

One of Marli's paintings in an ornate frame was an abstract design-like close-up of a face. Wu thought it looked like Max Beckman, George Groz, or Max Ernst, certainly a Bauhaus and German Expressionist influence there. He included her pictures in the background when he could. Marli's artwork and sense of aesthetics would later be instrumental in solving the great mystery that grew up around her.

In her sketchbook Marli had drawn an oil or watercolor sketch of an abstract landscape and a fish in pants sitting on a box. Wu wondered what all the men who had fantasies about Marli would think of her simple, unpretentious lifestyle. With her, what you saw was what you got. Like the murdered and unobtainable Laura that the obsessed detective discovered was obtainable after all, Marli was obtainable too.

Chapter Twenty-eight
The *Psycho* Killer

S onny found his next victim unexpectedly. Little time had passed, but it seemed like forever. He wondered if all that had happened so far hadn't been just a dream, a trick of the mind. He could remember before and after vividly, but the middle portion was blocked out. By early Tuesday morning, the long Labor Day weekend was just a memory. It was hotter than ever. Northridge reached a high of 104 degrees, San Gabriel reported 102, San Bernadino 101, Burbank 99 and Long Beach 98. An Inglewood woman was overcome by the heat over on Court Street near the Civic Center and was recovering at the hospital

Sweat trickled down Sonny's cheek and his long, thick neck. He wiped his brow and let out a long breath. That didn't work either. Smog was already crawling in, and it was getting to be a deadly problem. California's population had reached sixteen million people, and the total registered vehicles had reached eight million. Last year the legislature created the California Motor Vehicle Pollution Control Board to test emissions and certify emission control devices. The Federal Motor Vehicle Act had just been enacted. Maybe that would do something about all this air pollution. There had already been seventy smog alerts in the region this year.

Sonny fought to breathe. He had not shaved, and the faint stubble on his chin was itchy. He struggled to control himself as he felt the old familiar urge steal over him. He began to drive even more erratically and sped up, then slowed as he saw the roads were already clogged with cars and highway patrolmen were everywhere.

At 6:57 A.M. he pulled into the lab parking lot at Hollywood Boulevard and North Vermont Avenue. What had drawn him here? Did he actually intend to go to work at his monotonous job three blocks away at Hillhurst and Prospect Avenue? Though he had worked at the optical lab as a lens polisher for years, he was still a stranger there. Sonny began thinking about Griffith Park, where he intended to dump the body of his next victim. It had possibilities. Any corpse left there was usually never found.

One of Thad Brown's most difficult cases, and he had headed up the Black Dahlia investigation, had involved Griffith Park. In 1949 Hollywood showgirl Jean Spangler vanished. She had been a dancer with the Earl Carroll Theatre and the Florentine Gardens and had been an extra in films and television.

On October 9, 1949, a Griffith Park groundskeeper had come upon Spangler's purse on the left side of the road alongside Gate 2 off Fern Dell Road in Griffith Park. Gate 2 blocks off access to the "scenic route," which runs up the mountain and ends at Griffith Park Observatory. The groundskeeper noticed the carrying strap of her purse had been ripped loose as in a struggle. Thad Brown and his men were notified, and soon two hundred searchers had fanned out over Griffith Park. A fierce rainstorm forced them to call the search off and no other search was ever made. Her body was never found in the park though it might have surfaced years later as a Jane Doe and never been identified.

Sonny, knowing the impregnability of Griffith Park, concluded it was the perfect place to stash a body. He remembered how he had tied a dog to a tree there and it had died of hunger and thirst. Griffith Park was a big place, but Sonny had several specific sites in mind—Forest Lawn Memorial Park, Roosevelt Golf Course, and near the Hollywood

Reservoir. There was always Runyon Canyon Park just above Nichols Canyon. In his mind he could see himself putting the body in the trunk of his car. The corpse was light as air now. Then he would drive to a swampy area in Griffith Park and cover it with brush or board it up in one of the old abandoned structures.

Sonny was sweating profusely. His shirt was sticking to his back. He looked frantically around for a victim. There was no one, only a few workmen nearby.

Then, as he pulled up a few ticks before 7:00 A.M., he saw a familiar figure already in the lot. She shimmered in the waves of heat. Whoever it was, was moving toward him, a strong, sturdy figure. The sun was in his eyes, and so he waited. She would soon be close enough for him to tell. No matter who she was, he had found his victim.

Mrs. Magdalena A. Parra, the attractive and athletic technical inspector for the optical plant, closed the door to her car. Today was one of those occasions when she was early to work to beat the heat and outrun the morning rush hour traffic. It was probably the heat that made it difficult to sleep. Even her sleeveless silk summer dress seemed hot. It clung to her chest and hips. Magdalena hooked her black handbag over her arm and, swinging her hips, crossed the lot. She heard a horn honk and saw a 1958 Ford station wagon had pulled up to the curb. The driver was waving to her with a long spider-like arm. A frown crossed her face. Now she was just annoyed, but continued walking.

Sonny thought Magdalena looked extremely fetching today, though younger than he liked. He estimated she was in her late thirties (she was actually forty-nine). She took good care of herself. His spirits had lifted as she shut the door to her car and began walking toward Prospect. With a big smile, he hailed her from the open window. At first she didn't recognize him because he was in a strange car. Odd, she was frowning, thought Sonny. His gold-rimmed glasses gleamed in the sunlight. "It looks like we're both early," he called. She walked over to the car and recognized gawky Sonny leaning on the wheel. "Hot enough for you?"

Because the lab was still not open, he offered to take her to coffee. Magdalena had to think a moment. Not coffee, perhaps juice, something cold. She looked at her watch. It was still very early. She really hadn't fraternized with the introverted young man outside work before but didn't want to hurt his feelings by turning him down. He leaned over and opened the passenger door for her. Hesitantly, she climbed in and slid onto the front seat next to him. Sonny was sweating and he looked like he hadn't eaten in days.

At least the lab was air-conditioned. She was beginning to have second thoughts, but the car was rolling now. In fact, Sonny was accelerating. He looked wide-eyed. She tried to think of a way to calm him down and started to make idle chat. "What stifling weather," she said. "And the day has barely begun. What's it going to be like by noon?"

Sonny said nothing but turned in his seat and, grinning madly, suddenly shot out his arm toward Magdalena. Before she knew it his extraordinarily long fingers had locked around her windpipe and cut off her next word. He grabbed the nape of her neck and squeezed, but she immediately began to struggle and between reductions in the pressure got out some screams. His grin grew wider. It was so odd to see him smile and the eyes behind the glasses so big this close. She punched and screamed so hard, Sonny had to take his other hand off the wheel in order to clamp all ten fingers around her neck. He steered with his knees.

Out of control, the car began to weave from one side of Hollywood Boulevard to the other. It dented one car, bounced off. Houses rolled by. They passed two men working by a truck. Gathering speed, the car hit a curb, jolting Sonny into the dash. The car swerved to the center of the street and stalled at a thirty-degree angle. But this worked to Sonny's advantage. Now that he no longer had to pay attention to the wheel he was able to throw his entire body atop her and use his weight to hold her down. Sonny bore her slowly to the floor. This maneuver had worked in his previous attacks, but those victims had been older, weaker, and unsuspecting since he had come up on them from behind. Magdalena, suspicious and wary from the beginning, had been ready.

Under him Sonny could feel her wriggling, squirming and kicking like a wildcat. My God, what had he let himself in for? Sonny thought. This hadn't happened before. These younger women were powerful. Magdalena broke his stranglehold and began to punch back with her right hand, all the while screaming as loud as she could. Sonny, winded from exertion and the hot weather, was panting. Gradually, Magdalena forced Sonny to one side and was able to raise herself on one arm and reach for the door handle. Sonny pulled her arm back, but after several flailing attempts she managed to get the handle between three fingers and fling the door open. She squirmed halfway out then fell onto the pavement and rolled, but Sonny still had hold of her legs. She kicked him in the chin. He made one last grab, but she slid free and he got only her purse straps. She let go of the purse so she could escape and it fell back onto the seat. The few dollars it contained had fallen out. Sonny, furious at being thwarted, saw her beyond his reach and, hearing her rising screams and fearing others would come to her aid, jumped out of the driver's side door onto the road. He put both hands over his ears to blot out her screams and fled, leaving his Aunt Margaret's station wagon in the middle of the street with both doors open. Sonny ran southeast past Rodney Drive.

Mrs. Parra was screaming so loud that two truck drivers unpacking their load came running up to see if Magdalena was all right. Seeing she was unhurt, they leaped up and looked about for Sonny. Seeing him a block away in front of Lyman Place, they chased after him as he sprinted north, knotting their fists, bunching their muscles, and vowing to do a little damage. Within a minute the two freight men stopped and gave a cry of frustration. They had lost him. On the pavement were his discarded gold-rimmed glasses. He was close. They began searching again.

Chapter Twenty-nine
Martello

Willie Martello surveyed himself in the mirror—sleepy-eyed, thin-lipped with dark circles under his eyes, an amiable bear of a man with a huge heart. He liked to dress all in white as befitting his good guy status. Early in the morning, Willie centered his white cowboy hat on his head and stepped out into the blazing sun of the East Mojave. He sighed contentedly. May had plenty of wind, but the summer months were calmer, barely a breeze, which was fine with him too. Willie loved the heat of Nevada when the saguaro was flowering and fruiting among the desert ironwood trees. September was fine with him as well—always dry, over a hundred degrees by day, and never lower than the high forties at night. Willie studied his gambling resort—a series of three long, low buildings, its sign in the shape of a lucky seven on a curved arrow reading "El Rey Club." That was fitting since Willie was the seventh son of a seventh son and a very lucky man. In a small rectangle were the words *Bar, Casino,* and *Cafe,* stacked neatly atop one another. He might well have added the word *Brothel.*

Daisy Mae and her ladies had been working across the road since the 1950s, when Willie had decided to try out the idea to boost his cash flow. Willie ran the club, Daisy Mae ran the girls, and the two were very distinct from each other. Willie got a bad rap and though he was Searchlight's benefactor and sole employer, he was called "whoremonger." "From all accounts I've heard," historian and professional entertainer Andy Martello told me later, "Willie was not at all concerned about the brothel. The prostitutes were something of a necessary evil. The place wasn't frequented by the sheriff and was close enough to the military base that it seemed like a foolproof moneymaker. It isn't like he invented prostitution in Nevada and he always ran a family place . . . Given that Willie did so much for the town and never made a great living off his hard work (he put every dime back into the casino and town), I'd say a little tarnish on the teapot isn't too bad." When he was a kid growing up in Searchlight, Senator Harry Reid recalled how Willie would ask Mary's girls to clear out so he could invite the town's children, a dozen at a time, to swim in the El Rey Casino pool. By 1960, Willie, with $2 million in his pocket, was the wealthiest man in town.

Willie billed his combination restaurant-bar-casino-brothel as the "Gayest spot on I-95." To entice high rollers he offered free $4 gaming vouchers and round-trip champagne flights on Constellations and DC-3s from Long Beach to the Searchlight Airport, which he had privately constructed. The sixty-six-hundred-foot-long lighted airstrip was south of town near North Rancho Drive and West Carey Avenue. What Willie didn't know was that the average Constellation was far too heavy for the runway, a fact the city corrected before a tragedy occurred. The Dunes in Vegas offered similar free round-trip flights for their guests. The Hacienda near McCarran Field at the south end of the Strip also provided free flights aboard their DC-4, with in-flight entertainment, champagne, and gold-plated buckles on the seat belts.

Willie Martello and his brother Sonny co-owned the El Rey, but it had been Willie's notion to build in Searchlight after their brothers Albert and Buddy had relocated back there to raise livestock. Willie looked proudly at the little mining town around him. He had grand designs for Searchlight. Nobody was a bigger booster in spite of his lusty reputation. "We were trying to build a town," brother Bob said. "Every dime Willie made went right back into the club and the community." Willie, a native Californian, had arrived in Searchlight after World War II with only $13 in his pocket. At least he had had a free place to stay. Albert and Buddy were going broke trying to resurrect an old local hotel. Of course, there were always setbacks. A while back someone had placed a "jumper" on one of Willie's dollar machines to rig it, and he had his gambling license revoked for a year.

A miner had named Searchlight after a brand of matches.[7] The Martellos named their casinos after a popular brew (El Rey Beer). They had begun that custom in 1937 when brother Tony secured one of the first liquor licenses in California (after the end of the Volstead Act) and founded the first El Rey Club in Southgate, California. But in spite of Willie's efforts, the town remained small—about fifty people. In its boom days, Searchlight had had a bigger population than Vegas, but as the quality of mined ore diminished, gold and silver production dipped until only a few people straggled on in town, and Willie became Searchlight's primary employer.

Searchlight lies halfway between Needles, California, and downtown Las Vegas, fifty-three-miles southeast of the Strip at the juncture of I-95 and State Route 164, and situated in the Colorado River Basin in Clark County. Northeast of Searchlight lies Hoover Dam and Boulder City, and south is Kingman, Bullhead City, and Davis Dam in Arizona. From the southwest Searchlight basks at the feet of a jumbled mountain range. Fourteen miles downhill is a serene cove on the shoreline of Lake Mohave. The jagged clear-as-glass Mohave, a rip in the Columbia River, presents unsuspected desert waterfalls and hot springs.

Willie Martello priced his single, double, and family rooms from $6 to $20 a night, provided a live Vegas show, Tony Lovello's dance band, and Chef Luigi Scirocco's gourmet cooking. Willie was a classy guy. No one ever left the El Rey broke or hungry. He made certain of that. Tony Curtis's close friend, crooner Frank Sinatra, was a frequent visitor (es-

---

[7]An alternate origin of the town's name came from a remark made by a scoffer before the Colton brothers found gold in Searchlight: "If there's any gold here, it would take a searchlight to find it."

pecially when he played Vegas), and so were Martin and Lewis, and Betty Grable (now that her reliable venue the El Rancho had burned). Two Hollywood notables lived in Searchlight. The first was native-born Edith Head, tinsel-town's preeminent costumer (designer for Hitch's *Rear Window* and *North by Northwest*), who over her fifty-year career would work on eleven Hitchcock films and create the Hitchcock look.

The other local notable was Hollywood's first sex symbol, Clara Bow, the "It Girl." After a year of unhappy love affairs, a tax evasion charge, and huge gambling losses, Clara was abandoned by Paramount. She isolated herself from the public in tiny Searchlight and married cowboy star Rex Bell (later lieutenant governor of Nevada), who owned the Walking Box Ranch west of town.

Willie was friends with a lot of Hollywood Western film stars, among them Rory (as in "roaring blazes") Calhoun. For the last two years the six-foot-three star had been portraying Bill Longley, *The Texan*, on CBS-TV. Rory's show had been canceled last week, but Willie wasn't worried about him. He was a hard man to keep down. Only five years earlier, Rory's agent, Henry Willson, who had discovered him, and Universal International, who had Calhoun under contract, had sold him out. Willson informed UI that *Confidential* was going to run an exposé about the secret homosexual life of their joint client Rock Hudson. In exchange for not running Rock's story in the scandal mag, Willson offered to disclose information to them about Rory's hardcore criminal past. His theft of a nickel-plated revolver when he was thirteen landed him in the Pacific Lodge Reformatory. After he got out, Rory drove hot cars across state lines, a federal offense, got jailed in the Springfield Missouri Pen and San Quentin, and was paroled just before his twenty-first birthday. To Willson's dismay, his disclosure in *Confidential* had no negative effect on Calhoun's career, only solidified his bad-boy image. Rory got more TV and movie offers than he could accept. Robert Mitchum, whose marijuana arrest and conviction *Confidential* publicized to the same result, told them "Booze, broads, it's all true. Make up more if you want."

Rory was not only Willie Martello's pal, but a dear friend to a TV and film producer/director, quick-draw artist, and occasional stunt man named Jerry Schafer. Schafer was one of those guys who would tumble off a saloon roof at the drop of a cowboy hat (and still could). He had made his entry into show biz through stunts and using his six-gun. He recently won the world's fast draw championship. Schafer later told me,

Yes, Rory Calhoun was one of my closest friends. We met in 1957 way before the bull frogs wore britches! I did some stunts for him and helped him with his horse, Domino (falling on my head and jumping out of windows was a stepping-stone for me to get a foothold in the business). We became buddies then and when he got divorced from Lita Baron he moved in with me because she really decimated him financially. We also worked together in films. We lived together in England, too, when I produced *Belle Starr* with Betty Grable. Part of the time we spent in London, I moved in with Ava Gardner who had a flat near our flat which was located right across the street from the American Embassy.

In London, I introduced Rory to his wife, Sue Rhodes, a stringer for an Australian newspaper. She wrote a bestseller in Australia *Now You'll Think I'm Awful,* and wrote *When She Was Bad She Was Horrid.* The night Rory passed away we spoke on the telephone from his hospital bed in Santa Monica. The last words he said to me were "Jerry I love you!" The next morning Sue called me and told me Rory passed away after the call. I still keep his photo above my desk and look at him every day.

After doing stunts for five years, Schafer started his own live traveling stunt show and began writing thirty-minute shows and got about as far away from doing stunts as he could. He went to work at Republic Studios for Dick Powell at Four Star and became friends with Chuck Connors, Steve McQueen, and Robert Taylor, who were doing *The Rifleman, Wanted Dead or Alive,* and *The Detectives* series shows. In 1958, Schafer wrote and produced *The Legend of Billy the Kid,* his first TV production, a thirty-minute pilot in color. "That was a big deal at that time, color," he said. Schafer's script portrayed the fictionalized adventures of real-life Deputy Sheriff Pat Garrett and gunfighter William H. Bonney, "Billy the Kid." Schafer filmed at Republic Studios in North Hollywood, on location in Nevada at the Valley of Fire, and in Searchlight, where he met Willie Martello. When NBC-TV picked up Billy the Kid, they changed its title to *The Tall Men* and set it in 1870s New Mexico.

Schafer was also acquainted with an Israeli, Rayhavam Adie, who was interested in filmmaking. One day Schafer told Ray and his buddy Richard that he had just written a comedy film about a cowboy who gets bucked off his horse and hits his head on rock. Thereafter, every time he looked at any woman, she would appear to be completely nude to him.

While Jerry expounded his idea, Richard, who had been looking at him and smiling the entire time, said "Wow! That sounds like a great idea. Can you get away with making a film like that?"

"Sure, why not?" Jerry said. "As long as I make it on a secluded location." He thought he knew just such a spot.

"How much will it cost to make this film?" Rayhavam asked.

"The budget is forty five thousand dollars."

"Okay, I'll back it!" Rayhavam said, and pulled out his checkbook. "Who do I make this out to?"

That's when Schafer explained that he had to leave for London in four weeks. "I'd like to do the film when I come back," he said. "I entered into a contract to direct a musical comedy in England prior to writing the film."

"How long would it take to shoot the film?"

"I could do it in two or three weeks."

"I want you to shoot as soon as possible," Rayhavam said, "because my girlfriend has to return to Israel and I want her to appear in the film."

The deal (for lack of better words) specified that the backer had the right to do whatever he wanted with the film in Schafer's absence. They made an oral agreement on the spot . . . no lawyers, nothing in writing, just a handshake. To Schafer's amazement, Rayhavam tore the check out of his checkbook and handed it to him. Schafer didn't have a minute to waste. Schafer cast about for suitable Nevada locations, then realized Searchlight would be a perfect location for *The Wide Open Spaces*. He finished the script in a week, went to the phone and dialed SE 0603.

"Willie Martello, who owned the entire town," Schafer said, "had been trying to entice me to come to Searchlight to make a movie for a long time. Now was a perfect opportunity to do exactly that. Search-light, for all intents and purposes in the middle of nowhere, was a per-fect location to have nude girls running all over the place."

"Come on over," Willie said.

"God Willie was something wonderful," Schafer said, "a man amongst men, always smiling, always having something good to say, always ready for anything." Schafer considered Willie the luckiest man he had ever known, as golden as the El Rey's shiny gold matchbooks. Each "Lucky Match" had a winning hand stamped on it. Schafer hoped some of that luck would rub off on him. Excited, he made the trip from Vegas south-east to Searchlight in thirty minutes, half the usual driving time. "Wil-lie was ahead of his time in many respects," Andy Martello told me later. "The fact that so many films and TV shows began shooting in authentic western locations around that time proves the point."

When he pulled up in front of the El Rey, Schafer climbed out and patted Willie's back (to rub some luck off) and explained his idea for a Western nudie. "I had very little idea what the hell I was doing at that time," Jerry said. "It's the story of a guy who goes into a casino, gets hit on the head and when he wakes up finds himself in front of a bunch of topless women dealing cards." Willie listened intently. "The glamor girls are dressed for their job. They would be going about everyday activities one minute and naked the next." They could shoot interiors and exte-riors at the El Rey Resort and Casino. Willie agreed it would be good advertising for the town of Searchlight, which he lived to promote.

Schafer had hoped to make his comedy one of the first of the new sexploitation films. There had only been two nudies in release, *The Im-moral Mr. Teas* and *Not Tonight, Henry*, which had made millions for their filmmakers, but others were jumping on the bandwagon—*The Ad-ventures of Lucky Pierre*, starring burlesque comic Billy Falbo, made for $7,500, was due out. The nudie cutie waters were becoming crowded with sexploitation sharks before Schafer could even dip a toe in the pool. He would have to work as fast as possible if he was to cash in before the fad died out and still get to London on time. First, he needed five or six of the most beautiful women he could find. *Playboy* Centerfold

Virginia Gordon, a lovely brunet starlet, had just completed two nudie cuties: *The Ruined Bruin* due out in April and *Once Upon a Knight*, "The naughtiest Nudenik Scandal ever to come out of Hollywood." Schafer signed Gordon and flew her to Vegas. Enchanted by Marli Renfro's magazine appearances, he signed her too, quickly mounted a technical crew, and cast the remaining girls and the leading man, Larry Chance. "And before I knew it," he said, "I was about to make a film inside and outside the El Ray Casino in Searchlight, Nevada. To be completely candid, I considered what I did with *The Wide Open Spaces* as an embarrassment to me. I was new in the business and at that time, I'd do anything to make a film."

So would Francis Ford Coppola. What would become of *The Peeper*, which also featured Marli Renfro? Would Francis's first film ever see the light of the big screen? Would he ever see his name on the big screen as director? The UCLA grad student was hungrier than a shark. He was ravenous for recognition and money to finance his future films.

Chapter Thirty
Capture

"I t was just a personal argument," Sonny told the two burly truck drivers in the hot September sun as they cornered him at the end of a long dark alley. "Just a misunderstanding." He took a step back from the men, who had their sleeves rolled up and were sweating profusely. Sonny appeared ready to fight—huge hands opening and closing at an accelerated rate. He was licking his lips. "Keep away. Keep away," Sonny cried. "She and I are friends. It's okay." The gawky young man moved farther back into the shadows and stumbled into some trash cans, sending lids rolling out of the alley and down the slight incline into the street.

Spittle clung to one corner of Sonny's mouth, and his cheeks were sucked hollow. His bony chest was rising and falling rapidly as a bird's, and he was holding his arms straight out. His eyes were wide and staring, but without glasses he could barely see. The two truckers tensed, then relaxed as they realized Sonny had no fight left in him. They had no idea that Sonny was armed with a long steak knife and a box cutter hidden in his left pocket.

Not knowing of the danger, it was no trick for the two husky drivers to grab Sonny by the collar, give him a hard shake for making them run so far, lift him by his pointed elbows and stagger-walk him up the alley. They moved out onto the brilliantly lit street and began walking up the block to a substantial white apartment building where Mrs. Parra was waiting in the car. Her cheeks were spotted with red. In the background tall cypress bent in a wind bringing a little relief from the heat. The closer the three men got to her, the more furious she became and looked as if she might lunge at Sonny. "He tried to strangle me," she gasped as she leaped out. "Let me at him. He snatched my purse. Call the police!" Though the truckers had a tight grip on Sonny, he managed to pull back to avoid her fury. One driver stepped between them. "Sure, Lady, hold on. Get a grip."

"Call the cops!" she repeated, then stalked away and climbed back into the car, leaving the door wide-open.

The other trucker jogged to a booth on the corner. At 7:05 A.M. the LAPD complaint board, set up to respond to urgent crimes, logged his call. The complaint board officer, while talking, was recording essential information on a form. An officer on the dispatcher's mike was listening in too. Simultaneously the complaint officer passed the location to communications. Inside the all-white room a girl glanced at a map board showing the location and status of every radio unit by colored lights. Officers Eugene McGowan and Dale Baker of the Hollywood Division were nearby and about to go off duty. She put the essential data on the air and assigned their unit to investigate. McGowan and Baker rushed Code Three to investigate the altercation, and as they pulled up heard Mrs. Parra screaming to them from the front seat of the car, "Help me. He's crazy!"

The two radio patrolmen were young, very fit, and straight arrow, pressed and clean in spite of their long shift and the heat. Climbing out of their radio car onto the broad street, both officers ran to the station wagon, their hands on their service revolvers. Through the glass they could see the victim slumped on the front seat. In the shadow of the truck the drivers held Sonny, who was white-faced and shaking as he told the officers that he hadn't intended to steal the purse or hurt his co-worker. "Magdalena is a friend of mine," he screamed. "I've known her for a long time. We work together. I just put my arm around her in a friendly way and she started screaming and jumped out of the car and left her purse behind. That's all it was." Asked for his ID, Sonny fished his wallet out of his back pocket. "Take your license out of the wallet." The officer accepted the card and read Sonny's real name. It was Henry Adolph Busch Jr.

As the cops searched further, they discovered the steak knife and box cutter. In Sonny's right pocket were handcuffs. "You'll like ours better," said Baker and ratcheted police cuffs onto his wrists. By 7:10 A.M. the officers had gotten statements from the truck drivers, and ten minutes later were on the way to Hollywood Station. The attack, apprehension, and arrest had taken a short time. Baker rode in the backseat with Sonny. Sonny asked for a cigarette and the officer gave him one. As Sonny puffed, dragging deeply, he grew calmer and then started talking to Baker as if to confide in him and make him understand. "First, about that purse," he stammered. "You've got to understand that I wasn't trying to steal it. That was just an accident. It was just part of my trying to get that woman in my car."

He told them they could call him Sonny. When he felt Baker and his partner had understood he thought of something else and said, "I guess you'll see that's not my car. It belongs to my aunt." He went silent as if juggling his choices. Finally, he said, "You fellows don't want to talk to me just about the purse-snatching."

Baker said nothing, only nodded.

"I guess you've got me. I might as well make a clean breast of it. You'd find it out anyway."

"What are you talking about, Henry?"

"I'm glad you got me. I was going to take that woman up in Griffith Park and kill her. I've killed some women already." McGowan took his foot off the pedal, slowed and looked into the backseat. "In fact, there's a body right now in my apartment, over on Mariposa. I'll show you. There's another in one of my mother's apartment building on Virginia." The eyes behind the gold-rimmed glasses were blinking rapidly, and Sonny was sweating profusely. A cut one of the truck drivers had inflicted was bleeding. A crooked grin crossed his face and stayed frozen there.

At first the two cops thought that Sonny had probably seen "too many horror films," like the popular *Psycho*, but reconsidered. Changing direction they drove to Sonny's nearby apartment over on Mariposa and parked in front. While Baker guarded Sonny, Officer McGowan climbed out and sprinted up the steps to look for the building manager so she could let him into the apartment. A dark-haired woman with her hair in curlers answered the door. McGowan told her what he wanted and went upstairs with her. "He lives in the rear," she said. She got out a ring of keys, and jingling them, unlocked the door and let him into Sonny's apartment.

She stepped back and let McGowan walk inside. There was a very unpleasant odor, exacerbated by the heat. According to Sonny the body, if there was one, had been here a few days. A clock on a little table in the foyer was ticking placidly, but seemed very loud in the silent apartment. The officer observed a half-filled cup of tea on the kitchen counter. The rabbit ears on the twenty-one-inch black-and-white TV were standing erect in a V. On a wire rack beneath were a *TV Guide* and several issues of *Time*—"Automobile Trouble Shooters" and "Satellites in Space," and "Caryl Chessman's Execution."

The bulky green canvas, mounded on the floor, dominated the room. McGowan saw it was a brand new sleeping bag tied with white clothesline. Without opening it, McGowan kneeled and ran his hands carefully along the contours of the bag. He felt something vaguely shaped like a human body, pliable but rigid. Slowly he confirmed there was a corpse inside by touch—a head, features, shoulders—then rushed downstairs to the squad car so he could call headquarters.

At Hollywood Station a couple of miles away Lieutenant Charles Crumly, the acting detective commander, was just coming onto the day shift. He sat down in his swivel chair and turned so he could see the brick exterior of the police building through his office window. Everything in Crumly's spartan office was neatly arranged. On his desktop were a black rotary phone, two ashtrays, and two stacks of reports, and under the glass blotter were the name, office, and phone number of every man under his command. A second page underneath listed all the emergency numbers he might need if the city were in peril. A wooden file cabinet behind him held more information.

The hot shot call was patched through to Crumly, who listened a moment, then got his hat and coat, walked briskly to the door, and called two of his best men, Lieutenant Walter Colwell and Sergeant Edward Northrup. All three detectives drove immediately to the apartment house where Sonny was being held in cuffs in the back of the squad car.

"He says he killed a couple of women over the weekend," McGowan told Crumly. "One upstairs here and another over on Virginia Avenue. He's right about one—there's a body up there"—he inclined his head toward the top floor—"tied in a sleeping bag."

"Who's that in the bag, Sonny?" Crumly asked, leaning into the radio car and speaking like a parent to the child-like adult. At first the boyish figure in the rear seat wouldn't look at him, but then he blushed and his lips began to quiver.

"She's an elderly lady, Mrs. Shirley Payne," Sonny said at last. "She's about seventy-years-old, an old friend of my mother. I took her to see the movie *Psycho* on Saturday night, September third. Later in my apartment an urge came over me and I strangled her."

"An urge?" Crumly thought and shook his head. He doubted that. "What kind of urge?" Then he and Colwell went upstairs to see the still unopened sleeping bag. It was made of a dark, shiny kind of plastic and they had difficulty opening it. The zipper was caught. Both officers pulled and finally got it loose. What did she look like? How horrible was this going to be? It was worse than expected. Now they had to brief Chief of Detectives Thad Brown, who coordinated all action in the field. He was a very imaginative detective.

Thad, an avid mystery novel reader, once used a trick he had found in a book. When he found a girl shot to death, he saw she had tooth marks on her body. He stood and grabbed an apple from the mouth of a suspect. "Of course I gave him another apple to replace it—he was a big guy. But the tooth marks on the apple I took matched those on the body and we had our man."

Thad's approach to solving cases was simple: "Find the pattern and the man who fits it, be persistent and suspicious." And suspicious he was, especially as he heard the news of the arrest. How much of Sonny's story could he believe? He left his desk, donned a sport jacket with broad white flecks, and drove to the scene, which was now crowded with officers and interested bystanders. Brown walked to the patrol car, put his elbows on the sill, and leaned inside. Patiently, he waited to hear what Sonny had to say. The gawky youth was chain-smoking and stuttering so much it was hard to get the complete story. So jittery and malnourished, Thad thought, he didn't look capable of hurting anyone.

Now he had an unpleasant task to perform, a drive over to Virginia Avenue to check out the murder of Sonny's aunt Margaret Briggs. When he got there, Thad paused outside the white frame door and flagstone wall leading to her apartment and prepared himself for what must lay inside. Setting his teeth, he opened the door and entered.

Aunt Margaret was sprawled nude on the dining room floor, strangled and slashed with a knife, probably the pocketknife the two officers had confiscated from Sonny. There were too many cuts on her body to quickly count. Uncharacteristically Thad showed strong emotion, thin lips parting enough to let out a cry audible from outside. His temper began to rise, and he returned stiff-legged to the car, fists clinched.

Sonny was terrified at his approach. He told Brown he had intended to kidnap Magdalena Parra, take her up into the park and kill her too. "But I didn't do it, she got away from me," he said, "even though I had her down on the floor of the car, choking her hard. I'm glad you fellows caught me. I never went through such a battle. Now it's over."

"You've told us about these two murders, Sonny," Thad asked. "Is that all? Is there anything else on your mind? Did you kill anybody else?"

"Well, yes. I may as well tell you." He wasn't sure of the exact number because he sometimes returned to his apartment late in the evening without knowing what he had done earlier. "I do know one for sure," he said. "There was old Mrs. Miller back in May."

Mrs. Miller? Thad had her down as a possible Bouncing Ball Strangler victim. Was it all over at last? Brown's heart was beating fast now at the possibility they could wrap a lot of old cases at once. Across his stoic face spread the slightest sign of deep emotion and Thad's eyes grew cold with purpose.

Two days after the Labor Day weekend Thad stood in the hot sun, stunned. In the wavering heat he looked into the squad car and considered what Sonny had just told him. He had to admit that when he had heard of Sonny's arrest, he had first thought of the Bouncing Ball Strangler. That killer had been tall, gangling and young, but Sonny's complexion was not swarthy and he was thin. The witness had described the Bouncing Ball Strangler as husky. Still—it was possible. He didn't look like a man who had been eating regularly and perhaps he had lost weight.

The MO of the crimes was close enough that Mrs. Miller had been included among the powerful strangler–rapist's victims. Thad studied Sonny's fingers—long and thin as the Bouncing Ball Strangler's must be and hands as large. "Get him out here," Brown ordered. He smiled ruefully. He normally didn't give orders but put things as polite requests: "Let's do it this way," or "Maybe you might have him handle such and such?" In his heart he wanted to smash Sonny's face in. "Go on," Brown said evenly.

Sonny told the cops the entire story as they waited for Ray Pinker of the Scientific Investigation Department to lift the prints at both locations. At the same time, the men Thad had requested from downtown arrived at Shirley Payne's. He drove Sonny over toward Aunt Margaret's, stopped a half block before they got there, turned to look into the backseat and ordered, "Show us where Mrs. Miller lived, Sonny." Head lowered in shame, he took them to her door in the tiny bungalow court.

"After you killed Mrs. Miller, how did you leave her place, Sonny?" It was a trick question. Thad had not revealed to the press that the Strangler had left the back door ajar.

"I went out by the back door. I had left it partly open, I remember." That much was right. "Did you kill any more women?"

"I have no other slayings on my conscience, but I do have blackout spells sometimes. Mrs. Miller was the first. If you're thinking otherwise, well, you're wrong. If you hadn't gotten me, though, I'd have just gone on and on, killing and killing. In fact, I had another woman in mind besides Mrs. Parra to kill—my landlady on Mariposa, Elynore Riley." Sonny was sorry that he hadn't done her first since he hated that busybody. He thought about other victims and finally admitted he had raped a number of women he had picked up in bars. How many? He had assaulted eleven women and kidnapped a twelfth.

"But my memory is hazy," Sonny said and added that though his sex life had always been normal, he had gotten no sexual pleasure from his victims.

Hazy memory? Then, thought Thad, it was possible that he was the Bouncing Ball Strangler and didn't remember. They would see. God, he hoped so. After they had gathered the evidence, they booked Sonny at Hollywood Station on suspicion of triple murder. Before he was taken to his cell, Sonny took out the ten-dollar bill he had stolen from Aunty, unfolded it carefully and placed it on the desk in front of Lieutenant Crumly. Sonny smoothed it out. "Take five of it, and give it to my family," he said with tears in his eyes, "—use the rest to buy some flowers for Aunt Margaret."

On Tuesday afternoon Lieutenant Colwell and Sergeant R. R. Beck took Sonny Busch to Central Homicide. He was questioned by Captain Art Hertel in an office right down the hall from Thad Brown's.

Ever since the optician's arrest, Sergeant Beck had been watching for signs of remorse. Finally, on Tuesday morning, as Sonny was being booked into the County Jail, he saw another little crack in the iceberg persona. "I feel a little remorse now, but it is all done and there is nothing we can do now," said Sonny. He shrugged, smiled weakly, signed a confession, said he was sorry again, and was led away in cuffs to his cell.

Mother, dressed in a striped bathrobe, was led weeping from her apartment by a neighbor. The press was waiting outside.

On Wednesday afternoon, after a good night's sleep, Sonny underwent a four-hour-long lie detector test conducted by Lieutenant George Puddy. The examiner fashioned a measuring apparatus around Sonny's midsection, on one arm, and on the tips of two of his fingers. Telltale changes in Sonny's blood pressure—his heartbeat, the skin resistance set up by sweat gland activity—would transfer in squiggly or jagged lines on a chart by a moving recording pen. Puddy and Brown waited for the needle to swerve sharply, but that leap never came. "I picked up at least eleven women in bars, taking them to my apartment and attacking them," Sonny said. No movement of the inked needle. "A lot of people think I have a mother complex," he said after a moment. "They say that because I've always killed older women. But that had nothing to do with it. When I got that urge, I would have killed anyone, man or woman, young or old. Whoever was alone with me when I started to hear that noise in my head." The needle never moved. Sonny had told them the truth. But was it all of the truth?

Chapter Thirty-one
Thad and Sonny

T had sighed, frustrated. Okay, Sonny was telling the truth—as far as they knew, as far as the suspect knew, but had they asked the right questions? None of the queries had touched on the possibility there were more victims than Sonny was telling them about. Wasn't three plus thirteen enough? They had learned hardly any more than what he told them immediately upon his arrest. The results were not a total loss. That little bit more had cleared up a dozen cases—twelve rapes and a kidnapping. By *kidnap*, Thad assumed that Sonny meant poor Mrs. Parra, but now that he thought about it, Parra's had been an *attempted* kidnapping. To Sonny's way of reasoning it might not have counted.

"Some of his reactions merit further study," confided Lieutenant Puddy, who wanted to conduct a second lie test. Interviewing Sonny was like peeling back the layers of an onion. The DA's office charged three counts of murder and one of assault with intent to commit murder. Sonny wouldn't comment on the crime ring he had belonged to years ago, which had burglarized as many as a hundred Hollywood homes, and refused to name his accomplices. "They've served their prison time," he said, just as he had told Mother. "They don't deserve to be dragged into the limelight." Examiner Puddy believed Sonny was hiding more, but that afternoon Sonny was arraigned before Municipal Judge Louis Kaufman and held in County Jail without bail; in a press conference, Thad named Sonny as a mass killer. "If a murderer can get away with taking a thing as precious as a human life," he said, "then no one can expect to be safe from any crime."

An hour later the phone rang. Shirley Payne's son, Norris Wilkinson, in Las Vegas wanted to know what had become of his mother's three valuable diamond rings. "She always wore three rings," the son said. "They were missing when her body was found." Under intensive grilling, Sonny admitted he had given them to Ernie Shaffer after he killed Mrs. Payne. Detectives under Lieutenant Walter Colwell picked Shaffer up on Hollywood Boulevard to ask him about the rings. Shaffer told them he had panicked when he heard of Sonny's arrest in the papers. "I threw them in a trash can," he said. "He told me, 'I've done it again.' I asked him what he meant. He said, 'I've strangled another woman.'" I called the police on Monday, but I didn't give them any names. I just told them a fellow who lives in the area of Normandie and Sunset had committed some murders. Check your records."

"Well, congratulations, Mr. Good Citizen. Now you're an accessory to murder," Colwell said. Shaffer was booked and police announced they intended to seek a complaint against him on the grounds he had known about Sonny's murders and failed to report them. At first Shaffer agreed to take a polygraph test, but then backed down. "You guys are asking too many incriminating questions," he snapped. Meanwhile the heat was making everyone sick. Thousands flocked to the beaches as the mercury hit ninety-seven degrees by 1:55 P.M., then dropped slightly before climbing back to ninety-seven at 2:28 P.M. Within a few days, the temperature would finally fade to a "cool 89 degrees."

Jailers reported that in his cell Sonny was "like a zombie." Looking over Busch's interrogation, Thad Brown read that Sonny had seen *Psycho* just before the Labor Day slayings. Brown began to think he might have found the spark that had set off the dynamite that was Sonny Busch. Sonny didn't say that seeing *Psycho* specifically triggered the killings, yet mentioned the film each time he recounted his murders of Mrs. Payne and his aunt.

Reporters got hold of that information and played up the Hitchcock angle in all the papers—"mother fixation," "split personality," "shocking stabbing," and "Sonny has a mother fixation and split personality just like Norman Bates and even resembles him." "Did Movie Stir to Slay Three?" asked one paper in a headline. Another reported that, "Suspect Admits Hollywood Slaying After Seeing Hitchcock Thriller." The press named Sonny Busch the *Psycho* Killer.

Thad Brown was intrigued too and got Hitch on the phone. "I have absolutely nothing to say on the subject," the director said. The press spokesman for Paramount held off the reporters, saying, "Mr. Hitchcock has authorized me to state that the film *Psycho* was made purely for entertainment purposes and he cannot be held responsible for what someone may do after seeing his film." In a second statement Hitch said, "The movie couldn't cause a person to kill any more than any film where you see people killing each other. They see it on Westerns every night."

"I think it's awful," said Janet Leigh. "There must have been millions of people who saw this picture and nobody else was murdered." That was not entirely true.

Besides Sonny Busch, a Leroy Pinkowski had stabbed a girl to death and cited Hitch's movie as his inspiration. Hitchcock had a pat answer ready by then for both cases. "Those boys have killed before. I want to know what they saw those times, or did they do it after drinking chocolate milk."

Hitchcock declined to discuss any possible connection, but later made a comment in a debate with anti-violence guru and comic book censor Dr. Fredric Wertham. In 1954, Wertham's book, *Seduction of the Innocent*, detailed psychological damage purported to be inflicted on the nation's youth by comic books. Hearings before the Senate Sub-Committee on Juvenile Delinquency were held, which brought about the Comics Code Authority.

"Finally, there is the fact that Americans have made a cult of violence," Wertham said to Hitchcock. "Take a Los Angeles television station I know about. In one week's time, on programs appearing before

9:00 P.M., mind you, they showed 334 completed or attempted killings. And all that violence was displayed for children to see. This is a dangerous and vicious circle because a child's mind is like a bank—whatever you put in, you get back in ten years, with interest."

Hitchcock replied by referring to the *Psycho* Killer's murders, amplifying his stock answer. "Yes, but what about the so-called influences that are just afterthoughts? For example, there was a case in Los Angeles, I don't know whether the man is still in Death Row or not, but he committed—killed a woman and he said he did it after seeing *Psycho*. He had killed two other women before, so when the press called and asked if I had any comment, I said, 'Yes. I want to know the names of the movies he saw before he killed the other two, or did he kill the first one after drinking a glass of milk?" Hitchcock had Sonny's murders mixed—it was one strangling motivated by outrage over Caryl Chessman's execution, a man Sonny felt was innocent, then two murders and an attempted murder after seeing *Psycho*.

The two women Sonny killed that terrible Labor Day weekend had been cut with a knife after they were dead, an alteration in Sonny's MO made only after seeing *Psycho* an hour before. Up to that point, his murders had consisted only of strangling with his powerful hands. And Sonny had never wrapped a body before, as Norman did in a shower curtain, and never tried to get one into the trunk of his car to hide elsewhere.

"Violence, guns, killings, they are all around us," Wertham concluded. "And you know, Mr. Hitchcock, this affects your audience. All this exposure to violence desensitizes them. They want stronger and stronger stuff."

Hitch had famously said, "Television has brought back murder into the home—where it belongs."

Thad Brown was confident of a conviction in the Busch case. His two star witnesses were Magdalena Parra, whom Sonny had tried to throttle, and Sonny's landlady, Mrs. Elynore Riley. Both had been on Sonny's "Death List." "I guess I'm lucky to be alive," Magdalena said.

Finally, Thad went to talk to Mother. Sonny had talked about her constantly when he wasn't dozing. One big surprise lay ahead for Brown.

"Junior's never been normal," said Mae Busch. She alternately called him Junior and Sonny as she spoke and cried. "He's withdrawn and leads a secret life of his own."

"Secret life?"

"He's always been an outsider in the family. He has a terrible temper and he's always plotting. I could never do anything with him. My [late] husband had more patience with him than I had." The couple had operated Busch's Gardens for twenty years. "I guess I've been afraid something like this would happen someday. Junior was never violent toward me, but I've always felt afraid of him. I told my sister Margaret he might kill us someday in one of his fits."

Now Brown learned that Mae and Sonny had the same father.

Mother was actually Sonny's half-sister, though considerably older. Sonny's real mother had died when he was four years old, and when his father perished a few months later, the boy was sent to an orphanage in Scranton, Pennsylvania. Years later Mae Busch and her husband had given Sonny their name and raised him as their foster son. Now Thad understood a little Sonny's obsession with Caryl Chessman. When Caryl was nine, his mother was severely injured in a car crash, became paralyzed, and never walked again. He then developed debilitating bronchial asthma and rheumatic fever, which isolated him from his playmates. Sickly and alone, Caryl created a fantasy world to live in, and as a teen his criminal activities earned him respect for the first time among his peers. Chessman admitted his long string of offenses, twenty in one month in January 1948, but denied the offense for which he was placed on Death Row. Sonny too had been wrongly accused of a murder.

Mae, visibly upset as she spoke to Thad, said she refused to have anything more to do with Sonny until after her sister was buried.

Funerals were held on Friday, September 9, for two of Sonny's three victims. Mrs. Shirley Payne's at 12:30 P.M. and Mrs. Margaret Briggs's an hour later in the Wee Kirk o' the Heather at Forest Lawn Memorial Park. From his cell, Sonny said, "I don't care what happens now. I don't want my family to come here to see me in jail. I had to sweat it out alone for a long time, and that's the way it has to be now."

Janet Leigh and her husband, Tony Curtis, had attended the John

Fitzgerald Kennedy for President kickoff luncheon in California. "It was really a blockbuster," said Janet. The traffic jam had tied up over half of Beverly Hills as three of the Rat Pack, Frank Sinatra, Dean Martin, and Peter Lawford, attended. Janet participated in political rallies all over California, and November 8, 1960, was a jubilant date for her as JFK was elected the thirty-fifth president of the United States. The forty-three-year-old Massachusetts senator was the youngest president in history. After JFK won, Peter Lawford asked Janet to host a luncheon for Jackie Kennedy at the Curtis house. Tony felt very intimidated by Jackie's beauty, but she put him at ease.

"If my movie career was going great guns," Tony wrote later, "my personal life was in shambles . . . I wasn't sure exactly what [Janet] was going through. Perhaps she was having a midlife crisis; after all, she had married me when she was very young . . . her roles were getting better and better, but the bigger she became, the more discontented she was."

The LA Bouncing Ball Strangler, who targeted both young and old women, but especially elderly females, was still on the loose and no woman was safe from him. Sonny Busch was in custody and preparing to stand trial. Thad Brown thought about the two names Mother had for him, Sonny and Junior, as if he had two distinct personalities. What if it was Junior who had committed the other strangulations?

Thad got out the files. It made sense at first that Sonny had committed the crimes attributed to the Bouncing Ball Strangler. The rape–strangulation of elderly women was so rare, it barely showed on his statistical chart. Rape. Strangulation. It had to be the same killer. But then he remembered something that Sonny had said: "After I strangled them I disarrayed their clothes to make it look like a sex crime." "Make it look like?" Had Sonny restrained himself because he was related to some of his victims or because he had been interrupted? The Bouncing Ball Strangler *always* raped. Sonny sometimes didn't. Thad just didn't know what to think. If the two killers were separate, the Bouncing Ball Strangler was still out there stalking women. Who would be next, a young woman or an old woman?

Chapter Thirty-two
Freezing Water/Blazing Sun

T wo weeks before Jerry Schafer had to leave for London, he began shooting his "nudist clip-clop" in the windswept East Mojave Desert. Godforsaken little Searchlight would be a fantastic place to shoot a film—scrub-covered dunes, stately cactus, arid desert, abandoned mines, scaffolds and tailings in the center of town, even a ghost railway. The town unfolded against the backdrop of an impressive mountain range so magical that the great composer Scott Joplin had composed a haunting Rag in its honor.

Directly east of town lay Cottonwood Cove, a lovely expanse of the Colorado River, and the sixty-eight-mile slash of Lake Mojave, which was scattered with sandy beaches and sheer rock cliffs. Naturally, Schafer thought, there has to be a scene with the fully nude ladies splashing about in the frigid waters of Lake Mojave.

Marli Renfro had last been in the area in 1957 when she filmed a Lake Mojave Ranchos commercial. Back then, the producers, flush with money, had flown her, the cast, director William Brown, and a film crew to the lake in a couple of planes. This time, three years later, Marli was driven to the Lake Mojave shoot in a van. All of Schafer's female stars, reportedly carefully selected from 250 applicants, arrived in Searchlight about the same time, some in the same van. "If there were 250 applicants," Schafer said, "that's news to me. Casting was done very quickly." He had a shooting schedule of only seven days, the same time it took to shoot the *Psycho* Shower Sequence. It was still very early morning, and the long desert light set everything aglow. It was beautiful.

Marli studied the other women: Patti Brooks, an impish, pale-nippled nymph, was wearing a gingham shirt, blue jeans, and cowboy boots with a repeat olive leaf design. All the women wore boots because in many scenes they were to be their only costume. Blond and wacky Ginger Gibson's fancy tooled leather boots were entwined with rosebuds. Each pair was more elaborate than the preceding, but Marli's boots were the most embellished of them all with countless vines and flourishes. "I was wearing my own cowboy boots," she said. "I bought them when I was in Vegas."

The other girls were Barbara Martin, Sandy Silver, and Ginnie Gordon, whom Marli knew as *Playboy's* Miss January 1959. She and Ginnie had been photographed by the same photographer, Ron Vogel. Undressed, Ginnie would be spectacular—with classic lines and unshakable poise. Was there anything more beautiful than a woman? It would be fun to compare figures in person, Marli thought. She would have the opportunity because they would be playing topless blackjack dealers in the first scene and later perform totally nude in the desert and at Lake Mojave.

None of the "dudless quintet of dude ranch fillies" had been accustomed to the discomforts of location shooting—especially in the raw. Who was? It wasn't something that happened every day. Marli might be the exception. Remarkably fit from swimming, deep-sea fishing, dancing, horseback riding, hours of nude volleyball, and hiking in the wilderness, Marli was the total outdoors person. But it didn't really matter. All the women had set their minds to cooperating without complaint. It might not be so bad. There were natural wonders—hot springs, blue skies forever, low humidity, and low rainfall, the stunning lake and desert and scenic trails through passes where ghostly miners had ridden with saddlebags filled with gold.

Larry Chance (aka Don Kenney), the cowboy lead, arrived—ruggedly handsome, unshaven, and grinning at his good fortune to be involved with such lovely women. A minute later, the seven-man film crew and Jerry Schafer, the writer and producer of the film, pulled up and parked next to a huge Joshua tree and a wooden corral. Schafer, in a plaid shirt and dark pants, piled out and walked over to his actors. He seemed genial to Marli and looked very fit.

She studied the crew as they dashed for a patch of shade. The sound-man cut a dashing figure in his aviator glasses, knee-high boots, black shirt, tight-fitting jeans, and light windbreaker. He placed a huge generator on the ground and unwound a long cord attached to a microphone. The cameraman, in dark jeans, desert boots, and a baseball cap with a large dollar sign, zipped up his jacket against the rising wind. He screwed his bulky camera, the type seen in the Pathé newsreels that preceded shorts, cartoons, and features in theaters, onto a springy double-legged tripod. On its six legs, it looked like a tarantula stalking over the sand.

Schafer went over the shooting script. There were two interior sets (the inside of the El Rey Casino and the dilapidated brick jail) and considerable exteriors, all featuring Searchlight's rustic buildings, huge Joshua trees, mines, the El Rey Motel, the desert, and Lake Mojave as seen from frigid Cottonwood Cove. Schafer had broken the shoot into six or seven days—two or three days at the Casino, then the Jail Scene, the outskirts of town with the Cowboy's accident and a fist fight for two days, the desert (the second most difficult part—now that summer had passed, the area was prone to windstorms), and finally on the fifth and possibly sixth day the lake—the most difficult part. In June the lake water is about fifty-one degrees and in July and August around eighty-one. But this time of the year the water would be freezing. Yes, he would save that scene for last. There might be desertions, and he wanted to keep his voluptuous models happy.

The girls checked into the El Rey's motel. "It was nothing really fancy," said Marli. "We shared rooms; we ate there." There was a heated pool, though. Outside, Ginger was stripping down to pose for a men's magazine covering the shoot. Wearing only her boots, she climbed onto a wooden corral railing and sat there as Larry pretended to come up behind and goose her. She opened her mouth in shock and crossed her eyes. Just across the road from the motel were Mary's Girls. Willie would abandon his experiment in legalized prostitution in a year. Marli wondered what the girls must think of Ginger in boots and nothing else. She conjectured they must be thinking this was a very unusual kind of horse opera.

"We had breakfast before shooting the casino scene," said Marli. In the other room, Lucky Willie Martello, the proprietor, was preparing for his cameo as "The Pit Boss." He noosed his string tie, a long wide ribbon, and redundantly tied a kerchief over that. He fitted his trademark white hat on his head. In the other room, the girls were putting on clothes that would only have to come right off. Marli dressed in the identical El Rey costume as Willie, but without the white hat. "When the others are dressed in clothes, they all have El Rey bow ties on," she said. The ties came in two colors, brown and black. One side read "EL REY RESORT" in white letters and the other side "SEARCHLIGHT NEVADA." Willie was making sure his beloved casino and town got proper billing in every shot. Willie hadn't missed a trick. His drink caddies showed both a crown, the El Rey logo, and a searchlight.

"I had my hair up in a French twist, but a very casual French twist," Marli said. "I had it both up and down during the film." In her costume, Marli walked onto the set, which was the actual casino with a thick red carpet. Behind the bar was a framed picture of all seven Martello brothers as youngsters dressed in Native American costume. Only Willie, the rebel, was barefoot. Before there were telephone lines to Searchlight, Willie had had to send supply orders to Vegas by carrier pigeon. "It was a small room crowded with a craps table, a roulette wheel, slot machines and three blackjack tables."

Round lights set into the ceiling ran in rows and in front of the bar was a line of eight plush red stools. "I played Luci Mae, a blackjack dealer. In the scene I was dealing twenty-one. In the first hand I dealt Willie he got a blackjack." As Marli dealt Larry the Cowboy a card, her blouse vanished. No one else in the casino noticed except him. Willie looked nonchalant, but Larry, following the script, was in shock. "There's footage of us dressed and undressed, so that took up a lot of time. With Larry coming back in so we could be undressed for those shots, that was it. It took two days. I think they could have finished in one day. I don't know why they didn't. There wasn't that much and it doesn't take that long to film." Maybe the filmmakers were having too much fun.

"Actually, I shot in the Casino for three days," Schafer told me later. "We did B roll one day when Marli wasn't there." In the next shot, Patti, topless now, leaned over a pile of chips, her huge breasts completely obscuring them. At a table behind Marli, Ginger was completely naked from the rear, natural and zaftig.

"I had to use that girlfriend of the backer," Schafer said, "but I didn't use her as one of the nude girls. I told the backer I didn't think it would be good for her to appear nude in the film and thankfully he agreed so we placated them both by using her in the casino as a *dressed* dealer inside the casino. She wasn't exactly a Powers Model. It was insane! I shot the picture using masters whenever possible without doing any coverage—no two shots, no over the shoulder, no close shots, no nothing. All I could think about was getting it done before I had to leave for England at the end of the week."

Reporters from various men's magazines were getting it all down. Schafer still didn't have a distributor for his low-budget nudie or a name for the production company, which the writers variously listed as Decameron Productions, Searchlight, and Premier Pictures. The freelancers even made up their own titles. Max Harris, positive the film would be censored, called it *Meet Me at the Harem* (a moniker obviously not meant for Lone Ranger fans).

"A herd of bosomy beauties romp bareback and bare chested over the Nevada desert in the most 'adult' of adult westerns ever to wage a last-ditch stand against the TV scalping of box offices," he wrote. "Low britches at high noon . . . a vacationing glamour photographer falls from his horse and awakens to find the dude ranch a nude ranch where dears and antelope play in their rawhides. Each gal appears—by mirage or miracle—delightfully undraped."

While they were shooting that first day, a wild burro wandered into the Casino. Any domesticated burros who escaped into the Mojave eventually ran wild. Most of them would rather eat succulent desert grasses and forbes, but settled for browse in the scrub in the morning. At noon, the burros moved to lunch in the deep, shaded riparian depressions. In the afternoon, they migrated into desert washes to escape the blazing sun and biting winds.

Thus everyone was surprised when at 10:00 A.M. a wild burro wandered onto the set and nuzzled up to Willie who, without missing a beat, began feeding it. As soon as the burro, which apparently made a habit of eating at the El Rey, was full, he trudged solemnly out the door and back down into the desert to join the bighorn sheep, desert tortoises, and jackrabbits.

Finished for the day, the girls returned to their motel rooms and through sand-pitted windows watched a magnificent sunset. That night temperatures in the living ghost town were a mild forty-two degrees. Marli watched the shadows of twenty-foot-tall yuccas (Spanish for any desert plant that bears white panicled flowers) and heard night lizards scurrying from the trees' decaying bases. She fell asleep early and arose with the sun the next day anxious to get to work.

"After we filmed inside the casino there was a fight scene," Marli said. "Larry, the fella who sees the girls topless, runs for help and complains to the local sheriff, then brings him back to show him the nude women. They go into the casino, and of course we're all dressed. All of a sudden they start to leave and Larry gets a headache and he sees all the girls nude. So he gets in a fight with the sheriff and pulls a gun on him. Naturally he's arrested and chucked into the town's brick jail as a lunatic."

Behind the bars and crouching just out of camera range, the clapper board man slapped the boards, and Ginnie, a firm, athletic woman, an outdoor sportsman like Marli—muscular, powerful, and lithe—did the Jail House Scene. When extolling her virtues, caption writers tended to run though the "A"s—"adorable, animated, audacious . . . loves auto racing, aquamarines, ankle bracelets." Ginnie was born on All Saint's Day, in Chaplin, West Virginia, and her ancestors hailed from Alsace-Lorraine. She was so popular as a pinup (so far this year she had appeared in *Cloud 9*, *Hi-Life*, and two consecutive issues of *Adam*) that Hef demanded all future Playmates and pictorial girls sign exclusivity contracts forbidding them to appear nude in any non-*Playboy* project for the two years after their *Playboy* appearances.

They reset the camera and, as Larry Chance peered out from behind bars, Ginnie suddenly became completely nude. She had lovely nipples, rosy and perfectly circular, which in the sun took on a coppery color that matched the color of her lips precisely. Her breasts, thirty-seven-Ds, were natural, perky, weighty, and pointed straight out in a gravity-defying display. Ginnie redressed in a white, long-sleeved blouse, pulled on her tight jeans, re-knotted her El Rey tie, and left the jail to see Marli, Ginger, Sandy, and Patti posing on the hood of a black and white police cruiser for an *Adam* photographer. Marli was dressed in a long black dress. Patti's black toreador pants had laces on the sides that showed her nude legs and hips. Ginnie climbed onto the vehicle and they all mugged. Schafer shouted they were finished for the day, and the girls climbed down. Blond Ginger, in a short white shirt with black buttons, put on her sunglasses, stretched out on a slope of small rocks and ragged grass, locked her arms behind her head, and dozed. In the lingering twilight every noise was magnified. Marli sketched slender banana yuccas with their curved blue-green spines in watercolor and painted mound cacti with their overlapping red spines held as if clasping their bellies. Traces of scarlet flowers bloomed along their stems.

The next day, Schafer filmed the girls, nude except for their boots, at the El Rey Motel. As they huddled under the shade of a tall Joshua tree, Marli was next to Ginnie who was taller than her, five-foot six or more. The cameraman leaned forward to take a reading, placing a tape against one taut buttock after another. Each cheek, round as a melon, vibrated with energy. Most of the women were dancers and it was hard for them to remain still. To avoid interfering with the cinematographer's calculations the girls laced their hands on their heads and stood bolt upright. After he had his measurements, the girls folded their arms under their breasts, not out of modesty, but to warm themselves against the rising morning gale. "The hearty beauties brave a desert windstorm while the cameraman takes a light reading," scribbled the man from *Adam*.

Ginnie hated heights. "How high is Searchlight, anyway," she asked Marli. "Over three and a half thousand feet," Marli replied. Marli was not the only cast member with acting experience. Ginnie had wrapped *The Ruined Bruin*, filmed a layout for it for *Adam*, and was already contracted to play Vultura in *Surfside 77*, a comedy about an insurance investigator allergic to naked women, another repressed childlike hero, like the Cowboy and the Peeper. *Surfside's* director, Lee Frost, would later star Ginnie in *The Animal*, a parody of Hitch's *Rear Window* about a psycho peeper watching through a high-powered telescope. In his film, he would manage to evoke both Hitchcock and Coppola and lead the rather innocent nudie cuties into the darker territory of "the roughies."

The girls moved outside of Searchlight to the High Desert, so huge it encroaches into northwest Arizona. "We spent two days in the desert," Schafer said, "where we shot Larry Chance falling off his horse and some B roll riding scenes. Larry and I did a huge fight scene on some rocks." At 10:00 A.M. Schafer filmed Larry riding into town on horseback and leading a pack mule laden with canteens, mining equipment and grub. "Larry Chance, as the Cowboy, fell off his horse and hit his head on a boulder," Marli explained, "and had trouble seeing. From then on, whenever he had a pain in his neck, all of a sudden any women in view would be topless." When it came time to take a brutal spill, it would not be Larry falling off his horse, but ex-stuntman Schafer dressed in the Cowboy's black hat, red kerchief, gray denim jacket, and jeans. "Larry's on his horse leading the burro," Marli said, "when, according to the script, he sees a bunch of cattle going across the screen." "No cows," Schafer said. "I was lucky enough to have money to pay for the horse."

"I'm wearing red pants," Marli continued, "and walking a burro with another girl when Larry gets a pain in his neck and he sees me topless." Next he sees her totally nude among the rocks as a seductress. In a long sequence Marli waggles her butt, then undulates. Her nudity and red hair are startling among the rocks. A cool breeze comes up and her areolas, the size of quarters, shrink out of sight and leave behind erect, reddish pencil erasers. Larry, having seen Marli only in still photographs, was shocked to see how pliable her body was in motion.

Marli pulled on her red pants and, topless, affectionately nuzzled a white-nosed burro with her cheek and rubbed its ears. She was only imitating Willie Martello's interaction with the burro in the casino. Luckily, this burro wasn't a wild one because they often bite. It surprised Marli to see in the desert coyotes and roadrunners just like the ones in the Warner Brothers cartoons.

That evening, Larry and the girls watched the sunset. Marli wondered what the heat would be like tomorrow. In June and July, East Mojave temperatures average 108 degrees; some days in August reach 120 degrees on the valley floors. Now it was relatively cool, but Schafer decided to shoot underground the next day to avoid what promised to be an unseasonably hot day.

Marli and the others passed decrepit shacks among the cacti and spring yucca plants. They came to the rock-strewn Searchlight Cemetery: boulders in loopy rectangles and little crosses of sticks marking the graves. The girls started along rusted tracks, the remains of the Searchlight gold rush at its zenith a hundred years ago. G. F. Colton discovered gold ore west of town in the Duplex Mine. The Quartette Mining Company, north of the Duplex, doubled the area's total output, and helped build a twenty-three-mile-long narrow-gauge railroad, The Barnwell & Searchlight Railway Company. The line ran downhill to the company's mill and connected Searchlight with the main Santa Fe line from Needles to Mojave. Marli could almost hear the wail of the ghost train that had derailed forty years ago with its last shipment of gold and unique rare turquoise. It never reached the company mill on the Colorado.

"We followed the train tracks," Marli said, "and that day worked in the mines." Gold mines were all around them. South of Searchlight was the Berlock Mine. Eastward were Fourth of July Mountain and the Boston Searchlight, Oakland, Pittsburgh, Swickard, and Big Casino Mines. West of Searchlight the Parallel Mine swept away at a steep angle. All had played out long ago.

During the Mine Scene, Larry the Cowboy entered his mine and found the shaft and its entrance filled not with gold but with nude women. After they had the scene in the can, the desert wind whipped up to such a degree that it threatened to close down shooting for the day. The gale came roaring out of the west funneled by the bottleneck of the Tehachapi range between the town of Mojave and Edwards Air Force

Base. Santa Ana wind events run the opposite way as hot air from the desert blows into the LA Basin.

Around noon, the wind grew scalding and fierce. Sand and debris were flying everywhere, and little whirlwinds, known as dust devils, were twisting in the sand. Suddenly, a prickly cactus came tumbling along the sand, grew airborne, and hit Marli in her lower back. The wound was painful enough that Schafer suggested she return to the motel, but Marli wanted to continue. By evening she had not only erased the accident from her mind, but had to be reminded it had happened at all.

On the last day of filming, everyone—actors, writers, and crew: about fourteen people in all—traveled downhill to Cottonwood Cove. Schafer told the girls that today was the swimming scene where they all give the Cowboy one last shock. Marli considered herself only a fair swimmer, but then she tended to underestimate her abilities. "Okay, but I'm not really good, good, good," she admitted. She waded in and for hours they swam and dove in the icy water. The water temperature in July and August is quite warm, but it was nothing like that today. "It was in 1960 when I shot *The Wide Open Spaces*," Schafer said. "I'm sure of that, but like I said, I can't remember the exact dates. We spent a day at the lake."

"Well, as you can see," Marli said, "our nipples are really up so it wasn't warm."

Moving his tripod along the shore, the cameraman used the sun as hard backlighting on their hair, to highlight their bodies and separate them from the water background. The mountains were reflected in the clear water and Ginger, in up to her knees, was reflected full length. The cameraman loved working with water. It is always complimentary and never detracts from the figure. He noticed that the blue was terrific for the warm tones of the girls' skin.

The clapboard man in his garish shirt waded in and stood shivering next to Ginger. He had chalked the words "SEARCHLIGHT PR. Lake Girls, mid-lake Scene 3 Take 2" on his board. When the women came out of the icy water they tried to warm up before reentering—flapping their arms and running around. But between the sun and cold water, the girls were now sunburned *and* chilled. Patti, Ginnie, and Ginger decided to nude sunbathe on the shore. None of the crew seemed to notice. Marli decided to join them. By now the men had grown used to her nudity just as the grips on the set of *Psycho* had, but she put on her bikini anyway. "Marli is one of the few actresses who must dress to relax," Max Harris wrote. While the others looked about for suntan oil, she didn't. "I don't get sunburned," Marli explained. "You see, I was a nudist. I had a suntan all over. I didn't have any tan lines."

Marli lifted her black sunglasses and peered north toward Copper Mountain Canyon, Painted Canyon, and Box Cove. At its widest point, ragged Lake Mohave is not more than four miles across and its length is confined between the walls of Pyramid, Painted, and Black Canyons. Just offshore, Marli observed a fixed navigational light swinging sluggishly in the rising wind. She sat up on her elbows.

West Lake Mojave was teeming with striped bass, but Cottonwood Cove was packed with largemouth bass and rainbow and cutthroat trout. Marli loved fishing, would rather do that than anything. From time to time she saw a trout shatter the placid surface. Just below the surface, crappies and channel catfish swam in the cold water.

In the distance, a black thundercloud was dragging toward the cove. Moisture from the Sonoran Desert to the east was propelling monsoonal moisture west as Schafer got his crew going again. They were about to lose the day. The *Adam* reporter scribbled: "The girls shiver apprehensively before re-entering the water, so cold it literally turns them blue."

In the final scene, the Cowboy rows a white skiff to the middle of the lake where he believes he can avoid his "curse." When the boat capsizes, he comes up to beautiful nude girls swimming around him and becomes hysterical. According to Schafer's original script the Cowboy wakes up in bed in 1960. Was it a dream? *No!* There are the girls in his bedroom.

"It was a fun time," Schafer said later. "And one of the first of its kind. The ladies turned up topless. Wow, what a deal!!!! Shocking. There might even be a story to the picture." At the end of their six-day desert ordeal, Patti, Larry, and Ginger expressed relief in front of their motel that in spite of the boiling sun and ice-water baths, they had stuck it out to the end. "Thank God, it's over!" sighed Ginger.

But Marli liked the desert and thought it might the perfect place for her to live out her later years. They had finished nearly one year after Hitchcock had wrapped principal photography on Psycho, only Hitch had been nine days over schedule and Schafer had been right on the money: seven days and under budget, not that the budget had been that big in the first place.

"My editor got sick and wasn't able to edit the film," Schafer said. "The man who introduced me to the backer of the film told me that he knew a kid who was going to UCLA who was a brilliant editor and he asked me to look at his reel . . . and I did . . . and I was impressed. The kid was Francis Ford Coppola. Although I didn't meet him, I agreed that he could edit the film because I had to leave for England. Seven days after we wrapped the film I was on my way to England and Richard took over the movie and I pretty much had nothing to say about it."

Chapter Thirty-three
Coppola

I n the last months of Marli's incredible year, the general public gradually began to learn the secret of Alfred Hitchcock's shower that so
many Hollywood insiders, writers, and movie buffs either knew or
suspected. For a year, Hitch had denied there had been a body double for Janet Leigh in *Psycho*. So had Janet Leigh, as strongly as she
could until it was impossible to deny. The truth slowly leaked out in
the unlikely venue of men's magazines. A January *Mr.* article called
Marli "The Girl From *Psycho*." Even Hitchcock capitulated later to
the curious and provided a factual overview of the Shower Sequence
to François Truffaut, saying he used a naked model who stood in for
Janet Leigh. "We only showed Miss Leigh's hands, shoulders and head.
All the rest was the stand-in," he said. That had been Marli Renfro,
a famous not-famous face and figure. An essay in *The Dude* revealed
Psycho's secret too:

> When writer Robert Bloch and director Alfred Hitchcock . . . came
> up with the ultimate Grande Guignol, *Psycho* . . . little did you know

about their well-kept secret . . . Now did you really think that was Mrs. Tony Curtis in the shower scene? Wrong. Hollywood's best kept secret about the most astonishing double ever used in cinematic history is now revealed . . . No, that was not Janet Leigh you saw seeming cavorting in the nude while the knife went about its bizarre business . . . No indeed; it was Marli Renfro, girl double . . . The ebullient, effervescing Miss Renfro . . . has the particular physique that all West Coast ladies seem to be gifted with.

An October *Sir!* article, "Marli Renfro: Nude but No Corpse," mentioned her part in *Psycho*. Caryle Blackwell shot her as the *Modern Man* cover girl in a sunny garden, her red-blond hair blown by the wind and breasts threatening to burst from her low-cut blue knit sweater. Her face was everywhere—three pages in the April *Ace*, in *USA*, the May *Adam*: "Marli, An Essay in Perfection." Russ Meyer's friend Paul Morton Smith mentioned Marli's Western nudie and "exclusive coverage on what promises to be one of the funniest and most entertaining films ever to be shown." She was a full-color centerfold in July *Modern Man* and in August:

> The soon-to-be-released movie is the work of a stunt man turned film-maker named Jerry Schafer, who not only wrote, directed, and produced the bawdy affair, but also took the tumbles for the leading man. . . . If the film ever gets by the censor's scissors, the charge into theatre seats will be like the last minute cavalry charge saving the last minute TV scalping at the box office.

In September Marli was displayed as an "Uncovered Cover Girl":

> Shapely Marli Renfro is an outdoor gal, and although outdoor gals are not uncommon, shapely ones are, as a certain movie producer recently learned. Needing five alfresco femmes to populate an eye-popping reel titled *Meet Me at the Harem*, he searched for chicks who weather the sizzling sun wearing nothing more than lipstick. . . . She

performs some sightly scenes destined to jar even the most jaded viewers from their seats . . . Five beautiful nudes, plus one bashful cowboy equal sex in the sagebrush for the most hilarious horse opera ever filmed . . . The gambling casino is suddenly filled with naked girls . . . the sexiest hallucinations that ever bewildered a cowboy . . . Schafer's nonprofessional bit players behaved like true Western gentlemen in the midst of such unaccustomed nudity.

"I remember," Schafer said, "that a newspaper writer, Paul Coats, entitled his article: 'Billy the Kid sings: "There's Nothing Like a Dame."'" Magazines summed up the plot: "Schafer's hero is a bashful guy who can't stand nudity in any form. He tries to escape the lovely nudes, but they materialize everywhere—in a herd of cattle, a mine shaft, a gambling casino."

A photo story, "Marli Renfro in Scenes from a Barechested Western . . . a Rootin' Rawhide Reel," was published just as gossip spread that *Wide Open Spaces* was so bad that Schafer couldn't sell it. He admitted it was a very controversial film for the time, "one of the first major theatrical releases to feature topless women." With all this Western nudity in the can just screaming to be seen, the backer began searching for a way to salvage his investment.

A few days later, Schafer heard that Marli Renfro, who was in more scenes than anyone in his movie, had made another unreleased nudie called *The Peeper* with a young UCLA student, Francis Ford Coppola. The only thing *The Peeper* and *Wide Open Spaces* had in common was Marli. What if they expanded the redhead's part, named both her characters Lucie Mae and hired a director to transform two unsalable movies into one bankable film?

"I made a short twelve minute film called *The Peeper*," Francis wrote. "We tried to sell it, and the only buyer had this black-and-white Western about a cowboy who keeps seeing cows as naked girls."

This made Schafer laugh. "Very interesting comments from FFC," he said, "and honest inasmuch as his memory is concerned. But then, that's what makes him such a wonderful and talented director—always has been. However, the film was about a cowboy who got thrown off his horse and hit his head on a boulder. Thereafter, every time he saw a woman, she appeared to be naked."

"Some people saw [*The Peeper*] and offered to buy it," Coppola said later," but they themselves already had shot a vast amount of footage of a Western nudie . . . a film the distributors had but couldn't release (that I had nothing to do with) . . . It was unwatchable. They wanted to inter-cut my film with theirs to leaven it and thus make the package sellable. So they bought out the short, and gave me $500. So we devised a plot gimmick whereby both characters meet and tell their stories."

"Soon after shooting in Searchlight," Marli said, "I filmed another movie at a ranch south of Vegas called *Off with Your Shirts!* (I get the two mixed up sometimes, especially the people who were in them) and while I was waiting for it to come out, I get married. So I was surprised when the producers called me."

"Marli," they said, "we want to combine both films, *Wide Open Spaces* and *The Peeper*, because you are in both. We want you to do some tie-ins."

"Sure!" she said. "I'm excited."

"So they hired Francis to edit the film," Marli added, "and somehow tie the two pictures together and recreate the story line. It seemed like a difficult task, but he was a very talented guy. It wasn't the way he had planned it but the combined film would be Francis's first professional booking in the film industry as a director."

Francis excised a scene with Ginger wearing a white blouse, black jeans, and boots and Larry, clean-shaven and well-dressed. As Ginger pours coffee her blouse vanishes and Larry backs away in disbelief. He deleted a scene with a psychiatrist (similar to Simon Oakland summing up the plot in *Psycho* or the ending of *Mr. Teas* where the psychiatrist is a topless woman). "When the hero visits a psychoanalyst [Lou Scarcelli] for—of all the dumb things—a cure, the malady becomes contagious, and the doc also 'suffers' the illusions, thereby allowing the story to con-tinue through reel after reel of scenic western wonders and southern exposures." Francis cut the fight scenes in the casino and on the rocks along with all the dialogue in Schafer's film.

With the beginning and middle of the film in place, Coppola still had two different endings. In *The Peeper* the little man gets beaten by an outraged mob of feminists and do-gooders who invade the strip club; in Schafer's film the Cowboy swims away after seeing all the nude women around him.

"The producers called a few weeks later," Marli said, "and said, 'We're all set for filming the additional scenes,' and gave me the address. It was about that time I found out I was pregnant, so I'm getting ready to go to the studio and my husband says, 'No way. You're not going.' 'I don't show anything.' 'You're not going.' Just like that. I had to go on the day of my shoot to say I wouldn't be there. You have no idea how bad I felt. It was awful."

Without Marli's new bridges, director Jack Hill had to be hired to shoot fresh sequences as connecting footage to present the scenes as flashbacks and give the stylistically diverse sequences a sense of continuity. In the new story line, two hypocritical bluenoses meet at a Sunset Strip burlesque house to stage a blackout at midnight and shut it down. First they get drunk and tell Coppola's *Peeper* story and the story of Schafer's cowboy who sees naked girls. Francis spliced it together to encompass both story lines, cut it to sixty-eight minutes and retitled *Meet Me Tonight for Sure* as *Tonight for Sure!* "Sixty to 70 percent of it was not my work," he admitted, "but I was so eager for recognition . . . so thrilled to see my name on a film . . . that I shot the credit sequence and printed 'Directed by Francis Ford Coppola' up on the screen!" The final title credits read written by Jerry Schafer and Francis Ford Coppola and produced and directed by Francis Ford Coppola. "In fact I was the editor and had made the original short about a man eavesdropping on the photo session."

"Do you have any idea how many people have taken credit for my work or simply not given me credit at all?" Schafer told Andy Martello. "It isn't that big a deal. The only place I really want to see my name is when it follows the words: 'Pay to the Order Of!' I see, or at least I think I see what Francis was trying to do by putting the two stories together."

"Francis did direct quite a bit of *Tonight*," Marli said, "—with a stopwatch." The film featured a score by Carmine Coppola, Francis's father, who wrote music for his later films. After Roger Corman, king of low-budget B-movies, purchased the rights to two Soviet films with elaborate special effects, he needed some cheap labor to edit and dub them. "So I contacted the Film Department at UCLA," Corman said, "and asked them to send some students along. I talked to several."

"I heard in school that Corman was looking for some kind of assistant," Francis wrote. "I remember my phone was ready to be cut off, because I hadn't paid it and I called the lady who was handling affairs at Corman's office and told her I got the message late and wanted to be considered. 'I'll call you back and tell you what I think,' she said. 'Send over some of your writing.' So I'm sitting by the phone saying, 'Please don't cut off!' And sure enough it rang." The phone was cut off a couple of hours later.

"I talked to several and chose Francis," Corman said. Francis shot special effects scenes for *Battle Beyond the Sun* and a "girl-laden, sex-ridden, conglomeration of nonsense" from Germany. Francis was to film twelve minutes of three-dimensional color sequences to insert into the original black-and-white footage of *Mit Eva Fing die Sunde* (*The Playgirls and the Bellboy*). He got to film Meyer's bountiful discovery, June "The Bosom" Wilkinson, featured in *Playboy* in June, July, August, and October, and in November in a feature titled "The Bosom Revisits *Playboy*."

As Francis filmed Kelly Meyers, Sherry Daniels, and Linda Douglas sitting topless at their dressers, one girl came to him and said, "I'm only seventeen and my father is going to kill me." Francis said, 'Well, okay, leave your brassiere on." So there were these four girls, plus one who had a bra on," he said, "and I got fired because the producers were complaining they had paid the girls $500." The same amount Hitch had paid Marli to body double the most famous scene in movie history.

Chapter Thirty-four
The El Rey Fire

Marli had moved from Santa Monica in early summer 1961 when all the beach-goers began parking their cars in front of her house, leaving her a long walk home. She had really loved that house and listening to the waves crash. In her new apartment on Laurel Avenue, south of Sunset Boulevard, she had almost forgotten the long-delayed *Tonight for Sure!* Then on January 21, 1962, a late-night phone call reminded her of those happy days. The day in the desert around Vegas had begun cold—sixty-three degrees in the morning—and by night had plunged to forty-four degrees with blistering heat in between. Not far from the Strip, things got much hotter in tiny Searchlight. The Tony Lovello Revue, five musicians (Joe Veronese on drums), two girl singers, and a handful of gorgeous showgirls had just finished the first of three shows and left the stage to applause. Tony Lovello unstrapped his accordion, placed it on a chair in his dressing room, then sauntered into the busy kitchen to cadge a couple of thick hamburgers from Chef Luigi Scirocco, whom Willie had imported from LA.

As Tony entered, he saw the kitchen staff gathered around the big stove waving their aprons into a column of black smoke. A huge grease fire blazing under the hood leaped out of control and began crawling along the ceiling. Seeing the cooks' battle to extinguish the fire was hopeless, Tony raced down the hall to the dancers' area. "Girls, get out of your dressing room as soon as possible," he cried. "Throw all your costumes and belongings out the window!" They made from five to seven costume changes for each show so the pile of costumes on the ground outside was considerable. Tony yelled to his band. "Don't ask questions! Get to the bandstand and pack up!"

By now the pit bosses were gathering up money and stuffing it into their aprons and Willie was ordering folks to file out in an orderly fashion. Within ten minutes, the entire building was engulfed in flames. Searchlight's volunteer fire department, responsible for all fires within an area of twenty miles around the town, responded in two fire trucks. Arms of fire were shooting fifty feet high. In the flat desert the flames were visible for a great distance and attracted fire departments from Vegas and Boulder City. Three trucks responded and tried to contain the blaze, but had no better luck than the Searchlight volunteers were having.

Willie, his white suit streaked with soot, fought his way through the fire line and filmed the hottest part with his eight-millimeter camera. He might salvage something in the form of publicity—if he could get the film to the Vegas TV stations before their deadline. Only a trickle was coming from the firemen's hoses. The lines had failed or were out of water. Willie knew there was no chance of saving the El Rey and strode away as if washing his hands of the whole thing. As he passed the firefighters, he yelled out, "Oh, piss on it, boys. Just piss on it!" When he saw Tony and his Quintet, he ran over to make sure they were all right. "Come see me tomorrow and I'll pay you," Willie said. More bad news: $100,000 in checks and cash had been lost and he couldn't get his film developed in time for the Vegas television stations.

Within hours of the complete destruction of his casino his luck turned again. Willie sold the site and several other buildings where Mary and her girls had worked for $1.5 million to the First Capital Development Corporation, a Reno investment firm. They intended to build a

$1.7-million hotel casino with three hundred rooms there. Not only that, but the El Rey was fully insured, and Willie was repaid for the $300,000 loss. They didn't call him Lucky Willie for nothing. The next day he called Tony Lovello into his makeshift office across the street. "I want to pay you and the boys for the entire week," Willie said. "Pay off the whole contract."

"No, no, Willie," Tony said. "You have enough problems."

"Well, when I rebuild I'll invite you back."

After Tony left, Willie walked across the highway to survey the smoking ruins of his dream. All that was left was a concrete slab. Smoldering in the ashes were his hopes for tiny Searchlight. He had been the town's sole employer, its whole economy.

Marli hung up after hearing the El Rey was lost. The fire recalled to her the burning of the El Rancho Vegas. What was there about flaming redheads and burning casinos? She recalled the young couple that had extinguished the fire in her burning car. Marli laughed. Where was that couple when the El Rey burned? Schafer's still unreleased first nudie Western had outlived its setting.

Willie would rebuild the El Rey Casino, but it wasn't the same. He would run it for the next ten or eleven years, then let the property go to the city; they would turn it into Searchlight's new senior center.

Chapter Thirty-five
The Bouncing Ball Strangler

That had Brown just didn't understand. As he scanned the papers, his mouth tightened into a straight line. He lit his pipe and bit down hard on the mouthpiece. The string of rapes and strangulations of elderly women had ceased, but they had stopped for long periods before. Gaps were part of the Bouncing Ball Strangler's MO. Sure, the LAPD had had a number of false alarms and were making extra patrols, but was the Bouncing Ball Strangler still out there waiting to kill?

His crimes alone made him unique. It should be easy to recognize any future assault and murders he might commit. It was rare to rape and then kill senior victims. Brown went over the pattern in his mind. Something set the strangler off. What was it? Sonny Busch had undergone what is known as a build-up state just before his attacks—restlessness, a high level of anxiety, and increased motor activity. There had been that roar in his head. How did he select his victims—lovable silver-haired old ladies and beautiful young women? Brown centered the photo in its silver frame on his desk. His face grew grim as he cleaned the glass with a tissue and stood the frame upright again. Though Brown's department had advanced scientific methods, he had never forgotten his mentor, the detective who had broken him into police work. That old cop had only a seventh-grade education, but he knew people inside and out. "He taught me how to mix with the people in a murder case to figure them out," Thad said. "That's what counts in solving a murder—getting inside the suspect's mind. People murder people out of love, hate, greed, or revenge or because they're doped up or crazy, but a good detective has to get inside them to find out who and why.

"Solving murders under tremendous pressure requires the most intensive work it's possible to give. An effective investigation means death is reduced and society is protected. Just as the death penalty is a deterrent to crime, so is a well-constructed case that leads to a murder conviction."

That afternoon Detective Sergeant Beck received a call from the Hawthorne, New York, police in reference to Brown's probe of the eleven unsolved Los Angeles slayings attributed to the Bouncing Ball Strangler. "We need to know if Sonny Busch was in New York State on July 29, 1960," the officer said. "A sketch drawn from descriptions of a man seen at the murder scene of Carol Segretta, a twenty-four-year-old Hawthorne schoolteacher shot to death in her car, resembles him: gangling, bespectacled . . . " Thad Brown questioned Sonny about the Segretta homicide, but that period was a blank to him and without additional evidence he was never charged with her homicide.

Brown drove back to his office to think some more. Where was the strangler? He had been committing these crimes since 1956. Maybe he had outgrown his obsession. The Bouncing Ball Strangler had to be approaching thirty-five by now, and that was a common cutoff point for these new serial criminals, according to psychiatrists. Perhaps the strangler had learned self-control. "All of us go a little crazy at times." Wasn't that Norman Bates's line from *Psycho?* He might have committed suicide or been killed in one of his attempts or arrested for an unrelated crime. Perhaps an angry father or boyfriend had tracked him down and done the city a favor by blowing him away.

Brown almost wished he could do it himself. He still hated Sonny

Busch in spite of some sympathy for his mental turmoil, but what he had done was unforgivable. Brown picked up the silver-framed picture again and studied the sweet-faced, white-haired woman in it. His eyes misted over in a rare show of emotion.

Sonny's pathetic victims had reminded him of his mother.

Chapter Thirty-six

For Sure!

On October 25, 1962, Ginnie Gordon's birthday, Premier Pictures Company in New York finally released the bifurcated nudie film. Donald L. Velde Enterprises provided stills, a one sheet, a trailer, and twenty-two by twenty-eight lobbies with this tagline:

The Wild, Wild West has never been wilder . . . Beautiful babes . . . bashful cowboys! . . . The wide-open spaces suddenly grow crowded when delectable desert desserts roam the range and wide-eyed cowboys cry, Don't Fence Me In! Definitely & Strictly An Adult Western! The Adultest Western of Them All!

The reviews were enthusiastic:

Those lucky enough to see this unwoolly western in its entirety [at the Pussycat Theaters], where women are women without buttons or bows or buckskin, will witness something guaranteed to make the West really wild.

Karl Schanzer, who starred as *The Peeper*, would play in what Coppola often claimed as his debut film, *Dementia* 13, for Roger Corman. But Coppola's true first film was *The Peeper*, done before his graduate studies at the UCLA Film School, "the film debut the 'respectable' director wants us to ignore!" What did it matter? He was on his way. Ahead lay *The Godfather*, *The Conversation*, and *Apocalypse Now* and the rarefied heights that he would share with Alfred Hitchcock. *Modern Man* wrote of Coppola and *Tonight for Sure!*, "To accomplish this epic filming feat, producer-director Francis Coppola took over the entire town of Searchlight, Nevada, for two months of shooting shapely mammaries." The young filmmaker, who was never comfortable with onscreen nudity, had to have laughed. Well, he had never been to Searchlight, but at least they spelled his name right.

Thad Brown never caught the Bouncing Ball Strangler, though he had followed Sonny Busch's trial with great relish and made sure that the shambling young "Tony Perkins look-alike" got what he deserved. Sonny's trial began on Monday, December 5, 1960, in the court of Superior Judge Edwin L. Jefferson. Sonny's lawyer, Al Mathews, told the jury that his client "is a schizophrenic who slips from one personality to another." A hypnotist had placed Sonny under three times while he was in jail and the sessions revealed that Busch felt an irresistible pressure to kill arising from early life experience that included sensations of terror. Mathews attempted to have Sonny testify under hypnosis. Deputy D.A. Thomas Finnerty opposed the request and prevailed. Experts testified that Sonny has a split personality, but is "not legally insane." On February 1, 1961, Sonny Busch was found guilty by a jury of seven men and five women of the first degree murder of his aunt and the second degree murder of two other women. He was taken to San Quentin's Death Row to await execution. On June 3, the United States Supreme Court denied a hearing to Busch to halt his execution. On March 6, 1962, Sonny Busch's clemency plea was placed before California Governor Edmund "Pat" Brown. Arthur Alarcon, the Governor's clemency secretary, revealed that a neighbor who did not testify at the trial later told of hearing what appeared to be a quarrel in Mrs. Briggs's apartment before she was killed. "If this evidence had come out at the trial," he said, "Busch might have been sentenced for second-degree murder instead." Mae Busch traveled to Sacramento to make an emotional plea to the board. "I have tried in my own way to have the boy taken care of, but I failed." Governor Brown, who said he had "carefully reviewed the case," refused to save Sonny's life. Busch was scheduled to die on March 14, in the same gas chamber where Chessman had died. After the execution, Thad Brown tried to put the case from his thoughts, but on long, dark nights there would always be those unanswered questions and doubt in his mind.[8]

I was now a sophomore in college and working part-time for George Ross at the *Oakland Tribune* as a sports copyboy and getting another taste of the newspaper world. I liked the energy and rush and had begun to gravitate toward journalism; perhaps there was some way to combine art and writing, perhaps in books. In the January 1962 *Swank*, Marli appeared on the cover as "The nude Hitchcock can't scare," and on four pages inside, including two full pages of color photos, she was identified as "the nude in the shower scene in Alfred Hitchcock's classic thriller *Psycho*." In June 1962, *Cavalcade* devoted three pages to Marli "Henfro," which I added to my folder. *Adam 1963 Calendar* had her as Miss October. I was still collecting pictures of the beautiful redhead for my figure-drawing classes, for proposed paintings, and for a book about this very intriguing woman who had appeared in the single-most famous scene in movie history, the Shower Sequence in Alfred Hitchcock's *Psycho*. Critics have since said of Hitchcock's masterpiece:

> *Psycho* has the dimensions of great tragedy . . . one of the great works of modern art.

---

[8]Brown would be named interim chief of the LAPD in July 1966 after the death of Chief William H. Parker. He cleaned out his desk for good on March 13, 1967, and retired from police work.

One of the most crucial cultural artifacts of this era.

A genuine icon of cinema.

The "American dream" as nightmare.

Donald Spoto wrote,

> For *Psycho* describes as perhaps no other American film: the inordinate expense of wasted lives in a world so comfortably familiar as to appear initially unthreatening: the world of office girls and lunchtime liaisons, of half-eaten cheese sandwiches, of motels just off the main road, of shy young men and maternal devotion. But these may just be flimsy veils for spiritual, moral, and psychic disarray of terrifying ramifications.

Until 1963, I still saw Marli on the newsstands—in *Charm Photography, Famous Models, Glamour Parade, Bare,* and *Bold,* the first issue of *Purr-r* in 1963, even cover-featured with an article on Peter Gowland and film bombshells Yvette Mimeaux, Tina Louise, Julie Newmar, and Venetia Stevenson. She appeared in *Nudist Days* and *Nude Living* and the October *HQ* with short hair like Janet Leigh in *Psycho.* Marli was shown with balloons as "glory-gilded Marli," "childlike in spirit" and "full-blooded, yet strangely fragile." They tinted her black-and-white photos but others were in full color: sparkling green water, green umbrella against golden body, red hair and copper nipples, and lips the same color. Shown lounging on a tan trampoline, they captioned her "impressive body, her face sports a constant and wondrous smile."

When Marli saw *Tonight for Sure!* hers was the third name in the credits FFC had composed. "I'm in almost every scene," Marli crowed. "I couldn't believe it!" What a year 1960 had been for her—a film for Hitchcock and a film for Coppola, his first, two of the giants of motion picture directors. But *The Peeper* melded with the long-delayed *Tonight for Sure!* featured Electra and Exotica—strippers. Marli groaned. "Now people really will think I was a stripper."

She was more popular than ever—appearing in the November *High* just as her nudie cutie, *The Shirt Off Her Back*, opened in Dallas. She was in December *Modern Man*. Then Marli Renfro, one of the most popular and memorable models ever, inexplicably dropped out of sight. Marli performed in a stage comedy, *Ham on Wry*, in Hollywood. "That was really fun to do," she said, "but it came a few years after *Psycho* and those golden, wonderful days of 1960."

In 1960, Marli was *Playboy*'s cover star and layout model, appeared on the first *Playboy* TV shows, and became a Bunny at the first Playboy Club. As a dancer in Vegas, she saw the end of the Old Vegas as the El Rancho burned the day after *Psycho* was released. In Searchlight, she filmed the third nudie cutie film ever made (*Tonight for Sure!*), worked with Hugh Hefner, dated Lenny Bruce, attended nudist camps with nudist queen Diane Webber, and rode stallions along the Malibu Beach with Steve McQueen. Gorgeous red-haired model Marli Renfro captivated and en-slaved you to that iconic image that brought her in contact with other icons of the time—beautiful, talented people. I thought about her for years, impossible to get off my mind.

Yes, Los Angeles was a dangerous place in the early 1960s. No woman was safe. Though Sonny Busch had been put away, the Bouncing Ball Stran-gler, who targeted women, might still be on the loose. Or was he? Could he already be behind bars, unaware of his dual identity? The police just didn't know and so the hunt went on. And what of Marli, who felt oblivious to the forces swirling around her in the stark, hot California landscape? When Mr. recycled a photo spread on Marli called "The Girl from *Psycho*," it brought back my memories of her and my vow to write her story.

"I would not say, that I am exactly the girl whose part I play in *Psycho*," Marli explained, "but as a woman, I understand her." And that was the last time I saw her picture in a magazine. She disappeared from the public forum except in reprints. Sometimes I wondered, "What had become of her?" Had something terrible happened? Something horrible? I went on with my life, but I always wondered. In the pit of my stomach on long nights I had a very bad feeling about her.

*   *   *

Marli had promised herself a good hot shower and noted the shower stall in the bathroom beyond. She stepped into the shower. The bathroom was crowded with mirrors and reflective surfaces, dazzling white plastic tiles and a shower with a translucent curtain. Every bit of metal was polished to gleaming. She tested the water. It was a pleasant temperature. She got in and pulled the curtain behind her. In her ears was the roar of running water. Marli thought over the amazing year she had spent. The hot water raised clouds of steam. She looked up at the showerhead, and then started. What was that? A noise? The shower curtain billowed a little and the steam rose in clouds. Marli listened. No, it was nothing. The curtain died away and flattened out. She felt she had come full circle. She could almost see the sinister house on the hill. There was the roar of the shower and the water cascading darkly down the drain.

Chapter Thirty-seven
The Present

arli was dead. Wire services, magazines, a television show, and a book reported her ironic death as murder victim at the hands of a serial killer, the identical role she had played in *Psycho*. Even *Playboy* said so. In 2001, I had finally begun to write Marli's story just as news was howling out of LA about the trial of the murderer of the girl in Alfred Hitchcock's shower. It was hard to believe, and when I first heard the news, it knocked the wind out of me. The room virtually spun as I felt a tremendous loss. I had waited too long.

Over forty years after *Psycho* was filmed, I solemnly laid out the documents on my drawing table and sorted them into piles to make some sense of the loss. It seemed a senseless endeavor since her killer had been caught, and there was no mystery to solve or a criminal to catch. There was no girl to interview, nothing left to write but death and loss. Any book about the vibrant redhead would be a tragic book. The only mysteries remaining were who she had been, why she walked away from fame, and where she had been in the years before her death.

From the first page:

AP Online. Los Angeles, March 16, 2001—A thirty-four-year-old handyman has been convicted of strangling two women, including an actress who was a body double for Janet Leigh in the film *Psycho*. The man, Kenneth Dean Hunt, was found guilty of two counts of first-degree murder on Thursday. He could receive the death penalty at his sentencing set for Monday.

Mr. Hunt avoided suspicion in the 1988 killing of the actress Myra Davis, for 10 years, but in 1998 when the family of the second victim, Jean Orloff, 60, was preparing to have her body cremated, the authorities discovered that she had died of strangulation.

And also from the AP: "A handyman convicted of strangling two women, including the actress who appeared as Janet Leigh's body double in Alfred Hitchcock's *Psycho*, was sentenced Tuesday to life in prison without the possibility of parole."

CourtTV.com reported: "She wasn't a huge Hollywood star, but she was an important part of *Psycho*; she served as the stand-in for Janet Leigh during the infamous shower scene . . ."

"Stand-in?" I thought and placed a question mark after the word. Marli was a body double, a very different job. A stand-in, always dressed, was used to check lighting. A body double did nudity and performed. I looked at the next file, the most damning. *Celebrity Sleuth*, a popular men's magazine, had pictures of Marli Renfro and confirmed her real name was Myra Davis, an uncredited extra on *Psycho*.

"It's an amazing coda to the most affecting screen death ever," the *Sleuth* wrote. "For over ten years, Marli/Myra's 1988 rape and strangulation in her West Los Angeles home had gone unsolved. Then, in 2001, her killing was linked to a recent murder with a similar MO, and handyman Kenneth Dean Hunt was convicted of both crimes. He would have been 22 when he raped the then 71-year-old Davis. . . . Amazingly Marli was 43 at the time of the filming (nearly 11 years older than Janet)." Marli had certainly looked younger in her photos.

The magazine then made the case for her being the girl in Hitchcock's shower.

The famous frame in *Psycho's* shower scene where the knife touches the torso for the ONLY time. Compare to the belly of model Marli Renfro with the identical shape of the navel. The *Playboy* at the bottom of this page contains one more amazing irony: totally by coincidence, Davis's uncredited cover pose was out while the film was in its widest release.

The only visible nipple in the film (for 1/24 of a second), clearly matches those of Renfro in the shot below it, who was chosen because her thirty-six/twenty-three/thirty-six measurements were identical to Leigh's."

Sleuth added, "The second most revealing frame of the Shower Sequence is this side shot *Sleuth* has unearthed of this ultra-rare shot of Miss Davis in the shower, which she took in 1961 to prove her breast shape was identical. It is indeed."

Cold Case File wrote: "Police crack a cold case of murder when a mysterious woman calls to say that her boyfriend is the killer, and the murder of a woman in 1996 provides clues to the murder years ago of a stand-in for Janet Leigh in the movie *Psycho*."

There was an entire book about the case: "In *Body Double* we learn of the brutal murder of Myra Davis . . . the seventy-one-year-old former actress who served as the double for Janet Leigh in the movie *Psycho's* infamous shower scene," read the jacket flap copy.

. . . Miss Davis's body is discovered by her beloved granddaughter who although deeply traumatized tells police that she has had a bad feeling about a "weird" neighbor . . . mistakes are made and it is not until another grisly slaying of an elderly woman some time later that the cruel, sick killer is caught and brought to trial . . . shades of Norman Bates?

When movie buffs think of *Psycho*, the first image that comes to mind is the shower scene. Fans knew the stars, but few people realized they saw snippets of a performance by Myra Davis.

The back cover identified her as:

One of Janet Leigh's "body doubles" for the chilling shower-slay scene in Alfred Hitchcock's classic film *Psycho*. Now it was her own murder that had been played out with shocking brutality.

This book is about the true story of the brutal 1988 murder of Myra Davis, seventy-one, who was Janet Leigh's body double in the film *Psycho*.

Another headline stated "Man Guilty of Killing *Psycho* Cast Member." *The Guardian* reported, "Censors demanded the removal of one shot in which they believed Leigh's nipple was visible. But in actual fact it's stand-in Marli Renfro (aka Myra Davis) a gorgeous redhead glamour model."

"Caskets On Parade . . . *Playboy* Cover Models & Photographers," listed her name, though curiously not a date of death.

I looked over my folder of Marli's pictures, the candid snaps of her at the traveling nudist camp, her covers, movie stills, and her beautiful *Playboy* cover that had warmed my lonely studio and kept me inspired during those solo hours. I had fallen in love with Bronstein and Paul's puzzle cover. Marli had so projected her personality through her posing it was as if I had known her and had lost an old friend. I put the files away unable to go on.

A few years passed as I tried to put her story out of my mind, but couldn't. In 2006 I was at Kayo books in downtown San Francisco looking for old magazines when I discovered the July 1960 issue of *Playboy* with Marli's layout in a transparent dress. I walked to the front register and told the store owner about the part Marli had played in *Psycho*. "I'm going to write a book about her, Maria," I promised and went immediately home to start again.

After I had exhausted all the information about her from printed sources, I listened to the rumors, many conflicting. When raven-haired Bettie Page, a popular fifties pinup, disappeared in 1957, rumors spread that she had been rubbed out by the mob, become a nun, married royalty, or murdered her brother. None was true. Bettie had retired to Key West, Florida, where, a victim of religious mania, she threatened her landlady and was confined to mental care facilities. "[Bettie] served as a bridge between those naive 1950s," *Playboy* later wrote, "and the much more sexually open and explicit period that followed . . . in which sex was an accepted facet of a healthy, normal life. That's what made her a sexual pioneer, as well as a star."

I decided to interview the people Marli had worked with about who she had been. First though, I needed to find out about the *Psycho* Killer, who had been so affected by the shower scene. In Los Angeles, I visited the crime scenes in the Sonny Busch investigation and photographed them as if there might be a clue there. Mother and Aunty's homes had changed little, but Sunset Boulevard, the stomping grounds of Sonny and the Bouncing Ball Strangler, had.

Agent Joel Gotler, who worked out of a building designed by Charles Luckman on Sunset Boulevard, filled me in. "Sunset Boulevard now resembles urban sprawl," Joel told me. "It's just very crowded now, very congested. Dean Martin's Lounge was on La Cienega. The Source Restaurant, a very key place, that's gone. Ben Franks was a staple then and Greenblats was there forever, probably the best deli and best wine in the city. The Garden of Allah Hotel was torn down. A lot of Hollywood celebs, a lot of skeletons are buried in those stories. That's where Jennings Lang was shot in the balls when he caught his wife cheating with Walter Wanger. Hollywood Boulevard hasn't changed that much." After *Psycho*, I moved on to Marli's film with Francis Coppola.

First I spoke with Vegas juggler and comedian Andy Martello, an expert on Searchlight, Nevada, Willie Martello, and the El Rey Casino, where *Tonight for Sure!* was filmed. "The majority of the comments I received after I posted scenes filmed inside the casino online revolved around the question, 'Who was the redhead?'" Andy told me. "She's someone I'd love to talk to all these years later. Who is she?"

"That's what I'm trying to find out," I said.

Director/producer Jerry Schafer might know something. It turned out he and I had a connection. "Last night I spoke with my son Erik. We talked about you!" Jerry said. "Can you believe that? Erik told me that after the premiere of *Zodiac* you went to the Pacific Dining Car in downtown Los Angeles and he sat next to you during the meal." Jerry told me Gunilla Hutton was Erik's mother.

I met Gunilla when I was producing Jack Benny's show at the Thunderbird Hotel in Las Vegas in 1965. She was in an act called: "The Gwyer Sisters," a takeoff on the famous McGuire sisters of that era. There were three girls in the act; Iris Adrian, Peggy Mondo and Gunilla. Iris was a skinny cartoon voiced lady, Peggy was an overweight would-be opera singer and Gunilla was the good looking gal in the group and the only one who could sing on key. We were married in 1966 and had a son, Erik. Our marriage didn't work out.

Gunilla was booked as a regular on the TV series *Petticoat Junction*, which was shot in LA, and I was in Las Vegas. My career was bursting at the seams at that time and so was hers. Being apart was no way to have a marriage, so it didn't work out, but we were young and we had fun. We are still great friends. We see each other from time to time at family get-togethers with Gunilla and our son, Erik, and Christian and Amber, her other children. Some of her ex-husbands all come together at the same time in the same place. A few years ago, at a Christmas get-together Gunilla looked around at the crowd; then a big smile came over her face as she said: "Are there any men here I haven't been married to?" At that get-together I met Jamie Vanderbilt.

Jamie wrote the screenplay for David Fincher's Warner Brothers/Paramount motion picture, *Zodiac*, from my books, *Zodiac* and *Zodiac Unmasked*. I had attended Jamie and Amber's wedding. Gunilla was Jamie's mother in law.

"What about Francis Ford Coppola?" I asked.

"This thing with FFC has always amazed me," Jerry said. "Interestingly, I have never met him or spoken to him although we have many mutual friends and acquaintances. He became involved with my film after I had finished principal photography. It was a fantastic piece of shit film. I was still in England when the film was released and didn't get to see it. In fact, I didn't have any idea what had happened to the film and

I really didn't care. I never saw Richard or Ray again. They just disappeared from my life. To me it was like a grand illusion. From England I went to Sweden and did a film and then I went to Japan and directed a magic show for television.

"When I returned to the USA, I went to Las Vegas where I became the Entertainment Director for Del Webb's properties in Nevada in 1963 and I did that for nine years. I had dealings with Meyer Lansky who came into my life through his dealings with the Thunderbird Hotel which Del Webb sold to a company called Lance Incorporated out of Miami." As the entertainment director at the Thunderbird Hotel in Vegas, Jerry produced Judy Garland, Steve Allen, Jayne Meadows, Robert Goulet, Debbie Reynolds, and Sammy Davis and wrote *That Certain Girl*, the first original Broadway-style musical comedy to premiere on the Strip.

Jerry hadn't seen *Tonight for Sure!* Andy Martello got him a copy. "God it was awful!" Schafer said. "I couldn't look at more then about ten minutes of it. I had read an article that said the film was the brainchild of FFC. The work that he did on my film turned it into a completely different picture. It certainly wasn't what I had written or intended it to be. He shot additional scenes that had nothing to do with what the picture was originally about, and then changed the title. I see, or at least I think I see, what Francis was trying to do by putting the two stories together." Yet Jerry retains a fond place in his heart for his collaboration with Francis Ford Coppola. "It's hard to imagine that the fellow who put that together went on to become a famous director . . . but after the smoke clears away I remain a Coppola fan and always will be.

"Interestingly, the girl who doubled Janet in *Psycho* worked for me in the film. Her name is Marli Renfro . . . I don't know where she is today, but this is the little known information that I thought I'd pass along to you. Marli was wonderful in the film, a professional operator in every way. I really enjoyed working with her on that piece of shit I produced in Searchlight, and later that Francis Coppola took credit for doing . . . I'll never forget her . . . God, I love show business!"

In mid-December 2007, I was watching *Laura*, the story of a driven detective who investigates the murder of a beautiful woman and slowly falls in love with the dead woman through her portrait. He becomes obsessed with trying to solve her murder as, through the testimony of friends, he comes to know her. One night he falls asleep under her picture and is awakened when Laura appears alive. The murder victim was someone else killed in her place.

I couldn't get that out of my mind. I got up around 2:00 A.M. and went to my files. There was something wrong with those news reports and rumors. I suspected it hinged on the subtle distinction between the terms stand-in and body double.

Myra Davis's granddaughter, Sherry, reported in *Body Double*, "My grandmother loved her association with Janet Leigh . . . she was Janet's stand-in, but she was also the woman in the rocking chair, Anthony Perkins's mother." But Mrs. Bates in the fruit cellar scene was a stuffed dummy on a camera mount and was activated by a prop man turning a crank from underneath. Mrs. Bates needed no stand-in. "And you know that hand holding a knife, plunging it at Janet Leigh in the shower?" Sherry told author David Lassiter. "That was my grandmother's hand." That was inaccurate too. Stuntwoman Margo Epper, holding the knife, doubled for Tony Perkins as Mrs. Bates.

Even Sherry was puzzled by her grandmother's claim that she had functioned as "a body double in the famous shower scene in *Psycho*." "My grandmother would have never done any nude work. No, no, no, that was not my grandmother." Her statement had the ring of truth.

Then it came to me. I knew why the murdered woman had truly believed she was the girl in Alfred Hitchcock's shower. Myra had been truthful. She had been the girl in Hitchcock's shower. Now I remembered what Saul Bass had said about designing the storyboards for the Shower Sequence: "I used the stand-in for Janet to shoot it and at the end of the day had her stay a little longer." Bass shot twenty-five feet of test footage to see if his storyboard would work and that was what Myra recalled, not the actual filmed scene for the movie. Bass's footage was only for the designer's benefit to see if his ideas would work.

The woman who said she was Janet Leigh's body double in *Psycho*, Myra Davis, was actually a stand-in, and I found her listed as such. Unlike body doubles that did nudity or acted in scenes too dangerous for the star, stand-ins were always dressed.

I opened the file folder containing the crime scene photos of Myra's bedroom. In one photo her body lay atop a dark bedspread on an old-fashioned four-poster. At the head of the bed was an end table and lamp with a ruffled lampshade. Above the bed were eight pictures, staggered—four above, four below, all old-fashioned. All of them were of the murdered woman. The pictures! That was it. I remembered during Marli's photo shoots in her parents' apartment, Sam Wu had captured her art work on the wall. Marli, a woman of little vanity, always put her paintings up, but never a picture of herself. She hadn't even kept the famous photos of herself. The decoration in the murdered woman's bedroom showed no sign of any artistic knowledge or sophistication. This woman wasn't Marli Renfro.

The story I was writing wasn't just a story like *Laura*, it was *exactly* like *Laura*.

Marli Renfro was alive!

Someone else had died in her place, someone who had in all innocence claimed to be the girl in Alfred Hitchcock's shower. The compounded rumors led everyone to believe Marli Renfro was dead. I found her high school's website. The youthful photo at the top of the page was obviously of Marli Renfro in her youth. To my shock, she had written a letter in the summer: "I'm going up to Las Vegas with two girlfriends for a few days in October. We're celebrating our fiftieth anniversary of when we were chorus dancers at the El Rancho Vegas Hotel. Should be a lot of fun. Here's to health and happiness! Marlys Mouse, Marli Ruffles (take your pick)." But which October was the letter referring to? It was now December 2007. Had she already made the trip and gone? Perhaps I could get Marli to come to me. I began to lay out bait, making it well known I was writing a book about the girl in Alfred Hitchcock's shower. Would she bite?

Elaine Blandford was selling items on eBay, and on Saturday, February 2, 2008, I bought item #120215547535, an *Ace* 1961 magazine featuring Marli Renfro, one of dozens of different magazines she had appeared in. As I had done with similar purchases I attached a long note to Elaine that indicated I was writing a book about Marli. Blandford wrote back: "I look forward to mailing the magazine and do hope we share another eBay moment. I have prepared the magazine for the Golden Gate city and will email when your letter arrives." As I had hoped, she passed my information on to another buyer who was also interested in Marli Renfro magazines.

Then on February 15, I got this communication: "I understand you are writing a book about me. This is Marli Renfro."

Chapter Thirty-eight
Marli

My hands began to shake. I sat down, chills running through me. How could Marli not have heard the vastly exaggerated reports of her own death? Then I understood. Her frequent visits to her beloved La Paz were possible because, as she now told me, she lived on an oasis in the Southern Mojave Desert, an area of dunes and steeply sloped mountains with flat intervening valleys, an isolated area. Marli had never left the lava flows and dry lakes, the outreaching Joshua trees of the desert she had seen in Searchlight. These days she heard only the faint stir of palm fronds and the whisper of the sand, not the ugly rumors. In the spring she gathered blankets of wildflowers and lived her life. Highway 92 brought the playground areas of the Colorado River within easy reach and she took advantage of it with constant travel into the wilderness areas.

Marli told me she had called *Playboy* in 2001 and they had told her "Marli Renfro is dead." Apprised of that, she shrugged and let it go. "In 2008 I wrote Hef at *Playboy* a second time regarding one of his parties and his 'secretary' called back on my answering machine saying that they're filled up—blah, blah, blah. I think that if I'm invited they have to admit that I didn't die as they say."

In spite of her beauty and sexual attractiveness, Marli would never be self-centered enough to look for articles about herself. "I go through life aware but not knowing the significance of some things," she told me. Nor did she follow her field—that of Hollywood and the glamor girl. She didn't know who Bettie Page was and was unaware of Gay Talese's book about the sixties, free love, and all the happenings in Topanga Canyon that incorporated model Diane Webber in the changing mores. Marli had missed the *Cold Case* show about Myra Davis's death, the news reports of "her killer's" arrest, the *Celebrity Sleuth* article (the most damning), the book. Marli was too busy living to know she was "dead."

At last I heard the rest of her story.

Her only public appearance had been on *Oxygen*. "At the end of it, they discovered who I was and my secret," Marli said. "Teri Garr was on there (Teri's mom was wardrobe at UI), [and] John Ritter's wife. Somebody asked me how was Janet Leigh and I was just starting to say, 'She was cold . . .' and Teri Garr shouts out, 'She's a bitch!'

"October '60 found me traveling back to LA where I continued modeling and doing commercials," Marli continued. "Then I met my first husband, Ed Hilliard—he bowled me over. He owned a circus then a cosmetic company. We had two children—Eddie John and Erin Patricia, both precious persons.

"We divorced in November '69. I got an upstairs duplex a mile from my new job as Girl Friday at the Scenic and Title Artists Union, and had my children installed in a private school. I really liked that job at the union—lots of talent to be working with. In late summer '70, my dad's brother, Bob, invited me to spend a week in Pueblo, Colorado. I went and we traveled all around that area.

"While in Santa Fe, New Mexico, I fell in love with that city—went back home, gave notice to both my job and apartment and planned to move to Santa Fe. I had a VW bug and was going to tow it behind a Hertz truck. At the time, my parents were working and living in the California desert and I asked my mom, 'May I store a few things in your garage?' 'Sure' she said. So, on my trip out there my mom asked me, 'What's the hurry?' 'None.' So I moved to the East Sonoran Desert which became my home for the next fourteen years. It's funny how things work out.

"Two years later I met and married Bob Phillips and we were married almost ten years. Had a lot of laughs and good times. Rode motorcycles on short and long trips with Jim and Linda Todd, two dear friends. We divorced in October '80.

"Soon after I went to school and got a real estate license, a profession where you don't have to work nine to five, but you wind up working ten to twelve hour days. In 1984 I first went down to La Paz for five days. I went by myself and fished a couple of times with a grandpa and his grandson as my guides. I caught quite a few fish which I had the cafeteria broil for me—delicious! The Olympics were going on and it was in Spanish on TV. I had a year and a half of Spanish in high school which serves me okay. The people there are very happy you are learning their language and will help you. They also ask for your help in learning to speak English. I love it there, a very friendly place." Marli had found real contentment. She listened to the squeals of children at play in the village and smelled roasting pork and baking loaves.

"My son Eddie went to live with his dad when he was fifteen. When Erin graduated from high school in 1984 and went to Texas A&M, I moved to Phoenix—back to a city again so I could enjoy all the things a city has to offer—all the arts—season tickets to the opera and concert and classical music series." In October '86 Marli, along with a couple thousand others, auditioned to appear on *Wheel of Fortune*. She was selected and her show aired on December 26, 1986. "I had a lot of fun and won three out of four games."

A year later, she moved back to the desert and reentered the real estate markets. Marli had licenses for both Arizona and California. "After twelve years of being alone," she said. "I looked at couples who obviously liked one another and thought, 'I never had that.' My marriages were based on lust, not friendship. So I thought that a happy, long lasting marriage was not for me. I accepted that. Then in June '92 I met Mike Peterson and we became friends and married on November 14. We both enjoy traveling and fishing and sometimes act like we are ten years old and sometimes like we are 150. I'm still wondering when I will grow up.

"Mike retired and I quit in February '99 and we went traveling the US and Canada, driving a '93 Dodge diesel truck with a thirteen-foot aluminum boat on top and pulling a thirty-four-foot fifth wheel Avion trailer, a piece of cake. While in Florida we bought a park model at the Holiday Travel Resort in Leesburg, about thirty-five miles northwest of Orlando. After about eight months we came back west and spent the summer at Fish Lake, Utah. Mike caught a large Mackinaw and every evening we would take a drive to watch the deer come down from the mountains."

Over the years they flew down to La Paz, Baja Sur, and fished in the Sea of Cortez. They'd target dorado, cabrilla, and snapper. Their place in Florida is on a canal that leads to Lake Harris, where they caught huge black crappie. In the summer of 2007, they went on jet boat rides on the Rogue River up in Oregon. The scorching weather there made getting soaked palatable. She spent time on the Oregon coast and caught a lot of "mmm, delicious" Dungeness crab. They surf-fished and toured the redwoods on the way up and on the way down. On October 22, she had gone up to Las Vegas to celebrate the big anniversary of when she and her fellow dancers had been part of the chorus dancers at El Rancho Vegas Hotel.

Marli had begun to wonder about her contribution to *Psycho* and recently had gotten in touch with the Screen Actors Guild. "When I called to get stuff from *Psycho*, they said, 'Our records don't go back that far.' The woman looked anyway. 'You should be receiving residuals,' she said." In January 2008 she again contacted SAG. "He had to go in the Archives to find me," Marli said. "You're not on the new computer which goes back to '62," he told her. "They finally found me and they do have a section on residuals so I should look into that. On Turner Classics Network I'm mentioned as being in *Psycho*."

"No residuals or even a bonus from a film that made $15 million the first year?" I said. "That's criminal. Shameful. There should be an outcry and something should be done."

"In 2008, we sold our Florida place and moved back to California." In April, Marli and her husband returned from four days on the lower

Colorado across from Parker, Arizona. They had been checking on a resort. "We found it was really not us," Marli told me, "but it was nice to get away," she said. On March 6, 2008, she told me, "One thing, I don't think I ever met Saul Bass. When I first read that he was claiming to have directed the shower scene and also Janet Leigh saying that she did the whole thing, I lost respect for both of them and cared not to read or listen to anything they had to say as I would be suspect of its truth."

On Friday, March 7, 2008, Marli told me that all her photos and copies of her magazines printed during her glorious year, 1960, had been lost. "I used to have stacks of magazines and photos of me from the short period I was in the business," she told me, "but they were destroyed in the fire."

"The fire?"

She explained that her first husband, now deceased, had made her burn all her photos. "I am now collecting new ones. Robert, this is how I got to know about you. I was high bidder on eBay on a magazine in which I appear. The seller emailed me back saying it would be in the mail soon. I emailed back giving her my maiden name. She came back mentioning that you wrote her saying you were writing a book about me. By the way, the magazine you won from her, you outbid me as I was also bidding on it. Circles, circles, circles." She had ordered a DVD of *Psycho* "which should arrive any day." I told her that with the improved technology one can easily see that it is Marli Renfro in Alfred Hitchcock's shower.

"Well, Robert, take care," Marli said. "Here's to health and happiness."

Today Marli Renfro lives in a desert oasis in a modest two bedroom, which she is redecorating with her husband. I realized that Marli Renfro hadn't traveled far from Searchlight and the 1960s after all. She still lives among the shimmering dunes under the desert sun, the otherworldly Joshua trees, the long sunsets, images like herself that were impossible to grasp but remained indelible on the screen and page and within the mind forever like a once-glimpsed mirage.

BIBLIOGRAPHY

BOOKS

The Alfred Hitchcock Collection. *Psycho*. Widescreen. Special Features. "The Making of *Psycho*," Production Drawings, Universal City, CA: Universal Studios, 2000.

Anger, Kenneth. *Hollywood Babylon II*. New York: Dutton, 1984.

Auiler, Dan. *Hitchcock's Notebooks*. New York: Harper Entertainment, 2001.

Bloch, Robert. *Psycho*. Greenwich, CT: Fawcett, 1959.

Briggs, Joe Bob. *Profoundly Erotic*. New York: Universe Publishing, 2005.

Brill, Lesley. *The Hitchcock Romance: Love and Irony in Hitchcock's Films*. Princeton, NJ: Princeton University Press, 1988.

Caspary, Vera. *Laura*. New York: Dell, 1942.

Cowie, Peter. *Coppola*. New York: Da Capo Press, 1994. An excellent source for Coppola's student days and his first film.

Curtis, Tony, with Peter Golenblock. *American Prince*. New York: Harmony Books, 2008.

DeRosa, Steven. *Writing with Hitchcock*. New York: Faber & Faber, 2001.

Fischer, Steve. *When the Mob Ran Vegas*. Omaha, NE: Berkline Press, 2007.

Gottlieb, Sidney, ed. *Hitchcock on Hitchcock: Selected Writings and Interviews*. Berkley: University of California Press, 1995.

Gowland, Peter. *Peter Gowland's Figure Photography*. Greenwich, CT: Fawcett, 1954.

Hefner, Hugh, with Bill Zehme. *Hef's Little Black Book*. New York: Harper Entertainment, 2004.

Hitchcock, Alfred, and Robert Arthur, eds. *Stories Not for the Nervous*. New York: Random House, 1965.

Kraft, Jeff and Aaron Leventhal. *Footsteps in the Fog. Alfred Hitchcock's San Francisco*. Santa Monica, CA: Santa Monica Press, 2002.

Krohn, Bill. *Hitchcock at Work*. London: Phaidon Press, 2000. An excellent book that reveals for the first time Hitchcock's use of multiple cameras. A wonderful source and full of life.

Lacey, Robert. *Grace*. New York: Putnam, 1994.

Lassiter, Don. *Body Double*. New York: Pinnacle True Crime, Kensington, 2002.

Leigh, Janet, with Christopher Nickens. *Psycho*. New York: Harmony Books, 1995.

Muller, Eddie, and Dennis Faris. *Grindhouse. The Forbidden World of "Adults Only" Cinema*. New York: St. Martin's Griffin, 1996.

Nash, Jay Robert. *Bloodletters and Badmen*. New York: Warner, 1975.

Nevada Gaming Commission and State Gaming Control Board Exclusion/Ejection List, 1960.

Nevins, Francis M. Jr, and Martin Harry Greenberg. *Hitchcock in Prime Time*. New York: Avon Books, 1985.

Perry, George. *The Films of Alfred Hitchcock*. New York: Dutton, 1965.

Rebello, Stephen. *Alfred Hitchcock and the Making of Psycho*. New York: Dembner, 1990. The most faithful, comprehensive, and first book on the filming of Hitchcock's masterpiece, the bedrock upon which all *Psycho* mansions are erected.

Rothman, William. *Hitchcock the Murderous Gaze*. Cambridge, MA: Harvard University Press, 1982.

Spiegelman, Art, and Chip Kidd. *Jack Cole and Plastic Man*. San Francisco: Chronicle Books, 2001.

Spoto, Donald. *The Art of Alfred Hitchcock*. New York: Doubleday Dolphin, 1979.

———. *The Dark Side of Genius: The Life of Alfred Hitchcock*. Boston: Little, Brown, 1983.

———. *Spellbound by Beauty*. New York: Harmony Books, 2008. Relates the story of Hitchcock attempting to kiss *To Catch a Thief* actor Brigitte Auber in her car outside her Paris apartment.

Stefano, Joseph. *Psycho Script*, rev. December 1, 1959.

Talese, Gay. *Thy Neighbor's Wife*. Garden City, NY: Doubleday, 1980.

Taylor, John Russell. *Hitch: The Life and Times of Alfred Hitchcock*. New York: Da Capo Press, 1964. [Reissued: Pantheon Books, 1978.]

Truffaut, Francois. *Hitchcock*. New York: Simon & Schuster, 1967.

Watts, Steven. *Mr. Playboy: Mr. Hefner and the American Dream*. Hoboken, NJ: Wiley, 2008.

Webb, Jack. *The Badge*. New York: Thunder's Mouth Press, 1958.

Winecoff, Charles. *Split Image: The Life of Anthony Perkins*. New York: Dutton, 1996.

Woods, Paul Anthony. *Ed Gein—Psycho!* New York: St. Martin's Press, 1995.

Wu, Sam. *Sam Wu's Hollywood Figure Studios*, Greenwich, CT: Whitestone, 1967.

NEWSPAPER AND MAGAZINE ARTICLES

"Attacks on Eleven Women, Kidnapped 12th, According to Lie Test; Was Once Member of Burglary Ring." *Los Angeles Times*, September 9, 1960, p. 1. (Microfilm.)

"The Bellboy and the Playgirls." *Modern Man* 12 (December 1962): 21–23.

"Busch Loses Plea to Halt Execution, U.S. Supreme Court Denies a Hearing to Henry Busch." *Pasadena Star-News*, June 4, 1961, p. 6. (Available at www.newspaperarchive.com)

"Confessed Killer's Friend Held." *Pasadena Star-News*, September 10, 1960, p. 1. (Available at www.newspaperarchive.com)

"Defense Will Try Hypnosis in Kill Trial." *Tucson Daily Citizen*, December 5, 1960, p. 4. (Available at www.newspaperarchive.com)

"Devilish Daughters." *Celebrity Sleuth* 4, no. 7 (July 1991): 94–98.

"Deranged Man Admits Slayings." *Montgomery Post*, September 7, 1960, p. 5. (Available at www.newspaperarchive.com)

"Did Movie Stir Man to Slay Three? Hitchcock Denies Link with Killings." *Lowell* (Massachusetts) *Sun*, September 7, 1960. (Available at www.newspaperarchive.com)

"Dignitaries, Rank and File Attend Thad Brown Rites," *Van Nuys News*, October 15, 1976, p. 12-A. (Available at www.newspaperarchive.com)

"Down the Drain." *Celebrity Sleuth* "Women of Fantasy 15" (2005): 28–31. Describes Marli Renfro's death.

Duncan, Ray. "'I had to kill,' Says Strangler of Women." *Pasadena Independent*, September 9, 1960, p. 1. (Available at www.newspaperarchive.com)

"Friend of Confessed Slayer Busch." *Los Angeles Times*, September 10, 1960, p. 6. (Microfilm.)

Harris, Max. "Rawhide Reel." *Beau* (August 1967): 14–16. Photos of "Uncovered Cover Girl" Marli Renfro by Carlyle Blackwell on pp. 17–19.

———. "A Rootin' Tootin' Rawhide Reel." *Beau* (August 1967): 14–16. 17–19. Marli Renfro featured on pp. 17–19.

Hospodar, Paul S. "L.A. Police Job Opportunities." *Van Nuys News*, May 15, 1969, p. 2 A. (Available at www.newspaperarchive.com)

"Killer of Three Seized after Attempt to Slay 4th." *Oxnard* (California) *Press-Courier*, September 7, 1960, p. 2. (Available at www.newspaperarchive.com)

"L.A. News Roundup." *Pasadena Star-News*, September 8, 1960, p. 6. (Available at www.newspaperarchive.com)

"Like Mother, Like Daughter." *Celebrity Sleuth* 8, no. 6 (July 1995): 38–39.

"Man Admits Three Slayings, Made Plans for Two Others." *Kingsport* (Tennessee) *Times*, September 7, 1960, p. 1. (Available at www.newspaperarchive.com)

Maxford, Howard. "The Truth behind the Making of the Original *Psycho*." *Film Review* [Special issue #42] (2002): 12–18. "Call Sheet: Psycho." One of the published sources to list Marli Renfro as Janet Leigh's body double.

Meyer, Russ. "My Favorite Model." *Nugget* 5, no. 5 (October 1960): 56–59.

Playboy Cover to Cover, the 50's Searchable Digital Archive [DVD]. Bondi Digital Publishing, 2007. *Playboy's* first decade, every issue.

Playboy: The Hef Pages. Available at www.playboy.com/worldofplayboy/hmh. History and information about Hugh Hefner, *Psycho*, and pictorial essay featuring Marli Renfro and Janet Leigh.

"A Portfolio of the Past Delightful Dozen" *Playboy* 4, no. 1 (January 1957) : 57–61.

Rhoads, Jonathan. "The Lock on the Barroom Door." *Playboy* (November 1958): 25–30. Inspiration for the *Playboy* Club.

"Scene by the Sea." *Rogue* 5, no. 4 (June 1960) : 58–63. Photos by Ken Parker; Russ Meyer shoots June Wilkinson.

"Slaying Spurned by Chessman's Death?" *Eureka Humboldt Standard* (California), March 8, 1962, p. 1. (Available at www.newspaperarchive.com)

Smith, Captain Bouncer. "Sword Fishing off Miami Beach." Available at http://swordfishmiami.com.

Stamos, George. "Great Resorts of Las Vegas: The El Rancho Vegas Fire." *Las Vegas Sun*, April 1, 1979. Special series.

"Suspect Admits Hollywood Slaying after Seeing Hitchcock Thriller." *Lubbock* (Texas) *Avalanche Journal*, p. B-3. (Available at www.newspaperarchive.com)

"Thad Brown, Ex-LA Police Chief, Dies at 67." *Long Beach* (California) *Press-Telegram*, October 6, 1979, p. A-3. (Available at www.newspaperarchive.com)

"Use of Hypnotism at Murder Trial Sought." *Lubbock* (Texas) *Avalanche Journal*, December 5, 1960, p. 2. (Available at www.newspaperarchive.com)

Wilkinson, June. "MM Goes to the Movies—*The Bellboy and the Playgirls*." *Modern Man* (December 1962): 21–23.

———. "Scene by the Sea." *Rogue* 5 (June 1960): 59–61.

Wilson, Everett. "Hollywood's *Psycho* Strangler." *True Detective* 74, no. 2 (December 1960): 24–21, 88–92. This article was an important source for the rare case of Sonny Busch and Hitchcock's film.

AUTHOR'S FOLDER/SCRAPBOOK

Articles and photographs 1960–1963 concerning Marli Renfro collected during when the author was in college.

Ace. April 1961: "A Dog's Life," vol. 4, no. 6, pp. 42–44. Glamour Special, Sam Wu photos, Marli and Stumbles in her parents' apartment.

Adam. July 1960: "Behind the Camera," vol. 4, no. 7, p. 66, ; Marli Renfro cover and featured.

———. 1961: "Wide Open Spaces," vol. 5, no. 6.

———. November 1961: "Hollywood's Masters of Glamour," Thistle, Frank, vol. 5, no. 11, pp. 14–17, 40.

———. October 1963: Calendar; Marli Renfro as Miss October.

———. August 1961: "*The Wide Open Spaces*, A Movie Is Born" and "Jack Schafer," pp. 62–65.

Cavalcade. June 1962: "Magnificent Marli, a Pageant in Water Colors," pp. 17–19. Marli Renfro in four-color spread.

Debonair. December 1960: Marli Renfro, 3 pp.

The Dude. September 1961: vol. 6, no. 1, pp. 17–23.

Escapade. October 1960: "Marli for President," vol. 5, no. 6, pp. 32–37.

High. July 1959: Marli Renfro featured, centerfold.

Mr. January 1968: "The Girl from Psycho," pp. 57–60.

Modern Man. July 1961: Marli Renfro featured.

———. October 1961: "A Rootin' Tootin' Rawhide Reel," cover, pp. 17–19, 20–22, Marli Renfro mentioned in article on Peter Gowland, photos included.

"Mercy Asked for Youth Who Killed after Seeing Movie." *Corpus Christi Times*, March 7, 1962, p. 9. Story out of Sacramento, California.

Nude Living. 1962: Marli Renfro featured.

———. August 1962: "Secrets of a Nude Beauty," Diane Webber.

———. Ed and June Lange.

Nude Living Fact Finder. 1961: "Our Culture," pp. 2–29. Ed and June Lange, Elysium Inc. Los Angeles, California. An assortment of twenty, two-sided black-and-white and color photos of Marli at various nudist camps, odd sizes clipped from issues of *Nude Living*, contained inside acetate envelopes on black paper in art school binder.

Nudist Days. 1962: Marli Renfro featured.

Playboy. July 1960: Marli Renfro in a nude fashion pictorial.

———. September 1960: Marli Renfro cover.

Sundial. Ed and June Lange.

Swank. January 1962.

MOVIES

The Peeper. Completed at UCLA and combined with *Tonight for Sure!*

Psycho Special Edition. Universal Legacy Series. Bonus Features: *The Making of Psycho*: The Shower Scene—Storyboards by Saul Bass. A two-disc set with the digitally remastered picture and all-new bonus features. Disc 2, includes "In the Master's Shadow: Hitchcock's Legacy," "Hitchcock/Truffaut Interview Excerpts," and an *Alfred Hitchcock Presents* episode, "Lamb to the Slaughter." Copyright © 1960 Shamley Productions, Inc. Renewal 1988 by Universal Studios.

The Wide Open Spaces. Released as *Tonight for Sure!* through the Premier Company under the production company Searchlight in 1961 and distributed by Kinno International on VHS. Marli Renfro's personal copy.

WEBSITES, INTERVIEWS, AND OTHER SOURCES
Center for Gaming Research, University of Nevada, Las Vegas. A virtual exhibit. Includes "El Rancho Vegas History," "An Open Letter to Beldon Katleman from Tom Douglas," and "The Big Fire, the End of El Rancho Vegas." http://gaming.univ.edu/ElRancho/story.html.

Curtis, Tony. Address and audience participation interviews at JCCSF Goldman Center for Adult Living and Learning. Kanbar Hall, San Francisco, January 7, 2009.

El Rancho Vegas history and fire. www.onlinenevada.org/el_rancho_vegas and www.lasvegassun.com/photos?galleries.

Fabulous Las Vegas Mikey's. Hotel histories. www.lasvegasmikey.com/elrancho.htm.

Getlen, Larry. Interview with Hugh Hefner. Bankrate.com.

LAPD Historical Society. www.laphs.com.

Las Vegas History. www.earlyvegas.com and library.nevada.edu/speccol/photographs/0169_Frank_Watts.html.

Martello, Andy. Professional entertainer and historian of Searchlight, Nevada, in particular that of Willie Martello and the El Rey Casino. Andy is completing his book on the region. Tony Lovello and Kenny Laursen related their tale of the El Rey burning on this site. Andy has also profiled Las Vegas resident and producer, Jerry Schafer on his site. http://andymartello.blogspot.com/1990/01/el-rey-resort-casino.html.

Martello, Andy. Personal interviews. February 19, 25–26, March 5, April 17, 18, 20, and May 7–8, 2009.

Mojave Desert. http//digital-desert.com.

Monrovia High School Alumni Home Page. Includes a letter from Marli Renfro. http://www.madcatsalumni.org/'55.htm.

Renfro, Marli. Personal interviews from February 2008 through August 2009. By phone, post, and email. March 4, 6–8, 10, 11, 13–15, 20, 25–26, 2008; December 26, 2008; January 7–9, 2009; February 7, 2009; March 6, 2009; April 8, 11, 28, 2009; May 1, 6, 2008; August 25, 27, 2009.

Schafer, Jerry. Personal interviews on February 18–20, March 8, April 15–16, and June 2, 2009.

Summers Gross, Laurie. Personal interviews on March 15, 2009 and April 2, 2009. On tape and by phone. Visits by the author to Los Angeles Crime Scenes: July 12–16, 2007; October 7–10, 2007; April 15–17, 2008.

INDEX